D0101188

relational
leadership

Relational Leadership

A Biblical Model for Influence and Service

Second Edition
Revised and Expanded

WALTER C. WRIGHT JR.

Paternoster:
thinking faith

COLORADO SPRINGS · MILTON KEYNES · HYDERABAD

Paternoster Publishing
A division of Biblica
We welcome your questions and comments.

USA	1820 Jet Stream Drive, Colorado Springs, CO 80921 www.authenticbooks.com
UK	9 Holdom Avenue, Bletchley, Milton Keynes, Bucks, MK1 1QR
	www.authenticmedia.co.uk
India	Logos Bhavan, Medchal Road, Jeedimetla Village, Secunderabad 500 055, A.P.

Relational Leadership, Second Edition
ISBN-13: 978-1-60657-025-8

Copyright © 2000, 2009 by Walter C. Wright Jr.

11 10 09 / 6 5 4 3 2 1

Published in 2009 by Paternoster
All rights reserved. No part of this book may be reproduced in any form without permission
in writing from the publisher, except in the case of brief quotations embodied in critical
articles or reviews.

Scripture taken from the HOLY BIBLE, TODAY'S NEW INTERNATIONAL VERSION˚
TNIV˚ © Copyright 2001, 2005 by Biblica, Inc.™. Used by permission of Zondervan. All
rights reserved worldwide.

A catalog record for this book is available through the Library of Congress.

Cover and interior design: projectluz.com
Editorial team: Andy Sloan, Kay Larson, Dana Carrington

Printed in the United States of America

To the board, faculty, staff, and students of Regent College
who gave me the space to lead while serving them.

Contents

Foreword to the Second Edition

Walter Wright is the person who lured me into the study of leadership. In the 1980s he recruited me to co-teach a course on the subject in the Institute for Christian Organizational Development, a Fuller Seminary program that he served as the founding director. When he talked me into participating in that course I was still teaching philosophy at an undergraduate college, and the idea of leadership as an academic subject was a new one for me. When I started thinking about it, though, I realized that much of what I had been teaching my students for a decade and a half could be seen as a kind of philosophy of leadership. Plato's depiction of the ideal "philosopher-king" in his well-known dialogue, *The Republic*, was certainly an exploration of leadership. Once I got going I began to see a similar focus on leadership in other philosophers about whom I had lectured in the past: Aristotle, Machiavelli, Hobbes, Hegel—soon the list got very long.

And then there were the biblical materials. The very first thing that God says to human beings, we learn in Genesis 1, is that they are to exercise "dominion" in the garden he had prepared. The Old Testament books of Chronicles and Kings provide a series of stories about national leaders in Israel and Judah: judges, priests, prophets, kings, queens—some of them good leaders, some of them very bad, with a host of in-between types. And then there is what the New Testament teaches about leading—most importantly, the example of the One who came to show us all what it is like to be the kind of leader who stoops to wash the feet of his followers.

The more I got into this, the more excited I was about the subject of leadership. But, I must confess, I approached it all pretty much as a philosopher-theologian who was fascinated with ideas about leadership and how they might inform a Christian theory of leading. All of this was to change for me in a dramatic fashion, however, when at the end of the 1980s I actually became a senior administrator. To be sure, my intellectual preparation served me well. But I soon came to see the need for learning some new things about the practical—even "spiritual"—dimensions of leadership.

Like Walter Wright, I have learned much in my subsequent pilgrimage of leadership from the writings and personal example of Max De Pree. But I have also learned much from Walt himself. This book is evidence of the wealth of wisdom he brings to the subject of leading. At the heart of his understanding of relational leadership is his focus on the most basic relationship of all: the one that each of us has with our Creator. Here we are all called simply to be followers. The Christian message is clear on this subject: leadership at its healthiest must be infused with the kind of humility that recognizes that we are finite human beings who need all the help we can get in finding the right paths to walk as leaders. We are sheep who will inevitably go astray without guidance from the only true and reliable Shepherd.

It is in that very fundamental relationship, creature-to-Creator, we can find the direction necessary for all our other leader-follower relationships. And on the subject of these other relationships, Walter Wright is also a wonderful source of insight. He too is a philosopher, but of a different sort than I was trained to be. He is a lover of that variety of wisdom the ancients labeled *phronesis*, "practical wisdom." *Relational Leadership* is a marvelous "phronetic" book. In these pages he reminds those of us who sit in front offices, for example, that one of the most important persons in the organization is the one whose voice people first hear when they call the main phone number.

Walt guides us through the complexities of nurturing a healthy organizational culture and of dealing with conflicts. He alerts us to the temptations of power, and he instructs us in the nuances needed for being a mentor, a coach, a caster of vision, and the like. Most of all, he warns us against getting so absorbed in our public roles that we neglect those other areas of our lives—marriages, families, friendships, recreational involvements, faith communities—without a rich and vulnerable participation in which we become less than genuinely human.

I am grateful for all that I have learned—and am still learning—from Walter Wright. *Relational Leadership* has made the lessons that I have learned from him as a friend available to many others. May this new edition serve to enlarge even further the circle of "phronetic" leaders who have benefited from the practical wisdom that can be gained from these pages.

— Richard J. Mouw
President, Fuller Theological Seminary
Pasadena, California

Preface

Then the Lord said to Moses, "Write this on a scroll
as something to be remembered and make sure that
Joshua hears it." —Exodus 17:14

This fascinating statement occurs immediately after the biblical narrative describes Joshua's defeat of the Amalekites at Rephidim. What is this about? Joshua chooses a select team of warriors and leads them into battle. Moses ascends a nearby hill with the "staff of God" in his hands, holding up the battle before God with lifted arms. As long as Moses' arms are lifted up, the Israelites are victorious. When he tires and his arms droop, Joshua's troops are losing. And, like all of us, Moses gets tired. Aaron and Hur sit Moses on a rock and stand on either side, holding his arms up to God. And Joshua leads his army to victory, defeating the Amalekites.

Why is it important that Joshua remember this story? Because Joshua will be tempted to think that he is the leader, that he won the battle. And leadership never starts with us. It begins with God. We follow; and in the strength of that following we find others following our lead. The message of this book is that leadership is relational. It is grounded in our relationship with God through Jesus Christ and it finds expression in our relationships with one another. This study focuses on leadership in organizations, but it is about a life of following. It is always about God.

Things have changed since *Relational Leadership* was first published in 2000. God has not changed, and leadership continues to be a living relationship of influence and service. But the world around us has changed. September 11, 2001, shocked us all out of our comfort zones and dramatically changed the way we live, travel, and think about religion. A devastating earthquake in China followed a deadly tsunami in Indonesia and the destruction of Hurricane Katrina, awakening the world to the threat of climate change upon the earth. A "green" revolution is building.

And leadership is under siege. The world is presently facing a global economic crisis which many believe was caused by greed and fueled by poor leadership. Leaders of business and government are losing credibility and trust as homes go into foreclosure, prestigious companies fail, and small businesses strangle without credit. The church is not exempt, as highly visible, trusted leaders fall off of their pedestals.

Is leadership lost? No, it continues to beat in the hearts of men and women who look to the God who gives them life and follow their God into relationships of influence and service around the world. The need for leadership is greater than ever, and so is the reminder that God ordered to be written down in Exodus. We are not the leaders. We follow the God who is at work in this world.

The changes in this second edition of *Relational Leadership* come from conversations with many who have engaged the earlier version, from developing research in leadership, management, and organizational behavior, and from my own continued experience and learning. Working with the Max De Pree Center for Leadership at Fuller Theological Seminary for the past nine years, I have had the opportunity to meet and learn from business executives across North America and from nonprofit leaders around the world. This perspective has reinforced the principles articulated in the first edition and expanded my thinking about leadership development. This edition incorporates new or reworked thoughts about mentoring, coaching, emotional competence, team building, generational differences, planning, boards, and story as a leadership tool—framing the study within a model that underlines the connections of leadership that flow from our beliefs.

The revisions that follow reflect the evolving process of learning while leading. As we journey together may your thoughts wander creatively, your leadership deepen relationally, and your service to God be foundational.

Pasadena, California
June 2009

Foreword to the First Edition

We begin by following. There are no "born leaders." We start out by following our parents, our siblings, older children in the neighborhood. Later we follow teachers, coaches, bosses, managers, counselors, and guides. Eventually, writers and saints, preachers and prophets, some of them long dead, enter our lives as leaders and we follow.

And then somewhere along the line, whether we intend it or not, whether we want it or not, whether we realize it or not, people start following us. We become leaders. All of us. People see what we are doing and where we are going; it looks like we know what we are doing and where we are going. They follow. We are leaders before we know how to be leaders.

For some of us this is exhilarating. Leadership is a position of power; it is a place of prominence, we are looked up to, we are respected. We find we like being in charge; we like being followed—it increases our sense of worth, of importance. We look for ways to increase the power and use those who are following us to help us become what we want to be, to do what we want to do.

For others of us this is scary. Leadership is a position of responsibility; others are looking to us for guidance. If we say or do the wrong thing we are going to hurt people and if we get too involved with them they may well hurt us. We find we don't like being in charge; we don't like being followed—it interferes with our autonomy and our privacy. We look for ways to avoid the responsibility and have as little as possible to do with those who are following.

When we realize that we are inevitably all leaders in some degree or other, that "leader" is not a role confined to a job description, we know that we need help. For being a leader, whether in prominence or in obscurity, can fuel our ambition and a lust for power that ends up using people and organizations to enhance oneself. It is tempting to lead by coercion or manipulation and end up valuing followers primarily as a means to further my strategies and goals. Or leadership can frighten us into withdrawing into a privatized isolation; we distance ourselves from others and their need for love and compassion and justice, separating ourselves from the people who follow us. We end up leading by remote control, perceiving followers as irritants and a bother. We avoid them. And when we can't avoid them, we condescend to them.

Without wisdom, without intelligence, and without vigilance, being a leader can diminish or even destroy us and the people around us. Being a leader so easily and so often depersonalizes us and those around us, making us less instead of more. Leaders of every shape and kind—mothers and fathers, friends and neighbors, brothers and sisters, presidents and chairpersons, pastors and teachers, artists and athletes—which is to say, all of us, need help. The track record of leaders through the centuries, whether in politics or business, whether in education or religion, whether in family or community, is not encouraging. The seductions and pressures of unmentored leadership can easily ruin us. Yes, we need help.

Walter Wright has been paying attention to the nature of leadership for a long time and offers timely and seasoned help. He has thought, taught, prayed, conversed, and read widely and deeply in and outside the Bible on the nature of leadership and has worked what he has learned into his own life. And now he writes. Leadership, as Walt

Wright lives and writes about it, is not a role, not an assigned position. Leadership is a way of living that suffuses everything we do and are. Leadership is a way of being in the family and marriage, a way of being among friends, a way of going to work, a way of climbing mountains, and, most centrally, a way of following Jesus—all of which things he both does and reflects upon.

— Eugene H. Peterson
Professor Emeritus of Spiritual Theology, Regent College
Vancouver, BC

Introduction

L eadership—What is it? How do you do it? Who is a leader? Who is not? For forty years I have been trying to understand the answers to these questions because I keep finding myself in situations where someone expects me to be one (a leader) and know what it (leadership) is.

Several years ago, I was asked to give the Earle Douglas MacPhee Address for the closing ceremony of the 78th Banff School of Advanced Management. What does one say to a group of veteran executives who have just spent four weeks intensely studying leadership with some of the finest faculty in Canada? As they prepared for the transition back into their corporate settings around the world, it seemed appropriate to talk about the relational nature of leadership. Leadership is a relationship between a leader and a follower—ideally, a relationship of shared vision, shared responsibility, and shared leadership.

So I prepared my remarks from the perspective of the people who look to them for leadership—the people in their organizations for whose success they are responsible. The title as published on the Banff School website was "'Look Out!—Here Comes a Leader!' or 'Who Are You? Who Cares?'" Looking at a relational model for leadership, I focused on the character of the leader that adds value to the organization and contributes significantly to the shaping of the organizational culture. Who you are matters. What you believe and how that shapes your character does in fact make a difference to the people you lead. The relationships you build within your organizational setting deeply affect the way the organization's mission is carried out and the daily experience of those with whom you work. People do care who you are. It makes a difference. When the talk was posted on the Web, I received letters from a variety of sources affirming the importance of personal character and relationships. My thoughts must have been well received, because I was invited back the next year to give the closing address on the role of forgiveness in leadership.

This relational model of leadership has been evolving in my mind over the years as I work with people and for people. Many of the foundational elements were forged without reflection while working my way through college as a ramp supervisor for International Flight Service, a contract service provider at San Francisco International Airport. There, with little authority, a low-paid team of short-term employees, and tight airline schedules to meet, I learned the critical value of relationships. I could not do my job unless all members of my team did theirs and owned our overall objectives. Leadership was shared and responsibility was shared, even though I was accountable to senior management. And as a team we performed well and had fun together.

That sentence probably sums up the governing philosophy of a relational approach to leadership: as a team we performed well and had fun together!

After college I had the privilege of working with and for some great leaders. Calvin Schoonhoven, assistant to the president for Academic Affairs at Fuller Theological Seminary, believed in me and took a chance. With his encouragement I began to think about leadership within a Christian community. Glenn Barker, the provost of Fuller, took me under his wing and became my mentor for twelve years, pouring into me the model of servant leadership that he embodied so well.

David Hubbard, the brilliant president of Fuller, set a model of leader as theologian that still takes the measure of everything I do.

And then there was Max De Pree. The former chairman and CEO of Herman Miller, Inc., a Fortune 500 furniture manufacturer, and author of *Leadership Is an Art, Leadership Jazz, Letters to Zoe, Leading without Power,* and *Called to Serve* has probably shaped me more than any other single individual. When I was a young administrator at Fuller, Max was the chair of Fuller's board of trustees.

In 1981 I served as the founding director of the Institute for Christian Organizational Development at Fuller Seminary. Max taught a course in leadership for us each year. As I watched and listened to him, and later read his books, I found a man who incarnated a deeply caring relational approach to leadership. By all measures of success Max had been recognized for his leadership at Herman Miller, and I watched him bring that leadership to the board of Fuller Seminary. This was a man of character whose deeply held Christian values permeated his relational approach to leadership.

When I became president of Regent College, with great audacity I asked Max De Pree to become my mentor—and he agreed to a relationship that continues to this day. So each year I have the marvelous privilege of spending two or three afternoons with Max reflecting on what I am learning, what I am trying to do, and drawing from his continually increasing wisdom on the subject of leadership. If there is any visible model for the leadership in which I would like to invest my life, it is Max's model at Herman Miller. He integrated Christian beliefs with effective corporate leadership to make Herman Miller one of the most respected workplaces in America. Max has become known as an outstanding relational servant leader. That is the standard with which I want to measure my growth as a leader.

This book is a work in progress. It is a reflection of my current thinking about leadership as I try to do it and teach it. For over forty years I have been trying to live out the developing theological understanding of my Christian faith in a variety of roles in middle and top management. For nearly thirty years I have been teaching classes and workshops on leadership, attempting to bring the best of contemporary thinking about leadership into dialogue with my own study in biblical theology. I served as president of Regent College in Vancouver, British Columbia, for twelve years, and found everything I teach put to the test. For the past eight years I have directed the Max De Pree Center for Leadership at Fuller Theological Seminary, working with leaders, corporations, nonprofit organizations, and government agencies to develop healthy organizational cultures that promote human well-being en route to increased productivity—mission accomplishment that flows from men and women realizing their potential.

In many ways I have been writing this book for forty years. It forms the core of a course I teach, "Relational Leadership," but it keeps changing as new research and thinking is incorporated and new situations are confronted in the practice of leadership. The world around us keeps changing. Our organizations continue to change. The people we lead are changing. Leaders and leadership must change as well. Only God remains unchanged. And in Christian organizations, that is where it all begins.

In this study I start with one biblical writer's critique of leadership in a first-century Christian community. The five sharp challenges raised by Jude's letter form the outline for the presentation of relational leadership that follows. Also, throughout the book, I try to ground the practical application of leadership in the wonderful biblical case study of Colosse. In this real-life, down-to-earth community of Christians, we watch relational leadership worked out in the midst of human emotion and organizational conflict.

Building on the foundations laid in Jude and Colossians, I seek to set out a basic model of relational leadership as it has evolved from my reading and my daily efforts to exercise leadership in particular Christian communities. Many of my illustrations are drawn from my own experiences at Regent, at Fuller, and in churches. While I apologize for the narrowness of this sample, it is the actual arena in which these principles and practices have been tested. This is not just theory. It is a way of leading that I am trying to live and to which I am prepared to be held accountable.

Leadership is a relationship, and for the rest of this particular journey it becomes a relationship between you the reader and me the writer. May these thoughts and experiences stimulate your thinking about leadership and empower you to invest yourselves in the people for whose success you are responsible.

The Theology of Servant Leadership

This is a book about leadership, about biblical leadership, about servant leadership.[1] In these pages we will look at a model of leadership that begins with our relationship with God and moves out from there into relationships of service with those around us. This is a study of the theology and practice of servant leadership that takes as its starting point the book of Jude, which was a letter to Christian leaders.

What Is Leadership?

Before we begin this study, we need to clarify our definition of leadership. What is leadership? Who is a leader? Are we talking about the responsibility of persons who hold positions of leadership in an organizational context, or are we talking more broadly in terms that include us all? Is every Christian a leader?

In her little book *I Heard the Owl Call My Name*, Margaret Craven tells the wonderful story of a young Anglican priest who doesn't know that he is dying of cancer. A wise bishop assigns him to the isolated and difficult parish of Kingcome, a Native American village in British

---

1. Robert Greenleaf, formerly an executive with AT&T, was the first to apply the concept of leadership as serving to the business world in his book *Servant Leadership* (New York: Paulist Press, 1977).

Colombia. Mark Brian came to the village as vicar, thinking that his leadership was in his role, his position. Three years later he died in that village surrounded by a community of friends, knowing that his leadership was in his relationships and that he was led as often as he was followed. It was in his relationships with the village people that Mark was able to lead them, to make a difference in their lives. And it was these same relationships that enabled the village people to make a difference in Mark's life and ministry. He taught them about the love of God. They taught him about the quality of life and the meaning of death.[2]

If by *leader* we mean one who holds a position of authority and responsibility, then every Christian is not a leader. Some are—some are not. But if by *leader* we mean a person who enters into a relationship with another person to influence behavior, values, or attitudes, then I would suggest that all Christians should be leaders. Or perhaps more accurately, all Christians should exercise leadership, attempting to make a difference in the lives of those around them. This latter definition is the one put forth by the contemporary literature of leadership, followership, and management. In this study I will suggest that *leadership is a relationship—a relationship in which one person seeks to influence the thoughts, behaviors, beliefs, or values of another person.*

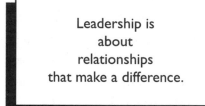

Leadership is about relationships that make a difference.

In their classic text, *Management of Organizational Behavior*, Paul Hersey and Kenneth Blanchard define leadership as "any attempt to influence the behavior of an individual or group."[3] The same definition

---

2. Margaret Craven, *I Heard the Owl Call My Name* (New York: Dell Publishing, 1973).

3. Paul Hersey and Kenneth H. Blanchard, *Management of Organizational Behavior*, 5th ed. (Englewood Cliffs, NJ: Prentice Hall, 1988), 5.

drives Howard Gardner's brilliant study of contemporary leaders, *Leading Minds*.[4] James MacGregor Burns, in his Pulitzer Prize-winning book *Leadership*, takes this one step further, arguing that transforming leadership is a relationship that raises the vision, values, and aspirations of both the leader and the follower to new levels of expectation.[5]

Jude and Leadership

While rereading the New Testament prior to writing the first edition of *Relational Leadership*, I came again to the book of Jude, a little letter right before the majestic and mysterious book of Revelation. Jude had never caught my attention in the past, but this time it jumped right off its pages.

As one whose entire life seems to be entwined with leadership—trying to figure out what it meant in my role as a college president and now in my role as a consultant, stopping occasionally to reflect and teach various topics in the area of leadership—I was amazed by the relevance of Jude's letter to the issues of leadership. These twenty-five verses form a powerful letter to Christian leaders today.

In this case, I do not mean only persons who find themselves in positions of leadership: organizational executives, pastors, politicians. Jude is writing to the ordinary members of the church and warning them about some of their number who are seeking to influence the community, claiming to be leaders but in fact pointing people in the wrong direction. He is dismayed by the self-serving behavior of some teachers who are seeking to provide leadership to the church. In the midst of that experience, he writes the powerful little letter we call Jude.

In particular, it was verses 12 and 13 that first captured my thinking. Jude describes the leadership of these false teachers in terms that Tom

---

4. Howard Gardner, *Leading Minds* (New York: Basic Books, 1996), 8.
5. James MacGregor Burns, *Leadership* (New York: Harper & Row, 1978).

Peters and Nancy Austin, authors of *A Passion for Excellence*, would use to describe the behavior of what they call "non-leaders."[6]

> [They are] shepherds who feed only themselves. They are clouds without rain, blown along by the wind; autumn trees, without fruit and uprooted—twice dead. They are wild waves of the sea, foaming up their shame; wandering stars, for whom blackest darkness has been reserved forever.
>
> Jude 12–13

Jude lists five powerful images of the non-leader who focuses on the use of power, images that will be central to my book. But before looking at these images, there are some other questions to be addressed, the first of which is *Who was Jude?*

As I spent more time with this little book, I began asking people if they knew who Jude was. Most people did not. The book is seldom referred to, and the average person couldn't tell you anything about the content of the letter, let alone the author.

Jude introduces himself in verse 1 as "Jude, a servant of Jesus Christ and a brother of James." According to early tradition and most contemporary scholarship, Jude is assumed to be the younger brother of James and the brother—or, if you will, the half brother—of Jesus.

I have a friend who is the third son in a successful family. His father is the president of a respected college; his mother is a published author; his oldest sibling is a highly successful pastor of a large church; and the second sibling is president of another college in the United States. The father and both siblings have earned PhDs and growing reputations.

My friend is a very talented and gifted man who, in his middle years, emerged as a nationally recognized Christian thinker and writer.

---

6. Tom Peters and Nancy Austin, *A Passion for Excellence* (New York: Warner Books, 1989), 354–59.

But as I watched him grow in the early years of his career, I saw an almost desperate need to live up to the expectations set by the other members of his family. He was driven to succeed. And succeed he has, as I had no doubt that he would. His natural gifts and abilities drew him into roles in which he continues to make important contributions. He is an established leader in his field and his reputation will continue to develop.

However, in the early stage in my friend's development I did not see his leadership emerging naturally and comfortably from his many

---

The Theology of Leadership

This study reflects briefly on the theology of leadership revealed in Jude's letter to his community. It is one point of entry into what could be a much larger discussion of biblical leadership running from Genesis to Revelation. This use of Jude, and the case study of Philemon and Onesimus below, are selectively limiting, grounding our thinking about relational leadership on two specific historical moments in the biblical narrative. There is much more that could be mined from the rich vein of leadership principles found in the stories and teaching of Scripture, such as:

- Leadership is for servants (Mark 10:35–45)
- Leadership is serving rather than ruling (1 Kings 11–12)
- Leadership is a gift from God (Romans 12:1–16)
- Leadership serves at the pleasure of God (1 Samuel 10:17–27)
- Leadership finds success in seeking God, not power (2 Chronicles 26:1–23)
- Leadership celebrates the coming King (2 Samuel 6:1–23)
- Leadership trusts God when risking decisions (Acts 15:1–29)
- Leadership is responsible for the growth of people (Ezekiel 34:1–10)
- Leadership is for the empowerment of others (Ephesians 4:1–13)
- Leadership manages partnerships (1 Kings 5:1–12)
- Leadership requires courageous followers (2 Samuel 19:1–8)
- Leadership reflects the character of God (Galatians 5:13–26)
- Leadership seeks continual renewal (Colossians 1:9–14)
- Leadership contributes to Christian community (Philippians 2:1–11)
- Leadership is responsible for the use of resources (Genesis 41:15–57)
- Leadership is responsible for the use of time (Luke 10:38–42)
- Leadership models integrity of character (1 Corinthians 13:1–13)
- Leadership envisions God's future (Revelation 20–22)
- Leadership leaves a legacy (2 Samuel 23:1–7)

gifts but rather from his aggressive need to achieve—his need to live up to the model set by the other members of his family. He pushed himself and lived with a fairly strong sense of self-judgment. He seemed insecure as he measured himself against his family. I do not believe he was centered in his soul at that stage in his life. From my perspective, as long as his leadership arose from his insecurity and his needs, it was less effective than it became when he relaxed and let it flow naturally from his many gifts and his dependence upon God.

Now it's one thing to have older siblings who have PhDs and are successful leaders of churches and colleges. But what if one brother was the head of the Jerusalem church and the other was the Savior of the world? Where does that leave you?!

That is where we find Jude. Jude who? The brother of James and the half brother of Jesus. Third in line, at least, within a family that he will never live up to. That is why I think it so wonderful that Jude starts his letter by dealing with what I call the psychology of leadership—or better yet, the theology of leadership.

Prerequisites for Servant Leadership

Jude brushes quickly over his legitimate status as a "brother of the Lord," identifying himself as a servant—a servant of Jesus Christ—and alluding to his status only in a secondary relationship to his brother James. In spite of the fact that as a brother of Jesus he would be accorded special recognition in the early church, he is anxious to point away from himself, something he criticizes the false leaders for not doing, and he moves immediately to his readers.

Centering

> To those who have been called, who are loved in God the
> Father and kept for Jesus Christ.
>
> Jude 1

Here Jude describes his readers in terms of three characteristics that I believe are prerequisites for leadership in the Christian community, three characteristics that set biblical leadership—the leadership of servants—apart from ordinary leadership. In fact, I believe Jude 1 addresses three critical questions that are foundational to any form of leadership anywhere:

- Who am I? Do I have worth? This deals with the issue of *identity.*

- Will I be here tomorrow? This deals with the issue of *survival.*

- Why am I here? This deals with the issue of *meaning.*

Peter Koestenbaum, a philosopher of business, sees these three questions at the core of every leadership relationship. In his book *The Heart of Business,* he examines what makes an effective leader. He asks what gives a person the character that causes others to accept his or her influence, the character that enables the person to make a difference in the world. Koestenbaum argues that effective leaders are centered in their souls. They have come to peace with the questions of identity, survival, and meaning. It is this centeredness that makes others listen to what they have to say, that gives them credibility.[7]

In their excellent book *Credibility,* James Kouzes and Barry Posner show that people follow leaders because they see a quality of character, a credibility worth trusting. People respond to this centeredness, this quality of character.[8] As Koestenbaum observes, "Centeredness is what makes people seem powerful, and its absence is what makes people perceive themselves and be perceived by others as ineffective and even

---

7. Peter Koestenbaum, *The Heart of Business* (Dallas: Saybrook Publishing Company, 1987), 352.
8. James M. Kouzes and Barry Z. Posner, *Credibility* (San Francisco: Jossey-Bass, 1993), 22.

impotent. . . . Centeredness is the source of authentic faith, belief and realistic self-confidence."[9] Good words from a philosopher.

So how do we get centered? How do we find that quality of character that people respond to? Look again at Jude 1.

1. Identity

In response to the question of identity, Jude answers that we are *loved in God.* Our value, our worth, our individual personhood is determined by the fact that God loves us, that he has entered into a relationship with us in which, out of his covenant faithfulness, he commits himself to our well-being, our growth, and our eternal existence. Who am I? I am one known and loved by God. I am one of his. Our identity is not in our work or in our leadership. It is found only in the understanding that we are loved by God. This is key to leadership for Christians.[10]

2. Survival

As for survival, it does not matter whether or not we will be here tomorrow. Jude responds that what matters is that we are *kept for Jesus Christ*; or better, we are kept by God for the return of Christ. It is God who will keep us secure in and for Jesus Christ. The fears and anxieties of today must fall into perspective before the truth that we are in the hand of God. Our lives are shaped not by our positions or accomplishments but by our relationship with God in Jesus Christ. Only that matters. Biblical leadership is grounded on our relationship with God.

3. Meaning

And then there is the age-old question of meaning. Why am I here? Jude's answer is short. We are *called.* We have been chosen by God to be his people, to be his servants. What is the meaning, the purpose, of my life? It is to be a child of God, to be his servant, to live my life for his

---

9. Koestenbaum, *Heart of Business*, 354–55.
10. Parker J. Palmer, "Leading from Within," *Insights on Leadership* (New York: John Wiley, 1998), 205.

glory and honor. We are not called to a position or a role. We are not called to a specific ministry, lay or ordained. We are called to live the resurrected life in such a way that it points people to God wherever we find ourselves.[11] Leadership for Christians is about God, not about us.

Centeredness is getting our lives in perspective before God. It is knowing that we are loved, kept, and called by God. Out of this identity, security, and meaning comes a person of character, a person who is believed, a person who can influence others and make a difference in the world—*leadership*.

In his little book on leadership, *In the Name of Jesus*, Henri Nouwen argues that biblical leaders must find their identity deeply rooted in God's love.[12] And they must realize that any valid leadership they seek to exercise must be grounded on a permanent, intimate relationship with the incarnate Word, Jesus Christ.[13] This is an important study and deserves to be read often by anyone who presumes to live out of a role or responsibility of leadership. Nouwen captures well the three temptations of leadership that seek to draw us away from God: relevance, popularity, and power. Only an intimate relationship with Jesus can anchor the biblical leader in the love of God.

This is the starting point for all who wish to exercise leadership as Christians, for all who seek to influence the people around them. We begin by focusing on our relationship with God. We center our soul in the hand of God—only then are we ready for leadership. Leadership for Christians starts with a vital relationship between the leader and God. Leadership begins by following. This is the essence of biblical servant-hood, of servant leadership.

I do not think this is easy, nor do I think it happens once for all time. It is a continual process. As often as we reach out into the world trying to make a difference, we also need to be focusing on God, centering

---

11. Os Guinness, *The Call* (Nashville: Word, 1998), 4.
12. Henri Nouwen, *In the Name of Jesus* (New York: Crossroad, 1989), 28.
13. Ibid., 31.

our souls. In recent years, the media around the world has been filled with stories of leaders whose uncentered lives landed them in trouble and tarnished their influence. But I do not have to look beyond my own mirror to see fear, anxiety, and insecurity. The more I take on, the more I am conscious of my dependence upon God, my need for his presence at the center of my being.

Each of us must work out with God our own centering procedure, our own way of investing in our relationship with God in Christ. For me, there are five necessary components.

Solitude:	Time when I listen to God without distraction—ranging from praying alone in my room to walking a mountain trail in silence.
Study:	Time for reflection on God's Word—ranging from reading Greek in the library to reading Psalms by the seashore.
Worship:	Time when I focus intentionally on the center—the presence of Christ—with humble gratitude, both in times of personal devotion and corporate communion.
Community:	Time to celebrate shared relationships and to balance my uncentered life with people who care—from family and friends to mentors and small groups.
Service:	Time to experience and share the love of God, to make a contribution, to exercise the gifts entrusted to me—to make a difference.

When a potter sits down to make something, she takes a lump of clay and places it in the middle of the wheel. She works patiently and intently to center that lump of clay before making any attempt to shape its future. Every potter knows that if the clay is not centered, the vessel he or she makes will be deformed. Even irregular, individualized pieces must start with a perfect centering.[14]

This is true for each one of us who wants to make a difference in this world. The shape of our future leadership is determined by the quality of our centering.

Hesed (KINDNESS OF GOD)

In verse 1 Jude started by focusing his readers on their relationship with God. Now, in verse 2, he shifts the focus onto our relationships with other people—our leadership. It is only out of centeredness, out of an intimate relationship with God in Christ, that we can reach out in relationships and attempt to lead others, to influence the way they think and believe and act. Henri Nouwen calls this the solitude of the heart—a process which first attaches one's self to God, thereby empowering one's relationships with others.[15]

In my mind Jude 2 bridges the gap from living in the hand of God to walking in the world in relationships. Jude is writing to a community where some people are leading for their own benefit and dividing the community in a destructive fashion.[16] As Jude exposes these false teachers as a model of ineffective and dangerous leadership, he also gives us some clues to the character of servant leadership. What are the characteristics of servant leadership, of Christian relationship? I believe that Jude lists three in verse 2:

Mercy, peace and love be yours in abundance.

These are the characteristics of leadership for people whose lives are centered in their relationship to God.

---

14. Mary C. Richards, *Centering in Pottery, Poetry and the Person* (Middletown, CT: Wesleyan University Press, 1964), in Charlotte F. Speight, *Hands in Clay* (Sherman Oaks, CA: Alfred Publishing, 1979), 217.

15. Henri Nouwen, *Reaching Out: The Three Movements of the Spiritual Life* (Garden City, NY: Image Books, 1986), 48.

16. Jude 18–19.

Jude 2 is easily passed over because it falls into the same category as "Hello" and "Dear friend." It is a greeting, a formal and almost common salutation. "Mercy and peace" was the standard Jewish greeting of the day. It referred to the covenant kindness of God (*hesed*) and the shalom, or sense of total well-being, that flowed out of this experience of covenant faithfulness. Jude adds the word "love" to his greeting, bringing Christian overtones into the leadership relationship. God's covenant kindness that results in peace or total well-being is most visibly modeled in the incarnation and sacrificial death of Jesus.

If we see this verse only as a "Dear friends" greeting, we will not spend much time with it. But it is more than a greeting. It is a prayer, an invocation that God will grant the readers an abundance of his mercy, his peace, and his love so that it will overflow from their lives onto others. These three components of Jude's invocational greeting, I believe, represent three critical aspects to the character of servant leadership.

Exercising leadership as servants involves love, peace, and mercy. If we are going to be biblical leaders we need to be lovers, peacemakers, and keepers of commitments. I only note these characteristics of the biblical leader in passing. They deserve to be unfolded and applied to our lives in detail. Yet as we move from our relationship with God to principles for leadership, we must acknowledge these three crucial elements of Jude's prayer so that we always keep them in the back of our minds.

- **Love:** We are to be lovers of people. Leaders must love the people for whom they are responsible, modeling the consistency of the love that God has poured out on us in Christ. Leadership is a relationship of love. It is an investment in the life of others for the purpose of their growth, their contribution, and their walk with God. Only people who care about people will be effective leaders today.

- **Peace:** We are to be peacemakers. In a world of conflict, leaders bring calm. In a world of brokenness, leaders offer healing. In a world of loneliness, leaders provide relationship. Leaders work for the reconciliation and healing of relationships, for the creation of strife-free environments where people are freed to use the gifts they have been given and to grow. Leadership is a relationship of shalom, a relationship that works actively for the total well-being of the persons being led.

Hesed, God's covenant love or covenant faithfulness, represents the commitment that God has made in relationship with his covenant people—a commitment to be our God, to be there in our future, to be for us. That alone would be enough to elevate the importance of this word in defining our approach to leadership, but it carries even more content. *Hesed* is God's commitment to be our God even when we fail to live up to our part of the covenant relationship. Even when we fail, God still commits himself to us and honors his end of the relationship by carrying our end also. That is where the "mercy" side comes in. We always fail. We cannot keep our end of the covenant relationship. We cannot live up to the requirements of being God's chosen people, his children, his servants. We try, and we fail. But God has committed himself to the relationship, he has committed himself to us in Jesus Christ; and because of his mercy, his covenant faithfulness, we can still be in relationship with God in Christ.

This is the model we have for being servant leaders who are full of mercy, who are keepers of commitments. It is promising to be there in someone else's future. It is committing ourselves now to be there in the future for another person, knowing that both of us will change between now and then. We commit to another recognizing the possibility, perhaps even the probability, that he or she will not live up to our expectations. It means giving another person the space to change and committing to that person on the other side of change.

This is an important theme for Jude. Near the end of his letter, Jude calls on his readers to demonstrate this kind of commitment, to maintain their relationships with those who have been influenced by the false teachers, even with the false teachers themselves—to be there for them, accepting and caring for them personally even while patiently standing against the false teaching and dangerous leadership they represent.

Leadership for Christians means committing ourselves to be there in another's future as a friend, as one who cares: regardless of the circumstances that occur between now and then, regardless of the path upon which our organizational roles may lead us.

- **Mercy:** We are to be keepers of commitments. Jude uses the term "mercy" in his greeting. This component of Christian relationships, of servant leadership, may be the most important. When we hear the word "mercy" we tend to think in terms of the English ideas "pity" and "compassion"—and sometimes "condescension" or "undeserving," with a touch of our own pride thrown in. The Hebrew word *hesed*, which is translated "mercy," means much more than this.

Leadership is for lovers of people, peacemakers, and keepers of commitment. These are not unique characteristics. Much of the current leadership research would also identify such qualities as important to leadership today. Yet because Jude grounds these characteristics of Christian servanthood in our relationship with God, he separates servant leadership from ordinary leadership. Relationships with those we seek to influence are characterized by love, peace, and *hesed*, mirroring what we ourselves have experienced in our relationship with God. Servant leadership is about a relationship with God that so shapes who we are that people see in us a person of character and commitment whose influence they choose to follow.

Is every Christian a leader? Yes, to the extent that we seek to influence others and make a difference in the lives around us. Are we exercising servant leadership? Yes, if we have centered ourselves in the hand of God and are leading out of a relationship with God in which we know we are *called, loved by God*, and *kept for Jesus Christ*, and if we are seeking to make a difference in the world by investing ourselves in relationships with those around us that are characterized by *mercy, peace*, and *love*.

Principles of Servant Leadership

You are probably familiar with the powerful words of Ezekiel to the leaders of Israel in Ezekiel 34. If these are not immediately familiar,

I encourage you to read them regularly. In a scathing denunciation of leaders who used their power and position to get fat off of God's flock rather than to shepherd them, Ezekiel reminds us all of our accountability to God for the exercise of our leadership. It is a strong message, but it strikes a note of accountability to God that anyone engaging in the leadership of others should keep in mind.

That is precisely the image that sits in Jude's mind as he writes against some would-be leaders in his community. Six hundred years after Ezekiel, nothing has changed. Jude, the brother of our Lord, challenges the self-proclaimed leaders about the same misuse of power that God had addressed through Ezekiel. Jude uses the language of Ezekiel as he addresses his community of believers, counseling them against the leadership of false teachers within their ranks who are flaunting their power and seeking to promote themselves as the leaders of this Christian community.

In his powerful critique of their leadership, Jude uses five graphic images of the non-leader, and in so doing, I believe, gives us five working principles for effective servant leadership.

Principle 1: Leadership is about influence and service

Jude's first image is of "shepherds who feed only themselves" (v. 12). These leaders use their power for their own benefit. As we see in Ezekiel and elsewhere, the shepherd is a common image for leadership in the Bible, modeling the care and investment that the leader must make for the growth and nurture of the followers. Jude, however, confronts the false leaders in the community to which he writes for precisely the same error that Ezekiel attacked. They are using their power, not for the nurture of the community, but to draw people to themselves, to put themselves on a pedestal above the rules and values of the community. They are getting fat off of the flock.

Servant leadership, on the other hand, is community-directed. It uses its power for the growth of those who are being led and the accomplishment of the shared mission of the community.

In its broadest definition, leadership is a relationship of influence. It is a relationship between two people in which one person seeks to influence the vision, values, attitudes, or behaviors of the other. This definition makes it clear that everyone exercises leadership. At one time or another, we all seek to exert such influence and thus engage in leadership.

When leadership is formally granted to a person by a group, community, or organization—when that person is given the responsibility of being a shepherd—that leadership carries with it the expectation that the influence will be directed toward two purposes: the accomplishment of a mission or objective shared by the leader and the followers and the care and nurture of the community or organization.

Personally, leadership is a relationship of influence. Organizationally, it is a relationship of influence with purpose: maintaining the community and achieving the shared mission. When leadership is truly exercised in our organizations and in our churches, the mission is being accomplished and people are growing into community.

Principle 2: Leadership is about vision and hope

Jude's second image is just as potent. Non-servant leaders are "clouds without rain, blown along by the wind." Imagine a farmer in a hot desert countryside trying to scratch out a living in the harsh climate. As he looks to the sky, he sees a cloud heading his way. The promise of rain looms large on the horizon. He has a vision of crops growing, of food on the table. And yet the clouds pass by, blown along by the wind, failing to deliver on their promise. The vision withers.

Another powerful image. Jude is accusing the false leaders of promising a future to the people but not delivering. They are too intent on following their own desires and pursuing their spiritual visions to empower the dreams of the people they claim to lead.

Leadership is about vision. It is about tomorrow, about hope, about mission. Leadership articulates a compelling vision for tomorrow that captures the imagination of the followers and energizes their attitudes and actions in the present. It gives meaning and value to living. Leadership in community focuses the dreams and commitments of the people on a shared vision of the mission that brings them together, and then leadership works with the people to see that that mission is accomplished. Leadership is a relationship of influence that points people to a shared vision that shapes their living today in such a way that the vision is realized.

Servant leadership offers hope, it offers vision, and it delivers on its promise. Servant leadership empowers people. It makes a difference.

Principle 3: Leadership is about character and trust

The third image is of "autumn trees without fruit and uprooted—twice dead." Trees without roots produce no fruit. This image, too, focuses on the expectation of results. The leadership of the false teachers did not produce growth. There was no fruit, no product to show for the leadership that was being exercised. And Jude is not surprised since the leadership of these non-leaders is not rooted in the love of God for his people. They are doubly useless—not grounded in a relationship empowered by God and therefore not producing any growth in their community.

As Jude recognized in his opening verses, leadership arises from character. Recent research has shown a direct link between leadership and credibility. Leadership is a relationship of trust. We listen to people we trust. We accept the influence of a person whose character we respect.

Leadership is grounded in the faith, beliefs, commitments, and values of the leader. Leadership that produces fruit is rooted in the character of the leader. It is impossible to provide consistent leadership out of insecurity. Leadership emerges from secure people, from men and women who know who they are and live authentically in the security of that knowledge. The person who lives securely in the knowledge of the love of God will be a person whose influence is sought, whose leadership produces fruit.

What is the fruit of effective leadership? Warren Bennis, the distinguished professor of leadership at the University of Southern California, says that the three things people want from leaders are direction, trust, and hope.

Leadership points people in the right direction, showing them how what they are doing contributes to the shared mission of the community. Leadership believes in people and fosters relationships of trust between members of the community. It points people to God and roots their identity, dignity, and security in their relationship with God in Christ. And leadership offers hope. It provides a vision that lifts the eyes of the followers from the path they are walking to the horizon of God's eternal perspective and reminds them why they have life—to enjoy a relationship with God!

Principle 4: Leadership is about relationships and power

The fourth picture in Jude's description of these leaders describes them as "wild waves of the sea, foaming up their shame" (v. 13). Jude focuses on the power in the waves of the sea and leaves us with the feeling of unbounded power, power without purpose, power that leaves a trail of debris behind it. The self-appointed leaders in the community were using their influence to make a big splash, but they were not going anywhere. They were not working for the mission or unity of the community or the development of the people; instead they were divisive and contentious, flaunting a lifestyle that denied the lordship of Christ.

Leadership is a relationship of power. It is the exercise of power. Power is the potential for influence. It denotes the character or resources that others see in you that cause them to accept your influence. It may be the authority of your position. It may be the spirituality of your character. It may be the benefits you can provide (or the harm you can do). It may be the knowledge or skills that you possess.

Power is at the heart of leadership. Power exists, however, only when someone sees in you a reason to accept your influence. At that moment you exercise power and have the opportunity to lead. But power needs purpose. Power without purpose leaves a wake of debris, a trail of litter. Tornadoes have power, but look what they do. Power needs to be leashed to purpose.

The power that permits leadership in communities must be directed to the mission that forms the community. Leadership must be responsible and accountable. Leadership is a relationship of influence with a purpose. Servant leadership points people away from the leader to the mission of the community and empowers their individual contributions toward that mission.

Principle 5: Leadership is about dependency and accountability

The fifth image offers another timely corrective to false leadership, describing such leaders as "wandering stars, for whom blackest darkness has been reserved forever." These leaders are like shooting stars, streaking onto the scene with flash and excitement but eventually fading and disappearing. There are short-term gains but no long-term perseverance. Such leadership may offer a quick fix but does not nurture the long-range health of the community. There is a lot of activity, but no relationship.

Leadership is about people. It is about relationship. Leadership is a relationship of influence with a purpose, the achievement of the shared mission and the nurture of the community. Leaders are dependent upon the people. They are not charismatic comets racing alone across the sky. Leadership is a relationship of dependency. Leaders need followers. They are dependent upon the community because, in the end, leadership is in the hands of followers. It exists only when someone decides to follow, decides to accept the influence.

Max De Pree, author of the best-selling book *Leadership Is an Art*, says that one of the responsibilities of the leader is to say thank you[17]— an acknowledgment of dependence. In the final analysis it is always the one who follows who determines if leadership is being exercised. It doesn't matter how much power or charisma you think you possess, how exciting you think your vision is. What matters is if someone chooses to accept your influence and alter his or her vision, values, attitudes, or behaviors.[18] Leadership is a relationship of influence with a purpose, perceived by those who choose to follow.

So what?

So what? What does this mean for you? What will you do with your power? Will you lead to empower others or will you use your power for your own benefit—to gain recognition and solidify your position and status?

Sometimes you may not think you have much power; you may think that you exercise little leadership. Remember, however, that if leadership is a relationship of influence and power, the potential for leadership is what others see in you. It is the strength, gifts, and resources that other people see in you that gives you the opportunity to lead—to influence their beliefs, their values, their behaviors. Knowledge is power; information is power; personal integrity and confidence of vision are perceived as power. The security you have in your own relationship

---

17. Max De Pree, *Leadership Is an Art* (East Lansing, MI: Michigan State University Press, 1987), 11.

18. Howard Gardner (*Leading Minds*, 38) notes that even the Stalins and Saddams of the world have to persuade even as they invoke instruments of terror to control their followers.

with God gives you a spiritual power that can impact the lives of those around you.

Will you be a servant leader? Will you make a difference in the lives of those around you? Whether you are in a formal position of leadership or simply engage others in relationships, you already are equipped to lead. Out of your biblical knowledge, your maturing relationship with God in Christ, your integrated Christian worldview, you can make a difference in the world.

Your decision is what you will do with this power. Will you use it for your own benefit—to feed yourself—or will you use your power for the growth and nurture of people? Will you empower others? Will you be caring, encouraging, and motivating? Will you acknowledge your accountability to God? Will you offer vision and deliver what you promise? Will you make a difference in this world?

God has given you gifts and abilities. You are increasing your knowledge and skills. This gives you the power to influence others, to make a difference in the lives of the people around you. You are a shepherd. And the prophets are waiting to pass judgment. How will you use the power that God has entrusted to you? This is a sobering question. And if Jude said no more we would be left with only an awesome challenge of what it means to be a servant leader and a sense of anxiety in the face of divine accountability.

But Jude does not stop here. He goes on to remind us of the continuing sources of power available to the servant leader who wants to make a difference.

Power for the Servant Leader

But, dear friends, remember what the apostles of our Lord Jesus Christ foretold. They said to you, "In the last times there will be scoffers who will follow their own ungodly desires." These are the people who divide you, who follow mere natural instincts and do not have the Spirit.

But you, dear friends, by building yourselves up in your most holy faith and praying in the Holy Spirit, keep yourselves in God's love as you wait for the mercy of our Lord Jesus Christ to bring you to eternal life.

Be merciful to those who doubt; save others by snatching them from the fire; to others show mercy, mixed with fear—hating even the clothing stained by corrupted flesh.

Jude 17–23

Where do we get this power to be servants who lead, to be shepherds who feed and nurture the flock? Jude concludes his letter to Christian leaders by reminding them of four sources of power available to servant leaders:

- **The content of God's Word.** Servant leaders are instructed to build "yourselves up in your most holy faith": that is, to be grounded in the content of the Word of God—the body of truth handed down by the prophets and apostles, the scriptures of the Old and New Testaments. Knowledge is power, and we have the Word of God that we might know God. Equipped with that knowledge, we have something to say to this world.

- **The communion of the Spirit.** The servant leader is to pray "in the Holy Spirit." In other words, he or she is to live in the presence and the power of God in Christ through the Spirit of God. In prayer, prompted by and empowered by the Holy Spirit, we have access directly to God—the source of all glory, power, and authority. It is in prayer that we find the wisdom of God, that we are able to see things from God's perspective. In prayer we center ourselves in the hand of God, and out of the identity and security of God's hand we have power to engage others in relationships of influence.

- **A covenant in Christ.** Jude reminds us of our covenant relationship with God in Christ when he tells us to "keep yourselves in God's love as you wait for the mercy of our Lord Jesus Christ to bring you to eternal life." For our part we are expected to keep ourselves in God's love, which Jesus has taught us means to obey his commands (John 15:10). The servant leader is obedient, seeking to live a life worthy of our God.

  If the sentence ended here, we would have an inadequate source of power. But Jude goes on to remind us also of God's part in this covenant relationship. God expects obedience; he offers mercy—mercy leading to eternal life. Remember, mercy is the covenant commitment to maintain our end of the agreement even when the other person fails. The servant leader is one who trusts in the mercy of God, who knows that God reaches out in Christ to provide the very obedience that we cannot live up to ourselves. It is this covenant commitment from God that gives us the confidence to be servant leaders. Otherwise the task would be impossible.

- **A calling to commitment.** The servant leader who has experienced God's covenant faithfulness, God's gracious forgiveness, is called to "be merciful"—to be a keeper of commitments in all leadership relationships. Servant leadership means committing ourselves to be there in another's future as a friend, as one who cares: regardless of the circumstances that occur between now and then, regardless of the path our organizational roles may lead us. It means committing ourselves to the relationship even when the other person follows a path that we cannot walk.

Jude calls the Christian leader to commit to those who are in doubt about the direction of their lives and to confront those who have chosen to follow false leaders. And if they do not respond, Jude calls servant leaders to continue to commit themselves to the relationship even as they stand against the beliefs and behaviors of their friend. Servant leaders are called to make commitments in relationships to others— caring commitments that earn the right to be heard, the right to influence. Leaders who care can make a difference in this world.

So here are four sources of power—with which to influence others and to make a difference in this world—for the servant leader. We are servants called to exercise leadership wherever God has placed us, shepherds who have been given power to feed. The prophets are waiting to pass judgment. What will you do with your power?

Jude knows that we cannot do much alone. But with God we can be leaders of influence, servants who make a difference. It is to the God who holds on to us that we point people when we seek to exercise leadership as Christians, as Jude says when he ends his letter with this well-known benediction:

To him who is able to keep you from stumbling and to present you before his glorious presence without fault and with great joy—to the only God our Savior be glory, majesty, power and authority, through Jesus Christ our Lord, before all ages, now and forevermore! Amen.

Jude 24–25

Belief Precedes Behavior

Why do we begin a study of relational leadership with the theology of leadership? We begin with theology because there is a direct connection between following and leading. There is no such thing as leadership without followership. Leaders and followers are bound together in relationship. Together they define the relationship that we call leadership. We only lead when someone chooses to follow, and any leadership we exercise is framed by our decision to follow. We are followers first—from infancy and childhood to the decisions that frame our adulthood, we select the paths we will follow.[19]

The God we choose to follow—the belief that informs our theology—ultimately shapes the person we become and the leadership we exercise. Theology matters; this is where leadership begins.

After he retired as chairman of Herman Miller, Inc., *Fortune* magazine Business Hall of Fame leader Max De Pree was interviewed by the company as they sought to create an archive of his leadership legacy. During the videotaping the interviewer asked, "How would you describe the qualities and principles of the Herman Miller culture that make it a special place? What should people know about the culture that your father, your brother Hugh, and you all sought to create?"

Max responded:

> It is easier to understand if you work backwards. . . . Your connections are important and your relationships are fundamental. . . . Why would you have good relationships? Because your values dictate to you that you ought to have good relationships. Where do those values come from? The values come from certain beliefs. Beliefs always precede behavior. Then where do you get your beliefs? Now you have come back to: Do you believe certain things about the way the world is? Do you have any convictions about where everything started? You can work your way back and you start with whether or not there is a God, and whether or not the words he left us were truly inspired—whether

---

19. Barbara Kellerman, *Followership* (Boston: Harvard Business Press, 2008), xxii.

we can count on them. And whether or not there is any truth to the existence of Jesus as part of the Godhead. . . . If you accept this particular pattern of thought about faith . . . what kind of encumbrances do you now live with? I think we start with a certain theology; we start with a God. That becomes a theology, which becomes a set of values, which becomes a kind of behavior, which produces a kind of relationship, which produces a kind of service or product.[20]

Beliefs always precede behavior. That principle, articulated by Max De Pree and put into practice by the leadership team of Herman Miller, goes to the heart of the matter. Leadership begins with theology. For Christian leaders, it starts with a commitment to follow: to obey Jesus' call to "follow me"—to follow the way set forth by God in the life, death, and resurrection of Jesus. As Eugene Peterson reminds us in *The Jesus Way*, the God we choose to follow determines what we believe, forms our values, and shapes our behavior.[21]

Our faith forges our character, who we are—the beliefs, promises, and commitments that define us as individuals in relationships. Our character is revealed in our values: our stated values—what we say is important—and our acted values—our behaviors. Both are important, but our behavior—our lived-out values—always reflects our true character. We need to be clear about what we believe, to state unambiguously the values for which we stand. Yet it is our actions that inform others about our beliefs and our character, because our behaviors always reveal what we truly believe regardless of what we say is important. That is why integrity is so critical to leadership.

---

20. Max De Pree, interview conducted by Bruce Buursma for Herman Miller, Inc. archives, November 4, 2004, Marigold Lodge, Holland, MI. Used by permission.
21. Eugene H. Peterson, *The Jesus Way* (Grand Rapids: Eerdmans, 2007), 22.

Integrity is the alignment of stated values and acted values. Integrity is doing what we say is important. Without integrity it is difficult for others to know the purpose of our lives, the direction of our leadership. With integrity of character grounded in our relationship with God we work out the purpose of life, who we intend to be, what we will be known for when it is all over. Character is the defining core of our being, the foundation for our leadership.

Leadership flows from character. Leadership is a relationship of influence. It is a relationship in which one person seeks to influence the thoughts, behaviors, beliefs, or values of another. For leadership to have been exercised both a leader—one who influences—and a follower—one who chooses to accept the influence—is required. The choice of the follower is critical. Unless the follower chooses to follow there is no leadership, and people choose to follow individuals who have integrity, individuals who are honest, credible, and dependable.[22]

Character is the heartbeat of leadership. It anchors the person and fuels the vision toward which leadership strives and the strategies that we employ to accomplish that vision. It also creates the trust necessary for relationships to thrive. As we will see later in this study, leadership is responsible to envision strategy and to nurture relationships that engage the contributions of others toward the accomplishment of the strategy. Both tasks of leadership are tied to character.

The strategic responsibility of leadership is well known. People in leadership positions are taught to cast vision; to articulate the specific mission of the organization or community; to clarify that mission in terms of goals, objectives, and plans. Leaders organize the resources available and delegate responsibility to those who follow, translating the vision into the ownership of individual actions. Success is measured by the outcomes, productivity, and accomplishment of the mission. Chapter 3 will explore how relational leadership influences through vision.

---

22. Kouzes and Posner, *Credibility*, 12.

The relational responsibility of leadership is also well known, but until recently has been given less attention. Through the relationships of leadership, values and beliefs are reinforced in the culture or character of the organization. Over time the organizational community develops its own unique culture—its way of working together—shaped significantly by the values of its leadership. That culture, whether stated explicitly in core values, norms, standards, and plans or assumed implicitly, clarifies expectations for those who work in the organization and constrains their behavior.

The experience people have within an organization is a direct result of their engagement with the culture, and it contributes significantly to their level of personal fulfillment and satisfaction. The values of leadership, embedded in the organizational culture, create the context in which people work and determine whether they will find meaning and achieve their potential. Chapters 4 and 5 will develop the leadership influence of values and relationships.

These connections are pictured graphically in the chart on the following page.

It all starts with theology. The God we choose to follow shapes everything else. Theology shapes character; character fuels leadership. Leadership is responsible for strategic vision and relational connections. Recent research in the field of emotional intelligence has demonstrated that the bottom half of this chart—the emotional-relational connections of theology, character, leadership, culture, and environment—is twice as important as the top half—the purpose, vision, mission, and organization—in predicting productivity and accomplishment.[23] Twice as important! We influence others through vision and organization, but the most significant influence of leadership flows through values and relationships. As Jude reminds us, leadership starts with theology—our

---

23. Daniel Goleman, *Working with Emotional Intelligence* (New York: Bantam Books, 1998), 320.

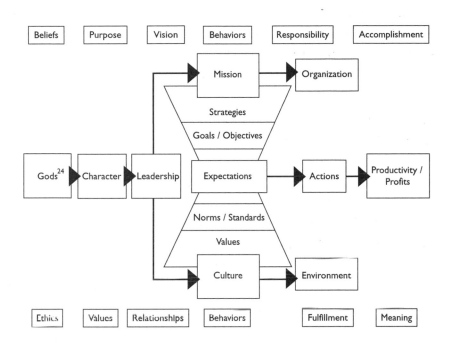

relationship with God—and it influences others through vision, values, and relationships.

Theology matters. In this chapter we've seen how Jude calls us to examine our leadership in light of the God we choose to follow, to ground our relationships with others in our relationship with God. This shapes everything else. In chapter 2 we will look at the character of a biblical servant leader and the leadership that flows from first being a follower.

---

24. The plural form of *Gods* is intentional. Those of us who follow Jesus tend to relax because we believe we know what God we have in the box. Research shows, however, that the behaviors of the people we lead are determined by the gods we follow, revealed through the values we demonstrate in the leadership relationship. Only a study of our behaviors and relationships can surface all of the gods we allow to control our actions. For most of us since Adam and Eve one competing god is ego—myself.

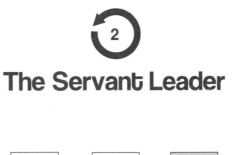

The Servant Leader

L eadership begins with God. And Jude provides us with an outline for approaching the topic of relational leadership: five biblical principles drawn from the struggles of his own Christian community. Each chapter in this study will explore one of these principles and apply it to the contemporary context of leadership and organizations.

These principles and the struggles they address are not unique to Jude's community. They speak to the core of the leadership relationship in every community of people that seeks to organize itself around a vision or purpose. The Bible is filled with stories of men and women and communities attempting to work out an effective model of relational leadership. My favorite biblical drama is the story of the Colossian church as we see it in Paul's letters to the Colossians and to Philemon—a community struggling with issues of leadership, relationship, diversity, and conflict. The story of the Colossian church is the story of human organizations. And each player in this drama has something to teach us about relational leadership and organizational community. As we move from the context of Jude's situation to leadership in the twenty-first century, I would like to locate each leadership principle in the real-life narrative of Colosse. The leaders, servants, and community there present a model for relational leadership that defines what it means to be leaders who serve. There is a place for each of us in the story of Onesimus, Philemon, Tychicus, and Paul.

Shepherds: Servants Assigned to Care for the Sheep

In the first chapter, I set the theme for this study by looking at Jude, the half brother of Jesus, as he critiques those who would be leaders in his Christian community. His little letter offers us two contrasting pictures of a leader. On the one hand we see Jude, humbly pointing away from himself—taking on the responsibility of a servant rather than claiming his legitimate status as a brother of the Lord. On the other hand we see the active and visible leaders of the community, using their roles for their own benefit and growing fat off of the flock—*shepherds who feed only themselves.*

In Jude's biting words, in the contrasts posed by his letter, we see the biblical model of leadership. Shepherds are there for the sheep! Shepherds by definition are servants entrusted with the care of the flock.

> Leadership is about service, about shepherds who care for the sheep.

They hold a position of responsibility and service, not of status and power. The sheep do not exist for the shepherd. The shepherd was hired because of the sheep.

Onesimus: Leader as Servant

Enter the narrative of the Colossian church. Step into the sandals of Onesimus. How would you feel? You finally got away from the work that was grinding you down, burning you out. Perhaps you did leave with some uncomfortable circumstances, but you took the step. You left to find yourself, to figure out what you are going to do with your life. Away from your home, far from the responsibility of your work, you have time to do some thinking. And some of that thinking may be life-changing!

In relationship with new friends, you begin to put the pieces of your life together. In the context of a new community, you meet the resurrected Christ and begin to think through the implications of his claim upon your life. A place like this—away from the pressures and responsibilities of your normal life—is a gift from God, a privilege to be enjoyed and cherished. It is an opportunity to grow and to be changed. You feel like a different person in this supportive community with these encouraging friends.

But now you have to go back. Back to your community, back perhaps to uncomfortable circumstances, to old responsibilities and liabilities. You go back a new person, or at least a renewed person. What does it feel like to leave this supportive community that nurtures your new growth and development, to go back to the people you left behind?

That's the position in which Onesimus found himself. He had left his life in Colosse, where he had been a slave on the staff of Philemon, a well-known leader in the Colossian church. Illegally he had run off, betraying his relationship of trust, and—probably to finance his trip— he stole from his master before he went.

Somehow, in his flight he ended up with the apostle Paul. We do not know the circumstances of how they met or how Paul ended up convincing Onesimus to become a follower of Christ. But we do know that a strong relationship developed between Onesimus and his new friend and mentor. He stayed with Paul, learned from him, cared for him, and was loved by Paul in return. A close bond was formed between the two. But somewhere in his education, somewhere in the discipling process, Paul and Onesimus agreed that it was time for him to return to Colosse—to go back to his community, return to his position as a slave to Philemon, restore the broken relationships, and learn to serve God and grow within that community.

Paul writes a letter to Philemon to pave the way for Onesimus' return, building strongly on his personal relationships with Philemon and Onesimus. He also writes a letter to the Colossian church to encourage them since they will provide the context of Christian community in which the reconciliation of one of their elders and his newly converted runaway slave must take place.

Paul then gives both letters and Onesimus to another friend and colleague, Tychicus, and sends him off to Colosse to make this all work—to show that Christian faith can be integrated into the fabric of life and work and relationships, that Christian community can deal with conflict and forgiveness and new beginnings. Paul hopes to encourage Philemon, Onesimus, and the Colossians to listen to and learn from each other as they work out how their common faith will lead them through their damaged relationships and pain.

Three things strike me about Onesimus' return to Colosse: he is stepping out of his comfort zone; he has a mentor to encourage him; and he is going back to serve.

Stepping out of the comfort zone

It must have been a painful experience for Onesimus to leave Paul and return to Colosse. Not only was he leaving the man who had introduced him to Jesus, he was leaving a mentor and a community of encouragement—a network of supportive relationships. He was leaving a place where he could grow, a place where he was loved, a place that valued him and his contributions, a place where his personal spiritual pilgrimage was understood. Onesimus was leaving the safety of a community that had shared his experience and nurtured his growth to go to one that was predisposed to receive him with hostility. He was leaving the comfort and security of the known to risk the unknown future.

Yet Paul and Onesimus agreed that he must leave the comfort of the community and return if he was to grow personally and make a difference in the lives of the people in Colosse. Leadership is about leaving your comfort zone and taking a risk to engage those around you.

The tradition of the early church frequently equates the Onesimus of our story with the later Bishop Onesimus of Ephesus. This cannot be proved. But if it is true, the runaway slave from Colosse learned well from his mentors and became one who was regarded as a leader and teacher in the church. From a slave of Philemon, mentored by Paul, Onesimus may have become the bishop of Ephesus, leading the leaders of the church.

Taking mentors with you

The second thing I see in the Onesimus story is the importance of encouraging relationships. Paul did not send Onesimus back to Colosse alone. He sent him with a mentor—Tychicus.

Tychicus is the least-known player in this Colossian drama. He is a friend and colleague of Paul who was with Onesimus during his conversion and growth. He knows Onesimus well, and we can assume that he has become an important friend to the converted slave.

When Paul sends Onesimus back to Colosse, he surely sends him out in the power of God. But he also sends with him a friend to support and encourage him as he returns home. Tychicus is there to encourage Onesimus as he faces Philemon: to confront Onesimus if fear makes him falter, to pave the way for him with Philemon and the Colossian church, and to pray for him and give advice as needed.

Again, the story has parallels for today. Whether taking up new responsibilities of leadership or continuing in service, we all need mentors and friends to guide and inspire, to challenge and support us as we live and work. All of us need a Tychicus to encourage us and hold us accountable for our growth and our calling. If you do not have such a relationship in your setting, I encourage you to find such a relationship and commit to one another to keep in touch and provide the caring encouragement, the listening ear, and the loving accountability that we all need. Leadership is risky business. It takes more from the servant leader than it gives. We need one another.

A number of years ago a very competent leader accepted the position of president at a Canadian theological school. Within six months he had encountered enough problems to drive him to despair. During Easter week he had a major conflict with his faculty and board. With no one to encourage him and hold him up before God, he walked back to his office and killed himself. That is extreme, and it is incredibly tragic. It is hard to understand, but it underlines the vulnerability of leadership as we leave our security and comfort and go out to serve.

We need to hold one another up before God and engage in encouraging relationships. Stop and reflect: Who is your Tychicus? Who stands with you as you exercise your leadership responsibilities? Who keeps you focused on whom you intend to be?

Going back to serve

The third thing we can learn from Onesimus may be the most important. He is going back to serve. In our familiarity with Bible stories, we look at what God has accomplished in his grace and often forget the feelings or anxieties of the person. We hear about Onesimus the bishop and assume that God is sending Onesimus back to Colosse to become a bishop. Maybe this is true, but Onesimus certainly does not know it! Paul is only asking Philemon to receive him as a brother *and* reinstate him as his slave.

Onesimus is going back to serve. He does not go back a free man. He goes back as Philemon's servant. The very act of returning to Colosse was an acknowledgment of this status and a willingness to serve. Maybe Onesimus did become a bishop. But he did not go back to Colosse to be a bishop and do something great for God. He returned to be a servant.

Herman Hesse, in his novel *The Journey to the East*, describes a quest to discover the high council of a secret order in the East. The main characters are seeking to meet the leader of this society and be introduced to the fundamental truth of life. Throughout their journey they are guided and assisted by a servant assigned to care for them, carry their luggage, and ease their passage. At the end of the journey, when they finally arrive at the grand throne room of the society, who should walk out in the golden robes of the league president but their servant![1]

Onesimus returned to Colosse after a time of instruction and growth with Paul and his friends. He left comfort behind, and returned to Colosse with a friend to take his position as a slave to Philemon and a servant to his new master, Jesus Christ. That is the calling of the biblical leader! We are called to be servants of Jesus Christ who care for the people who have been entrusted to us and point them to God in every act of leadership and service that we undertake. Leadership is a relationship of service—a relationship in which influence and leadership flow from service, not from position or status.

Leadership: A Relationship of Influence

What is this thing called leadership? The leadership model that I work from has become popular over the last three decades. Researchers, consultants, and corporate and nonprofit executives have observed a transition in leadership models evolving in the West in recent years. This "new paradigm," as it is sometimes labeled, reached popular acceptance with the publication, in 1982, of *In Search of Excellence*.[2] Tom Peters and Robert Waterman were the first to put the new research

---

1. Herman Hesse, *The Journey to the East* (New York: Noonday Press, 1956), 98. It is with this story that Robert Greenleaf launches his foundational work on servant leadership in *Servant Leadership* (New York: Paulist Press, 1977).
2. Thomas J. Peters and Robert H. Waterman Jr., *In Search of Excellence* (New York: Harper & Row, 1982).

findings in a popular form that captured the attention of leaders, particularly in North America. Since the appearance of their book on the management bestseller lists, a steady stream of publications have continued to present a model of leadership that is relational, vision-driven, and value-shaped. Peter Drucker, Peter Block, Warren Bennis, Max De Pree, Steven Covey, James O'Toole, Charles Handy, Peter Senge, Daniel Goleman, Ronald Heifetz, Jean Lipman-Blumen, James Kouzes, Barry Posner, Barbara Kellerman, and many other names have become familiar to readers of leadership literature.

While many of these writers are committed Christians and support a relational approach to leadership because of its recognizable grounding in biblical values, the model has emerged primarily because it works. It treats people with dignity, offers hope, and gives meaning, but the bottom line for most organizations is that it has proven effective in addressing the organization's mission. I want to look at a pragmatic model for leadership that I believe is founded on strong biblical principles. The beliefs, convictions, and commitments that shape our character—the God that we choose to follow—frame our relationships of leadership and the vision and values we influence.

We need to remember that we are talking about an intentional model for leadership—a proven model—but not necessarily one that can be found consistently lived in many organizations. It sets out the principles against which we can measure our leadership and against which we see our shortcomings. I sought to live out at Regent College everything I talk about here, but those who have been to Regent know that we experienced all of the struggles of any human community. Nevertheless, before God we kept trying. Now, at the Max De Pree Center for Leadership, I work with a team of principals committed to encourage business and nonprofit organizations as they seek to live out this model.

I should also underline here that I am writing out of my experience and reading which has been heavily centered in North America.

Moving to Canada in 1988, I observed subtle but distinct differences between Canadian and American attitudes toward leadership. I do not pretend to know much about the cultural assumptions and structures that shape leadership in other parts of the world. If you work in a different cultural setting, or even if you serve within a particular ethnic subculture within North America, please remember that, like most writers, I see things from a particular perspective, and you will need to work with me to translate these ideas into the appropriate context for your setting. However, I do want to explore some guiding principles for leadership that I believe are both effective and biblical.

So, what is leadership? What is leadership all about? What is a leader? In this chapter and the next (on vision) I will focus primarily on the leader. In the remaining three chapters I will try to be a little more practical and look at strategies for serving as a leader.

People have been defining leadership for years. The variety of technical and anecdotal definitions is extensive and often more confusing than clarifying. Gary Yukl, in *Leadership in Organizations*, defines leadership as "the influence process whereby intentional influence is exerted by the leader over followers."[3] Paul Hersey and Kenneth Blanchard, in their vintage text, *Management of Organizational Behavior*, see leadership as a broader concept than management. If management is working with and through individuals and groups to accomplish organizational goals, "leadership occurs any time one attempts to influence the behavior of an individual or group, regardless of the reason."[4]

> **Leadership is a relationship of influence.**

---

3. Gary A. Yukl, *Leadership in Organizations* (Englewood Cliffs, NJ: Prentice Hall, 1981), 3. See also Howard Gardner, *Leading Minds* (New York: Basic Books, 1996), 8–9.

4. Paul Hersey and Kenneth H. Blanchard, *Management of Organizational Behavior* (Englewood Cliffs, NJ: Prentice Hall, 1988), 5.

Leadership is a relationship

Leadership is first and foremost a relationship between two people. Even in a group or organizational setting where we may be responsible for leading a number of persons, we are still leading in the context of specific relationships. Leader and follower, or as John Gardner, the author of *On Leadership*, likes to say, leader and constituent—two people engaged in a relationship.[5] That is the specific context of leadership.

Leadership is influence

In the definitions to which I just referred, leadership is defined as the process of one person influencing another. It is a relationship of influence in which the leader seeks to influence the behavior, attitudes, vision, values, or beliefs of another. It is an intentional relationship with a purpose—a relationship of influence.

In his taxonomy of leadership research, Gary Yukl identifies eleven different forms of influence used by leaders today.[6] Knowing the specific types is not nearly as important as recognizing that we lead or influence others in a variety of ways. Leadership is more than telling someone to do something. In fact, research has shown that leaders who seek to lead primarily with the first three types of influence described below may be quite effective when they are physically present, but they lose their ability to influence and lead the follower when they are not present. Yukl's influence types can be described as follows:

- **Legitimate request**

   The leader is directive and requests that the follower do a particular thing. The follower recognizes the authority or "right" of the leader to make the request and responds accordingly.

   Example: An executive asks an assistant to prepare a report, and the influence is accepted. The report

---

5. John W. Gardner, *On Leadership* (New York: Free Press, 1990), 2.

6. Yukl, *Leadership in Organizations*, 10–17.

is prepared because both know the assistant was hired for such a purpose and that the request is legitimate.

- **Instrumental compliance**

  The follower believes that the action requested by the leader will provide a specific desirable outcome promised by the leader. The leader in this case is still directive but needs to convince the follower to act and has the ability to reward the carrying out of his or her wishes.

  Example: If my students turn in a paper for my class they can receive credit for the course.

- **Coercion**

  Here the follower acts to avoid adverse outcomes implied in a failure to act. The leader again needs to convince the follower to act and possesses the ability to punish the follower for not complying.

  Example: Failure to turn in the paper for my class will result in a failing grade for the course.

- **Rational faith**

  The follower acts because he or she has faith in the expertise or credibility of the leader. The leader is believed to have the knowledge or competence to be followed. This type of influence may be a directive request, a consultative dialogue, or simply the offering of advice.

  Example: The church board will listen to the pastor on worship issues because he or she has been trained in spiritual leadership and worship.

- **Rational persuasion**

  The follower is convinced that the action desired by the leader is appropriate and the best way for the follower to accomplish his or her own personal objectives. With this type of influence, the leader moves away from directive leadership and moves into consultative dialogue, seeking to persuade the follower that this is a good thing to do.

Example: Kevin agreed to take on a research project for the trustees because he could use it for his doctoral dissertation.

- **Inspirational appeal**

  In this type of influence the follower responds because it makes him or her feel good and supports his or her values. The leader is making an appeal to the values of the follower.

  Example: The pastor urges a member to visit a parishioner in the hospital as a Christian service to the congregation.

- **Indoctrination**

  Here Yukl talks about a situation in which the follower internalizes values or beliefs that will cause the action to happen as natural behavior. This type of influence is almost completely nondirective. There may not even be a visible link between the efforts of the leader to pass on values and beliefs and the response of the follower acting out of those values. And yet it may be one of the most powerful forms of influence that we use as biblical leaders.

  Example: In many ways, while church leaders might not like Yukl's label, "indoctrination," this is what we are about in Christian education, confirmation, preaching, and the teaching of theology. We are seeking to embed a set of values and beliefs that will cause Christlike behavior to emerge naturally throughout a person's life.

- **Information distortion**

  This is another uncomfortable label, but a frequently used influence type. Here the follower receives only the data that will stimulate the desired action. The rest is screened out by the leader. When information is selectively given, it can produce a desired action. When we offer only one recommendation to our people, omitting possible alternatives, they will probably choose what we recommend.

  Example: Telling you the office lock does not work and someone entered the church and took a purse will get one response. Telling you the purse was taken by one of the preschoolers in the church because there is not enough supervision will provoke a different response—even if both are true. That is what Yukl calls "information distortion." And we use this type more often then we are probably comfortable admitting.

- **Situational engineering**

  Here the leader changes the follower's situation to make a particular action more advantageous.

  Example: The placement of desks in an office will either facilitate or discourage conversations. Passing the offering plate from person to person on Sunday morning is more conducive to increasing the offering than having people stop by the treasurer's office on the way out.

- **Personal identification**

  This type is similar to rational faith. Here the follower copies the actions or behavior of someone who is respected and admired. This relationship is what mentoring is about when formally acknowledged. But note that this kind of influence is going on all the time whether we know it or not. People watch leaders and learn. Our actions and behaviors teach as much about our beliefs and values as our words. People who admire leaders will copy their behaviors and be influenced by them without the leader necessarily knowing.

Research has shown that this type of influence, this building of personal relationships often called *referential power*, is the most effective leadership when the leader is not with the follower. It is leadership that lasts. I often tell faculty members that they teach as much by what they do between classes as by what they teach in class. People watch people they like and are influenced by their behavior. Leaders are models.

Example: One day as I was buying a cup of coffee at Regent's coffee bar I overheard a student in line behind me commenting to another student, "Look, the president is paying for his coffee." I'm not sure what concept of leaders they had that would cause them to think otherwise, but the point driven home again for me was the fact that people are watching—even watching little things like whether you pay for coffee like they do or expect special treatment because you are leader.

• **Decision identification**

This one is also important in relational leadership. When people are involved in the planning and decision-making process, when they feel like part of a team, they take ownership of the action. Participative management, team building, and letting people share in decisions that will impact their lives and work creates an ownership of outcomes that greatly facilitates appropriate actions. With this style of influence we have moved completely away from directive leadership into the realm of participation and delegation.

Now, why bother with defining influence types? Again, let me repeat that knowing these eleven types is not what is important. What is important is recognizing that leadership is much more than giving direction. We influence in relationship. We influence by our decisions and our actions. *Leadership is a relationship of influence.*

Leadership exists by the choice of followers

This important principle is often overlooked. I am regularly surprised by leaders who assume that they are leaders because of their position or because they want to be leaders.

David Hubbard, the former president of Fuller Seminary and a friend and mentor of mine, liked to tell a story about his grandson Jeffrey. Once when David and his wife Ruth were walking in the park with Jeffrey, they began to stroll off in one direction while Jeffrey was still playing. Seeing them leaving, Jeffrey came running, his chubby little legs churning, calling out, "Wait for me. I'm the leader!"

Having the title of leader does not mean you are providing leadership. We can exert every one of the influence types we have just reviewed, but unless someone *chooses* to accept that influence, we have not led. It is very important for those of us in leadership to remember that our followers always have a choice and that our leadership is always dependent upon their choosing to follow.[7]

Leadership is a relationship; and, like all relationships, it requires at least two parties: a leader and a follower. Both players are critical to the relationship. Both are necessary if leadership is to be exercised. And

---

7. Jim Collins, *Good to Great and the Social Sectors: A Monograph to Accompany Good to Great* (New York: HarperCollins, 2005), 13.

both provide leadership.[8] Followers also seek to influence outcomes. In recent years the literature of management and leadership has begun to recognize the lack of attention paid to followership.[9]

The leadership relationship has been explored in depth from a leader-centric perspective, almost as though the followers have nothing to do with it. Yet, as Barbara Kellerman observes at the beginning of her significant study entitled *Followership*, "Leaders themselves are following their followers more closely now than ever before." She closes her book with the suggestion that "followers are more important to leaders than leaders are to followers."[10] In a relationship of influence everyone has some influence, and the exercise of leadership is determined by the choice to follow.

My grandson Brendon is eight years old. He has no title, no positional authority, but he has immense power to influence my behavior. Through the loving relationship of grandparent and grandchild he regularly exercises leadership, influencing what I do and say. When he was only five years old he illustrated brilliantly the reality that leadership is a relationship of influence, not a position or a person.

My son and his family live north of San Francisco, in Marin County, and have a guesthouse on their property. One summer the CEO of a company in San Francisco and his wife and daughter stayed in the guesthouse for several weeks while their own home was being remodeled. During this time they took a vacation to Hawaii. The CEO asked Brendon if he would feed their cat while they were away. The CEO offered ten cents per day. Brendon thought for a moment and responded, "No, that isn't enough for me to have to remember it every day."

The CEO countered, "OK, I'll give you twenty-five cents a day."

---

8. Joseph Rost, "Followership: An Outmoded Concept," in *The Art of Followership*, eds. Ronald E. Riggio, Ira Chaleff, and Jean Lipman-Blumen (San Francisco: Jossey-Bass, 2008), 56.

9. Robert E. Kelley, "Rethinking Followership," in *Art of Followership*, eds. Riggio, Chaleff, and Lipman-Blumen, 11.

10. Barbara Kellerman, *Followership* (Boston: Harvard Business Press, 2008), 46, 242.

Brendon replied, "No, that still isn't enough to have to do it every day."

So the CEO asked Brendon how much he wanted. Brendon suggested one dollar per day, and negotiations began. They settled on fifty cents per day to feed the cat while the CEO's family was on vacation.

On the morning of their trip, the CEO took Brendon out to the guesthouse, showed him the cat food and the bowls, and restated the agreement: "You will feed the cat every morning and I will give you fifty cents per day. Do you have any questions?"

Brendon looked up at him with his large blue eyes and innocently asked, "Did you want water also?" . . . That was another fifty cents per day!

Neither position, authority, age, nor charisma are the determiners of leadership. Leadership is exercised whenever one person influences the vision, values, attitudes, or behavior of another and the other person chooses to act. Leadership is dependent upon the choice to follow, whether CEO or five-year-old.

Leadership style is adapted to follower competence and confidence

Leaders are dependent upon followers who choose to accept their influence. This dependency of the leader upon followers is what makes the leadership relationship so important. Leaders must adjust their attempts to influence and shape their leadership to the follower they want to influence.

Paul Hersey and Kenneth Blanchard have developed a leadership model that sees leadership as a relational continuum with four distinct styles of leadership behavior tied directly to the specific follower. Their excellent book, *Management of Organizational Behavior*, describes this model, often called contingency leadership or situational leadership.[11]

---

11. Hersey and Blanchard, *Management of Organizational Behavior*, 171.

Situational Leadership®

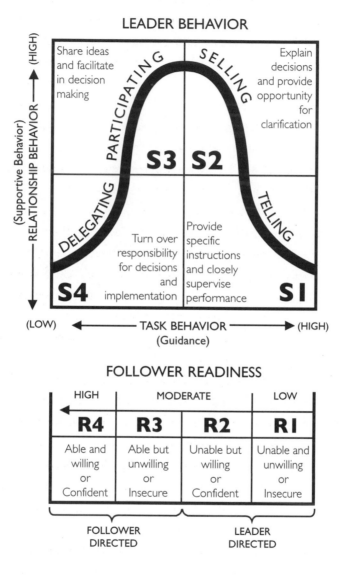

LEADER BEHAVIOR

Share ides and facilitate in decision making	Explain decisions and provide opportunity for clarification
PARTICIPATING SELLING	
S3 **S2**	
DELEGATING	TELLING
Turn over responsibility for decisions and implementation	Provide specific instructions and closely supervise performance
S4	**S1**

(LOW) ◄——— TASK BEHAVIOR ———► (HIGH)
(Guidance)

(Supportive Behavior)
RELATIONSHIP BEHAVIOR (HIGH)

FOLLOWER READINESS

HIGH	MODERATE		LOW
R4	**R3**	**R2**	**R1**
Able and willing or Confident	Able but unwilling or Insecure	Unable but willing or Confident	Unable and unwilling or Insecure

FOLLOWER DIRECTED   LEADER DIRECTED

Note: Situational Leadership® is a registered trademark of the Center for Leadership Studies, Inc. All rights reserved. Reprinted with permission.

The model has two axes representing two continua. One relates to the amount of task-directive behavior the leader uses and the other measures the amount of relational support the leader provides. Task-directive behavior ranges from telling someone exactly what to do to full delegation, in which the person makes his or her own choices. Relational support behavior ranges from standing alongside someone, "holding their hand" and encouraging him or her, to standing back and trusting the follower to do it without you. When these continua are plotted on horizontal and vertical axes, the model makes it possible to identify four quadrants or leadership styles. Hersey and Blanchard label these telling, selling, participating, and delegating.

A *telling* style of leadership is highly task-directive with little relational encouragement. The *selling* style remains fairly directive but engages in much more relationally supportive behavior. The *participating* style is much less directive but retains a high level of relational support. Finally, the *delegating* style is quite nondirective and provides minimal relational support, trusting the follower to run with the task.

The most important element in this model, however, is not the four leadership styles themselves but the direct relationship between leadership style and the maturity of the follower.

Hersey and Blanchard identify four levels of maturity in followers. At the lowest level, the followers don't know how to do the task and lack confidence in their ability to do it, so therefore they are not willing to accept responsibility for the task. When followers are low in competence and in confidence, the model suggests that the most effective leadership style will be telling: directive explanation of what needs to be done with little relational encouragement or hand-holding that might reinforce their unwillingness to take responsibility.

At the next level of maturity, the followers still don't know how to do the task but they are willing to learn and want to accept responsibility for the assignment. Hersey and Blanchard call for a selling or consultative style of leadership when the followers are low in competence but high in confidence. Here the leader remains directive, telling the followers what they need to know to do the job, but engages them relationally to reinforce their willingness to accept responsibility.

At the third level of maturity, the followers basically know how to do the job but lack confidence in their ability to do it alone. Contingency leadership adapts to a participating style that becomes nondirective but participates in close relationship, encouraging and believing in the person to bolster confidence.

The highest level of maturity assumes that the followers know how to do the work and are willing to accept responsibility to see that it is accomplished. The best style of leadership now, say Hersey and Blanchard, is delegating. There is no need to be directive since they know how to do the job, and hanging around in close relationship only creates a dependence upon the leader. We need to get out of their way and trust them to lead out in getting the work done. The leader steps into the background but is available when the follower seeks assistance.

This is only a model—a representation of two competing responsibilities of leadership: the accomplishment of the task or mission and the care and development of the followers. It is not a precise formula for resolving the complexities of human relationships! Contingency theory or situational leadership can be helpful in clarifying leadership responsibility or it can be used as an excuse for poor leadership.[12] The importance of the model is that it graphically represents several key leadership principles.

- **Leaders must adapt their leadership style to the maturity of their followers.**

  The way you choose to lead is not up to you. It is determined

---

12. James O'Toole, *Leading Change* (San Francisco: Jossey-Bass, 1995), 7–8, worries that contingency leadership allows leaders to default to their most comfortable directive style whenever they find themselves in a complex or difficult situation, which is most of the time. When this happens, O'Toole says, contingency leadership is ineffective.

by the maturity level of the person you seek to influence. A preference for a relational, coaching style of leadership may have high value to the leader but not necessarily be effective in every case. Difficult followers may need a more disciplined, directive approach to get them moving. Highly relational leadership could be perceived as too "soft" and ignored. You may need to step out of your preferred style. Similarly, a high-achieving follower could perceive an extremely relational style as suffocating and lacking in trust—exactly the opposite of what was intended.

If leadership is exercised only when a follower chooses to follow, it behooves leaders to understand the competence and confidence levels of the persons they seek to influence.

- **Followers range back and forth on the maturity continuum.**
  People do not stay at one level of maturity. A problem at home or on the way to work can reduce a person's confidence level. A change in the way things are done can reduce their competence level. A very simple example of this occurred when computers were introduced in offices. Suddenly, mature secretaries who had been operating efficiently in quadrant four without much direct supervision lacked competence and in many cases lost confidence as well.

  The leader needs to recognize these shifts and not be surprised by them. When the situation changes, the maturity level changes; and the leader needs to adapt to the appropriate leadership style. The secretaries needed explicit instruction in the use of computers before their competence and confidence could be brought back up to the highest level.

- **The goal of leadership is to move people up the readiness continuum.**
  The aim of leadership is to increase the competence and confidence of all our people so that we can delegate leadership to

them. This is one of the purposes of leadership. We want to grow people. We want to invest in them to move them all, if possible, to the highest levels of maturity so that they can serve as leaders in their particular areas.

Success in leadership is measured by the growth of your followers: not by how *many* followers you have, but by how much each person grows under your leadership. In Christian circles we call this process discipling.

The importance of the contingency model of leadership is the reminder that leaders must be adaptable. You must be able to change your leadership style to match the maturity level of your followers in order to grow them. Leaders who are not adaptable tend to keep followers at a one static level of maturity.

A Complementary-Empowering Model of Ministerial Leadership

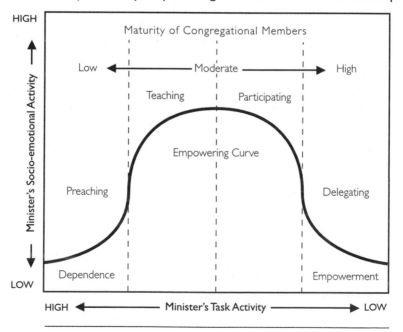

Jack Balswick and I modified this model from our biblical understanding of leadership into what we called a Complementary-Empowering Model of Ministerial Leadership.[13] We reversed the task continuum and changed the labels to preaching, teaching, participating, and delegating.

In addition, we added two primary elements to the situational model. First, we wanted to underline what we called the *empowering curve*—adjusting the relationship between the leader and the follower to move from dependence to empowerment. This means moving decisions from the leader to the follower because, in many ways, the power to decide is the power to lead.

In the *preaching* style, the leader decides and tells the follower what to do by proclamation. The *teaching* style acknowledges the relationship. There is consultation, and the leader decides only after hearing the opinions of the follower. In the *participating* style, the leader and the follower make the decision together. And in the *delegating* style the decision is delegated to the follower to make.

The second point Jack and I wanted to make focuses on adaptability. As Hersey and Blanchard have underlined, leadership must be adaptable. Leaders must be able to range from telling to delegating in their leadership behavior. For some that is natural, for others it is hard to learn. Some leaders simply work best in one style, with one level of follower maturity. While such leadership may be effective, it does not grow people.

Drawing on the biblical concept of community and gifted members, we suggested that it may be better to have a complementary leadership team rather than expecting one leader to work effectively with all four styles. A leadership team of clergy and laity, paid and volunteer, can ensure that someone is available with the requisite skills to provide

---

13. Jack O. Balswick and Walter C. Wright Jr., "A Complementary-Empowering Model of Ministerial Leadership," in *The Best in Theology*, vol. 4, ed. J. I. Packer (Carol Stream, IL: Christianity Today, 1990), 323.

leadership to followers as they are growing through the four stages of maturity. This reduces the burden on a single leader. In the church, a charismatic preaching pastor may need to pass members on to good interactive teachers, who in turn prepare them for coaching by discipling mentors who lead them to the point where they can carry out a piece of the ministry under the supervision of an organizing manager.

Both Jack and I believed (and still do) that leadership teams are often more effective than solo leaders. I will come back to this idea of team building later in this chapter. But before we talk about teams, let me underline a few more principles about leadership.

Leadership is a transforming relationship blending humility and will

In his Pulitzer-Prize winning book *Leadership*, James MacGregor Burns argues that there is an exchange that takes place in every leadership relationship.[14] He calls this exchange *transactional leadership*. He sees the leader and the follower exchanging something. Both gain from the influence type utilized. The followers perceive that it is to their advantage to undertake the requested action, and the leader has set up the request in order to achieve that for which he or she is responsible.

Burns sees this exchange present in every leadership relationship. But he desires more. He argues that great leadership is *transforming leadership*, in which the leader and the follower grow in the process. The relationship lifts both to a higher plane of maturity or morality. Burns wants the leadership relationship to accomplish more than simply making an action happen. He wants the vision, values, and beliefs of the follower to be transformed and enlarged; and in that process he believes the leader's vision, values, and beliefs will also be enriched. Transforming leadership is leadership that makes a difference in the lives of those involved beyond the task that is being completed. It lifts

---

14. James MacGregor Burns, *Leadership* (New York: Harper & Row, 1978), 4.

our eyes up from the task at hand to the horizon before us and to a vision of what we can accomplish together.

Achieving such a transformational relationship requires leadership focused on the accomplishment of the mission and the contributions of the people. Jim Collins, in his highly acclaimed study *Good to Great*, argues persuasively that effective leadership deflects attention from the leader to the shared vision of the organization and the people who will make it happen. Humility is the hallmark of what Collins calls "Level 5 Leadership." Recognizing the critical dependence that leaders have upon followers, Level 5 leaders are appropriately humble about their own contribution, defining their role with visible modesty and thereby enlarging the role that followers play in the organization's success. This humility is blended with a strong professional will to achieve—not to achieve as a leader, but to succeed as an organization. This humble, often self-effacing leadership style teamed with a passion for organizational accomplishment can transform an organization from "good" to "great," realizing the potential of the followers, the leader, and the organization.[15]

Leadership is emotionally empowering

Peter Block is a management consultant who has taken this vision a step further in what he calls *empowerment*. In his best-selling book, *The Empowered Manager*, Block calls for leadership that moves people from dependency to empowerment.[16] He wants to free followers (and leaders) to accept responsibility for their work, for their own lives, and not to become dependent on leaders. Block recognizes that we—leaders *and* followers—easily slip into dependency relationships, looking for others to solve our problems, to accept responsibility for our lives. As

---

15. Jim Collins, *Good to Great* (New York: HarperCollins, 2001), 17–38.
16. Peter Block, *The Empowered Manager* (San Francisco: Jossey-Bass, 1987), 15.

we journey through life, with all its ambiguities, it is easy to abdicate responsibility to someone we think has the answers.

Block sees two emotional forces competing within us: dependency and autonomy. Our dependent side wants to be taken care of, wants someone to give us answers and remove the risk of deciding. Our autonomous side wants control—of ourselves and frequently of those around us. We live and work in the tension of these two emotions.

This tension has been developed in important studies by Daniel Goleman and Jean Lipman-Blumen. Harvard psychologist Daniel Goleman reminds us, in *Primal Leadership*, that effective leaders understand the powerful role of emotion in human relationships.[17] The primal task of leadership is to handle both our own and other people's emotions. Managing emotion is twice as important as intelligence or competence in predicting effective leadership.[18]

We are relational beings who are motivated by powerful emotions as we journey through life. Recent brain research reveals that leading effectively is less about competence than about fostering positive feelings or emotions in the people we seek to influence.[19] Primal leaders understand this. They respond to our needs and address our fears. They empathize with the conflicting forces driving our ambiguity about life, relationships, work, and calling. They take on themselves the risk of uncertainty and offer hope—a vision for the way forward. And we follow leaders who promise a path through the problems before us. We *want* to follow them. We *want* them to show us the way. Yet the very emotion that leads followers to accept influence can lead to the dependency that Block warns against.

---

17. Daniel Goleman, Richard Boyatzis, and Annie McKee, *Primal Leadership: Realizing the Power of Emotional Intelligence* (Boston: Harvard Business School Press, 2002), 5.
18. Daniel Goleman, "What Makes a Leader?" *Harvard Business Review* (November–December 1998): 94.
19. Daniel Goleman and Richard Boyatzis, "Social Intelligence and the Biology of Leadership," *Harvard Business Review* (September 2008): 75.

The tension at the heart of leadership is about choosing to follow without abdicating responsibility for personal growth. Effective leadership resists dependency and empowers followers to own responsibility for their choices and actions. Primal leaders do not offer to answer all of our questions—creating dependency—but they do define the reality in which we must seek our own answers—encouraging empowerment— and they care about us enough to walk with us through that reality.[20]

When followers become dependent, leaders become toxic. Toxic leaders also appeal to emotions. They understand the powerful forces raging at the emotional level of life and relationships; but, as Jean Lipman-Blumen notes in *The Allure of Toxic Leaders*, they promise what they cannot deliver: to keep us safe, to validate us as special, and to ensure that we will always be included.[21] They manage the followers' emotions for their own benefit, taking advantage of the human desire for certainty and need for security. And again, people may follow willingly because leaders guarantee a trail through the jungle. This toxic side of leadership is the other side of dependency, and it can emerge innocently from a wonderful vision of service.

Our passionate commitment to the plight of those around us—to an urgent missional need—can compel us to conviction and clarity sharper than we can sustain. The enthusiasm of our dreams may suggest promises we cannot complete. Toxic leaders define reality clearly. As Peter Block warns, however, they interpret a reality that encourages our dependence upon the leader.[22]

Block seeks leadership that calls people from dependency and empowers them to take responsibility. He wants leaders to model and encourage empowerment. For Block that means deciding on a vision for excellence in your area of responsibility and encouraging everyone

---

20. Max De Pree, *Leadership Is an Art* (East Lansing, MI: Michigan State University Press, 1987), 11.
21. Jean Lipman-Blumen, *The Allure of Toxic Leaders* (Oxford: University Press, 2005), 29.
22. Block, *Empowered Manager*, 22.

else to have such a vision as well. It means believing that followers can grow and develop, that they will accept responsibility for that growth, and that they can live and work empowered by their own visions. Block, like Burns, wants leaders to see in others their potential to be more than they are today and to invest in a relationship with them that gives them the space to become everything that God intends them to become—from a Christian perspective, we might add, a relationship that gives them the space to use and develop the gifts that God has given them.

Max De Pree tells a marvelous story about an empowering factory supervisor. A young man who operated one of the machines in a Herman Miller plant had an automobile accident on the way to his girlfriend's house. He suffered serious injuries, including some brain damage. He obviously could no longer perform his job; and when he came out of his long stay in the hospital he lived with his parents.

Several months after the accident, his supervisor was walking in downtown Grand Rapids and saw the young man hobbling along with a walker, next to his mother. The supervisor greeted them and asked the young man why he wasn't at work. The young man's mother became quite upset, pointing out that her son would never work again. He was permanently crippled and would not talk anymore because of the emotional trauma. The supervisor found out that the young man was living with his parents, both of whom were retired.

The supervisor then told the young man and his mother that Herman Miller had been holding a job for the young man and expected him to be at work the next Monday morning! If his mother did not think he could do the job, then the supervisor expected the mother or the father to cover the job for him. And he said that he would be at their home Monday morning to pick up one of them for work!

When Monday arrived, the young man did come in to work. Over the next weeks either he or his mother or father was there every day, filling the position and drawing the paycheck. However, there was still the problem that he would not talk. The supervisor went to two of the women who worked in the same department as the young man and told them about the situation. They agreed to bring an extra lunch each day and eat lunch with the young man to see if they could get him to talk. Slowly he began to open up to them and then to others at the plant. This progressed for a period of several months, until the young man was able to return to his original position as a machine operator.

Several months later, the supervisor was surprised one morning by a car honking outside his house. He went out and found the young man driving his own car, specially fitted for his handicaps, and expressing deep joy and pleasure that he had his job, his income, and now his own car again.[23]

This is empowering leadership: one person using his or her position in the marketplace to serve and nurture another, one person empowering a follower to accept responsibility for the rest of his life, one person seeing in another the potential to be more than is visible today and committing himself or herself to the development of that potential.[24] *This is what servant leadership is all about.*

Servant Leadership: Relational Strategies for Growing People

We have defined leadership as a relationship of influence—a transforming relationship in which the leader invests in the growth and development of the followers, empowering them to become what God has gifted them to be. Now let's look at three practical applications of this empowering model for servant leadership: mentoring, coaching, and team building.

---

23. This story was told by Max De Pree in a public lecture and is used with his permission.
24. The movie *Schindler's List* is another graphic presentation of this kind of empowering leadership.

Mentoring

There is a lot of talk today about mentoring and coaching. Basically this pertains to moving your people along the maturity development continuum: making personal investments in your followers to move them along the continuum toward leadership. Mentoring and coaching are about empowering people.

Traditionally, *mentoring* has been the more formal term, denoting an intentional, exclusive, intensive, volunteer relationship between the leader and the follower. Mentoring is a relational experience in which mentors empower others by sharing themselves, their knowledge, and their experience. Normally the mentor and the follower, the mentoree, agree together to engage in an intentional relationship in which the mentor has the mentoree's permission to guide him or her along a career or personal development path. This guidance occurs in an interactive learning relationship structured around formative questions that can be initiated either by the leader or the follower.

I want to underline the importance of the interactive nature of this relationship, because this is what makes mentoring such a powerful teaching format. Research has shown that, while knowledge can be transmitted in a variety of forms and media, learning occurs in interactive relationships. Mentoring is an interactive learning relationship, providing a significant point of connection in an increasingly fragmented world.

For me, mentoring began with Donald Bubna, a pastor in San Diego. Don came alongside me as a mentor during my teenage years and patiently discipled me into leadership roles in our church and through decisions about the direction of my life and calling. Don was the first of a string of mentors who made themselves available to me during my leadership journey.

What started with Don Bubna continues today with Max De Pree, a wise leader with whom I meet regularly to reflect on my life and leadership. I have been in a mentoring relationship with Max for over twenty-five years. I have always admired his consistent integration of faith and leadership. Max lives out of a value-shaped character that I would like to emulate. Our relationship is primarily follower-controlled. I am one of a privileged few persons that Max engages in such relationships, and I have access to him for a half-day two or three times each year. These meetings are usually set up at my initiative. I bring the agenda to each meeting and draw on his wisdom—what he is learning these days and how he would reflect on my current successes and struggles. His profound insights always send me away with a different perspective on my leadership efforts. I have written in detail about this journey elsewhere, distilling what I learned about leadership and mentoring from these rich resources.[25] But let me summarize here briefly.

Mentoring is a teaching-learning relationship between two persons. It is intentional when a mentor comes alongside a person—as Don Bubna did with me—or when a mentoree recognizes a need for learning and seeks out a resource mentor—as I did with Max De Pree. Mentoring is exclusive in the sense that it is focused on the growth of a particular mentoree as perceived by that mentoree. It is a relationship shaped by mentorees who accept responsibility for their own development. Mentoring is intensive in that it normally has focus. The mentoree's learning needs define where mentoring is desired, and mentoring relationships intentionally focus on the mentoree's developing vision, values, perspective, knowledge, or skills. It is voluntary; mentorees choose mentors to guide them along a particular portion of their journey. Like leadership, it is always about choice. Both mentor and mentoree choose to commit themselves to this learning relationship. Mentoring happens when one person chooses to listen to and learn from another.

---

25. Walter C. Wright Jr., *Mentoring: The Promise of Relational Leadership* (Milton Keynes, UK: Paternoster, 2004).

Mentoring is a relationship with a purpose. There is no formula, no ideal model, and no program of steps to success. It is a relationship connected by a shared interest in learning and growth, and it must be constantly nurtured and recreated. It has purpose and structure defined by the learning needs of the mentoree and shaped by the wisdom and experience of the mentor. It is more than leadership. Good leaders seek to be mentors and create space for people to grow into their potential. But leadership, as noted above, nurtures personal development in the context of organizational objectives. Mentoring, on the other hand, may nurture organizational competence, but always in the broader context of personal development and growth.

Not every leadership relationship is conducive to mentored learning. It requires a level of promise and trust. But effective leaders bring wisdom, competence, experience, and a deep commitment to the growth of followers. This makes them valuable resources for a follower on a learning journey. Mentors offer a safe place to gain perspective; they provide reflective space. They bring their strengths and weaknesses to the relationship and allow mentorees to learn from both. Mentors provide perspective and wisdom. They critique ideas, provoke thinking, challenge assumptions, and uncover theology. They share their hopes and dreams and model what it means to lead.

Before I reached out to Max De Pree, I was richly rewarded by a manager, Glenn Barker, the provost at Fuller Theological Seminary. For twelve years I had the gift of Glenn teaching me what servant leadership was all about. He was my organizational supervisor, the corporate vice president of the institution. Yet he was much more than that. He took me into his head and his heart. We talked about everything: his vision and passion for the institution, his hopes, dreams, plans, frustrations, theology, family life, and relationships. For twelve years I was privileged to walk with a gifted and successful relational leader. Everything he did, every decision he made, everything he believed and valued, was on the agenda for discussion—the ups and downs, the successes and failures. What an opportunity for learning!

At its heart, leadership is a relationship. In the management of organizations, the development of leadership is greatly enhanced by mentoring relationships because relational leadership and mentoring share a common goal. Both are committed to the growth of men and women to realize their potential and become leaders who influence the people around them. Relational leadership is about growing people. It is about promise and hope. It is about men and women realizing their potential and developing into leaders. Not every mentor is a manager. "But all—absolutely *all*—effective supervisors and managers *should be* mentors."[26] Mentoring is leadership influence focused on growth. It is the promise of relational leadership, the commitment to a person and a future.

The promise of mentoring requires that mentors give thought to why they choose to invest in another person. Mentors, like mentorees, must understand themselves and their motivations. The work of Daniel Goleman and others in the area of emotional intelligence suggests that effective leadership and mentoring are grounded on certain emotional competencies.[27] Effective leaders and mentors rate high in self-awareness, self-control, social awareness, and relationship management. They have accurate self-assessment and corresponding confidence. They manage their emotions with transparency, adaptability, learning, initiative, and optimism. They have high empathy for the feelings of others and great understanding of the relational dynamics of community. And they are good at building relationships. The heart of the relationship will always be tied to the health of the follower or mentoree.

Over the years, as I have gotten older and, hopefully, a little wiser, I have accepted relationships in which I play the mentoring role. Randy, a minister, set up meetings once or twice each year. We met at his initiative for six years. Leslie, an educator and family counselor, set up

26. Chip R. Bell, "Mentoring as Partnership," in *Coaching for Leadership*, eds. Marshall Goldsmith, Laurence Lyons, and Alyssa Freas (San Francisco: Jossey-Bass, 2000), 133.
27. Goleman, Boyatzis, and McKee, *Primal Leadership*, 164.

regular meetings over a ten-year period of her life. Doug, a minister in Alaska, flew to see me once or twice each year to test his learning. We met monthly while he was a student at Regent College. Now we try to work around his trips. Brent was an administrator on the Regent staff. We both understood our relationship as organizationally defined as well as a mentoring relationship. In that context we met weekly in our managerial relationship plus regularly over lunch, in a mentoring relationship, to reflect on his growth. In these times of reflection, in fact at any time, Brent had the right to ask about anything that I was doing at Regent and now at the De Pree Center.

In all of these relationships, I am a learner as well as a mentor. As Leslie completed her doctoral program and Brent worked through an executive MBA program and went on to direct a Canadian foundation, I had the privilege of learning from their learning as well. Sharing yourself usually teaches you something about yourself in the process. It is a good learning experience.

And it is good for your health! Recently the work of Richard Boyatzis and Annie McKee was published in *Resonant Leadership*. Building on current brain research, they studied the impact of leadership on leaders. They found that the unique demands of leadership create "power stress." The exercise of power in relationships—the instrumental, missional twist that power brings to the leadership relationship—causes a dissonance in the brain that elevates stress and has a negative impact on our physiology. It eventually leads to burnout. Leadership is bad for your health. But there is an antidote: renewal. Boyatzis and McKee found that caring relationships, relationships in which we invest in another with no purpose other than to encourage that individual's growth and development in order to become the person he or she wants to be—what I am calling mentoring relationships—are key to renewal and mental and physical health.[28]

---

28. Richard Boyatzis and Annie McKee, *Resonant Leadership* (Boston: Harvard Business School Press, 2005), 205–13.

Mentoring is good for our health. If we are going to engage in leadership relationships, current research suggests that we also need to be investing in mentoring relationships to offset the stress that leadership causes. Mentoring grows followers and heals leaders—a very important strategy for relational leadership.

Coaching

Coaching has evolved significantly over the past two decades. When I first started thinking about coaching it was less structured than mentoring: more a style of management than an individual intentional relationship. It is a way of approaching all of your leadership relationships with a servant's heart, with the mind of a mentor, with the behavior of a player-coach.

Coaching is a developmental approach to leadership—more participative than directive. It sees the leader as servant and friend, not as ruler or boss. Coaches walk with their people, teaching as much by their actions as by their words. Recognizing the emotional-relational reality of organizations, coaching levels the hierarchical structure of the organization and puts the leader among the people. Coaching moves people along the maturity development continuum by walking alongside them.

In their book *A Passion for Excellence*, Tom Peters and Nancy Austin include a long list of traits that they believe describe a good coaching leader.[29] Like Peters and Austin, I see coaching as a way of being with people that encourages and empowers them to realize their potential. Their list includes

> Leveling the hierarchical structure of the organization, coaches walk with their people, teaching as much by their actions as by their words.

many characteristics that I have appreciated in managers and sought to apply in my leadership. Good coaches have high performance and

---

29. Tom Peters and Nancy Austin, *A Passion for Excellence* (New York: Warner Books, 1989), 357–59.

character expectations, and they challenge those who work with them to want to do their best. Because they care about people, they create loyalty in return. They affirm often and publically, and when correction is required they communicate it privately. They encourage ownership of decisions and results, delegating responsibility more than directing behavior. Coaches provide space for learning and growth, and follow up with the forgiveness necessary to learn from mistakes. Second chances are common. I remember one manager calling this approach "the second-mile lifestyle."

Coaches are good listeners, with natural emotional-relational capacity to understand and empathize with others. Coaching leaders are humble, focused on helping others succeed. And they communicate clearly their vision and values. They expect results and commit themselves to help others achieve those results.

Coaching, as Peters and Austin describe it, is a participative approach to leadership in which the leader sees himself or herself as a member of the team, working for the good of the mission, serving the community. The leader is there for the people, not the people for the leader.

Coaching has become more structured over the past two decades. Research in neuroscience has defined the fields of emotional and social intelligence, and specific competencies related to leadership have been identified and popularized by Daniel Goleman and his colleagues.[30] Around the same time, personal trainers became popular, bringing to physical health and exercise what accountants, lawyers, and therapists brought to financial, legal, and mental health. As we increasingly learned to look to specialists for coaching in these arenas, it is not surprising that executive coaching emerged as a professional contractual relationship focusing on leadership development.

---

30. Daniel Goleman, *Working with Emotional Intelligence* (New York: Bantam Books, 1998); Goleman, Boyatzis, and McKee, *Primal Leadership*.

Richard Kilburg defines "executive coaching," in his book with that same title, as "a helping relationship formed between a client who has managerial authority and responsibility in an organization and a consultant who uses a wide variety of behavior techniques and methods to assist the client to achieve a mutually identified set of goals to improve his or her professional performance and personal satisfaction and consequently to improve the effectiveness of the client's organization within a formally defined coaching agreement."[31]

Executive coaches recognize that organizations are struggling to recreate themselves. The conceptual and operational model of management that plans, organizes, staffs, leads, and controls within predictable systems values dependence and fears autonomy. Now organizations are adapting to systems theory, instant communications, flexible manufacturing, terrorism, and the rise of educated, liberated, independent, or interdependent men and women.[32] Kilburg observes, "Leaders, managers, and players at every level in any organization will need to formulate and implement different strategies for survival. These strategies and implementation methods will be based on the fundamental idea that individuals and any sized collective of them increasingly will be self-organizing, self-directing, and self-regulating. Everyone working in organizations will gain mastery of the concepts and skill of reflective self-awareness."[33]

Coaches, like mentors, recognize that effective leadership begins with accurate self-assessment. Leaders need to be in touch with their own strengths and weaknesses, their internal motivations and fears, their beliefs and vulnerabilities. Both coaches and mentors spend time encouraging leaders to mine their experience and reflect on their decisions and actions in order to understand how their feelings affect

31. Richard R. Kilburg, *Executive Coaching: Developing Managerial Wisdom in a World of Chaos* (Washington DC: American Psychological Association, 2000), 65, 67.
32. Ibid., 53–55.
33. Ibid., 55.

them and their behavior. When we know our abilities we are able to lead from our strengths with confidence. Self-management builds on self-assessment; when we know what is going on inside us we can try to manage our emotional reactions.

Self-managed leaders are transparent, living their beliefs and values with integrity. They are more comfortable with ambiguity, more flexible in the face of change or conflict. Attention to emotional control has been shown to increase learning, initiative, optimism, and thus achievement. With healthy self-awareness and control we are more likely to cultivate the necessary competence in social awareness and relationship building. A healthy sense of self increases our empathy for others, therefore helping us to read the emotional responses of followers and the emotional currents flowing through organizations. This ability to extend our emotional reach seems to increase the desire to serve, to see leadership as service to others. Emotionally healthy leaders are relationally influential, investing easily in others and fostering the kind of teamwork that produces healthy organizations.[34]

The Emotional Competency Inventory (ECI) and the Emotional and Social Competency Inventory (ESCI) 360 degree assessment instruments, published and licensed by the Hay Group in Boston, are very effective tools available to leaders and coaches.[35] Based on Daniel Goleman's and Richard Boyatzis' work in emotional and social intelligence, these instruments gather powerful feedback from leaders, followers, and peers about the personal and social maturity of the one being assessed. Leaders can use these exercises to strengthen their own relational influence, to develop emerging leaders, and to understand

---

34. Goleman, Boyatzis, and McKee, *Primal Leadership*, 253–56.

35. See http://www.haygroup.com/tl/Questionnaires_Workbooks/Emotional_ Competency_Inventory.aspx. Here the Hay Group Transforming Learning website notes, "The 360 degree element of the tool means that we collect data from you, your manager, peers, direct reports, and others to give you a complete and accurate picture of how you compare to a target group of successful leaders and managers."

the emotional maturity of their team. After participating in this 360 degree assessment, I have used it as a valuable coaching tool with pastors and executives. Principals in the De Pree Center use it to strengthen the working relationships within management teams. Feedback on our emotional maturity is a prerequisite for effective leadership; people taking time to provide us with that knowledge is a wonderful gift to our own reach for potential.

Mentoring and coaching are about encouraging leaders and followers to realize their potential as they increase their leadership maturity. There is significant overlap between the two strategies. I often make a distinction between mentoring as a relational work of love focused on leadership development within the context of personal growth and coaching as a contractual relationship targeting specific skills and accomplishments within leadership development. Both mentors and coaches ask questions focused on growth. However, I tend to categorize mentors as the persons who ask us defining questions about theology, character, leadership relationships, organizational culture, and personal meaning, while I assign to coaches questions related to leadership vision and skills and organizational mission, structure, and productivity. The former is usually a work of love without financial compensation; the latter is often a business relationship with specific contractual definition. While I do willingly—and, I trust, helpfully—engage in coaching commitments, I find a deep level of satisfaction in the mentoring relationship with its focus on human potential before God.

Team Building

Linked closely to the idea of the leader as a coach or servant is the idea of the followers as a team. In many ways these are two perspectives on the same relationship. Good coaches produce strong teams. How does the leadership relationship look from the perspective of the team?

In the early 1970s, Larry Csonka, who played professional football for the Miami Dolphins, was considered the best fullback in the National Football League. About this time, the World Football League was developing and offering large contracts to the stars of the NFL to entice them to jump to the new league. Csonka told Don Shula, the Dolphins' head coach, that he was considering accepting the offer. Shula responded that it would be a bad idea. However, when Csonka was elected All-Pro fullback again that year he notified Shula that he was leaving Miami to join the WFL. He said, "I'm All-Pro. I'm the best there is, and I'm worth the money."

Shula replied, "No, Larry, you are only All-Pro when you have me for a coach, Bob Griese for a quarterback, and the Miami Dolphin team blocking for you!"

Csonka did jump to the new league, and he basically disappeared from the professional football scene. He was good, but his effectiveness was made possible because he was a member of a great team.[36]

John Gardner, former US Secretary of Health, Education, and Welfare and author of books on leadership, renewal, and excellence, argues that the best leaders form a team with the talent and skills to complement their own.[37]

Today the literature of leadership and management is focusing more and more on team approaches to leadership: coaching, participative management, work groups, and task forces. The effective leader needs to be able to build and motivate a team of people who take ownership for their unit's results and participate in the decisions that affect their work experience. A recent article in the *New York Times* talks about the newest iteration of leadership as CEO Version 3.0: the necessary evolution from empire builders and fix-it men. The demands of

---

36. I first heard this story from Max De Pree, who heard Don Shula tell it at an event in Puerto Rico.

37. Gardner, *On Leadership*, 10.

leadership today call for team builders—leaders who can make people feel like they are working together.[38]

I have favored a team approach to management for years. I have tried to develop teams with "manual" laborers as well as with high-level "knowledge" workers, like the faculty at Regent or the principals of the De Pree Center. I am a strong believer in team leadership, since I know from experience that a team has both more hands and more wisdom than I do, as they see things from a variety of perspectives.

After years of working with teams as a middle manager, I was once asked to lead a workshop on team building. To prepare for this workshop, I asked all of the members of the current team I was leading and all former members of our organization who were still in the area to join me for lunch. I would buy them lunch if they would tell me what it meant to be on an effective team. I asked them to list the characteristics of a good team while I simply took notes. Since that meeting I have tried to keep up with some of the research on team leadership and have found that the elements listed by my team members are supported by the literature on team building.

Here are the elements that people (not only those at that lunch meeting, but teams and leaders in general) identify as important to their experience of working on a team.

- **Ownership of mission and strategies**

   This was a major point. Team members see the office as their unit. They own the goals of the unit and the way we do things. It is their operation, not just mine.

- **Shared visions and dreams**

   I think out loud about everything we are doing. The team knows where we are going and why. This transparency is important because it gives team members a chance to participate in the ideas and dreaming

---

38. Nelson D. Schwartz, "C.E.O. Evolution Phase 3," *New York Times*, November 10, 2007.

long before a decision is made for implementation. This participation creates the ownership they listed first. The dreams and plans become *ours*, not *mine*.

- **Communication of information**

This is basically the same thing. No secrets, no surprises. Information is friendly. The more the team knows, the more it can help. I have always shared nearly all information with my staff, unless it is harmful to their relationship with another person. Open communication and sharing of information develop trust.

Leaders are often nervous about sharing sensitive information or information about possible plans that someone might work against. In forty years of management, only once has a staff member betrayed my trust and used information inappropriately. When this occurred I simply spoke with the person and asked if that meant I could no longer share information. The person was immediately apologetic and vowed that it would not happen again, and it never has.

As president or executive director, however, sharing information can be a little more problematic. Sometimes when I think out loud people hear "policy" and begin to react accordingly. I regularly have to add a preamble in conversation: "We are just thinking and brainstorming; this may not be the way we should go at all." Occasionally my openness about my agendas and thinking does mean that people who disagree can begin to build opposition while I am still trying to test the idea. But I believe that is a risk worth taking. It may create a few more headaches for leadership, but it communicates trust and it earns trust. There may be some who do not like the direction I am leading, but everyone knows where I am going.

- **Relaxed relationships**

This may be more a matter of personal style than a requisite for team management, but it does seem to show up on Peters' and Austin's list of characteristics of a good leader and it does facilitate the relationship building underlined by research in emotional intelligence and leadership. I want to enjoy my work, and I encourage my teams to enjoy themselves as well. I try not to take myself or anyone else too seriously since everything I accomplish is directly tied to their contributions. I try to encourage talking and relaxed relationships while maintaining a professional environment. I want people to look forward to Monday, not Friday! I want them to come to work on Monday eager to see their friends and catch up on the important issues in their lives.

I believe that a team of people who like to be together will be more productive. Recent research in neuroscience confirms this. Leaders who laugh and smile trigger mirror neurons in members of the team, causing spontaneous laughter and pleasure and bonding as a team; and bonded teams perform at a higher level.[39]

- **Approachable leadership**

The team wants to see the leader as open, available, and approachable. This one often needs special effort. Leaders, by virtue of the position they hold, are perceived as distant, busy, and unapproachable. An open door can help. I also continually remind the team that they have access to me any time. I am there to help them get their jobs done. I must be available. I try to communicate that I am available to talk about work or about life.

In an insightful article in *Leadership*, Ben Merold identifies four elements that are critical for effective, approachable team leadership: prayer, fellowship, compassion, and vision. Merold recognizes that time spent together before God and in one another's company facilitates team decision making.[40] I have found over the years that thirty minutes reflecting on our relationships with God and with each other at the beginning of a meeting enables a team to accomplish all of its business in less than ninety minutes. Skipping that reflective relational

39. Goleman and Boyatzis, "Social Intelligence and the Biology of Leadership," 75.
40. Ben Merold, "Walking in Step," *Leadership* 29, no. 2 (2008): 31.

time usually lengthens the meeting significantly. Compassion directs the organizational vision to the care of the community and away from the leader.

- **Trusting relationships**

    The relational side of the team is important. In every office in which I have worked, and with every team I have been part of, we have spent a lot of time talking about life unrelated to the office operations or the organizational mission. Some years it seemed like we hired only newlyweds, and I felt like a marriage counselor much of the time. When people trust you to be their leader, even in the limited arena of their work, they are trusting you with a part of their lives. The work relationship is strengthened if a relationship of trust is developed with them as people.

    Hewlett Packard calls this MBWA (Management By Walking Around). I have watched Max De Pree walk through the factory at Herman Miller, addressing people by name, asking about family and outside activities—clearly a friend who cares. I like to connect with members of my immediate team regularly just to see how they are doing. In my middle management days the president would often catch me sitting slumped in a chair and talking to one of my staff. Sometimes I felt that he thought I was loafing. But I considered keeping up relationships with them and maintaining high motivation to be important work, since I had delegated so much to them (which is precisely why I had time to sit and chat).

    One caution here. The need to socialize and encourage strong relationships cannot be allowed to interfere with the work. Part of having a trusting relationship with the team includes their being able to tell you that this is not a good time to talk if they are to finish the assignment they are working on. Even coaching leaders need to be sensitive about intruding into people's time. A strong trusting relationship, however, will find the proper balance.

Trust is an important component of team unity. The team must trust the leader, and they must know that the leader trusts them. And they must trust each other. In their excellent book, *Credibility*, James Kouzes and Barry Posner argue that trust is the foundation of leadership.[41] We often talk about trust being earned. But trust is also given, and it is a fragile gift that must be cared for gently.

- **Vulnerability**

Team leaders must be vulnerable. They must be open enough for others to learn from their mistakes. It is hard to fail in front of your staff, but trust and community will be built if you are big enough to admit failure. I have had to apologize many times. My team members have always known my weaknesses and fears as well as my strengths and dreams. They already know that leaders are not perfect; they are just waiting for us to recognize it!

This was brought home to me sharply in an incident involving a water cooler, an incident about which I later wrote a short article for *Leadership*.[42] A number of years ago two programs for which I was responsible were merged into one office operation, combining staff and reassigning responsibilities. The Doctor of Ministry (DMin) program staff moved into the office facilities of the Leadership Institute. An excellent team was forged, but there was one problem. The old DMin team had had their own water cooler in their office; the Institute team used one across the hall. Early in the relocation process, members of the DMin team approached me requesting a water cooler with a small refrigerator for our office. I pointed out that I did not think this was necessary since we had access to one across the hall and were short on space. Wanting to be a good participative manager, however, I del-

---

41. James M. Kouzes and Barry Z. Posner, *Credibility* (San Francisco: Jossey-Bass, 1993), 22.
42. Walter C. Wright Jr., "Watercooler Management," *Leadership* 10, no. 2 (1989): 132.

egated this decision to the combined members of the new staff team. I told them to do the necessary research and make the decision.

A week later they came to me with a recommendation to buy a certain model of water cooler and handed me the papers that I needed to sign to implement their decision. Again I expressed my reservations about the project, but I signed the papers.

Several days later I walked into the primary reception office for our combined unit and saw a new water cooler boldly bubbling in the corner. I did not like it. From my perspective it turned a professional office reception area into a staff lounge. I told the staff how I felt— basically that I thought they had made a bad decision, reiterating again that we really did not need the water cooler and that it did not fit the "professional ambiance" of the office.

As often happens, this was the point when the leadership role shifted to another member of the team. A person who had worked with me for several years—and who had not even supported the water cooler recommendation—took me aside and confronted my behavior. She accused me of acting out of character with what I believed and taught. She asked whether I had really delegated the decision or whether I was playing some "parenting" game, expecting the "children" to agree with my opinion—and since they did not, I was pouting. (These are my words; she was much more loving and discreet.)

She was right! I had not delegated completely. I had delegated the decision only as long as it went my way. That is not delegation—that is bad management. When I delegated the decision to get a water cooler, I transferred my authority to determine the outcome and placed it in the hands of the staff. It was their decision, and my behavior now denied that I had really delegated the authority to decide.

Fortunately, someone cared enough to confront me and call me to account according to my own stated management values. I apologized to the whole team and acknowledged that it was their decision, that I was out of line, and that I would support their decision completely.

This was the first time that some of the team had seen a manager apologize. But I was wrong and I needed to say so. That experience greatly strengthened the new team that was coming together. And I believe the water cooler is still to this day bubbling and gurgling away as a monument to completed delegation and vulnerable leadership.

— SIMILAR TO HOW TRINITY IS DESCRIBED IN THE SHACK

- **Delegation**

Complete delegation, not my example of water-cooler delegation, builds people. It gives them confidence because it says "I trust you." Delegation is the process of moving the decision point from the leader to the follower. It is the act of giving power and authority with responsibility to the follower, allowing him or her to serve as leader for that decision. Delegation is empowering: the most empowering action a leader can take is to follow. In his classic book, *Leadership Jazz*, Max De Pree points out that delegation is a gracious act of involvement that grows people, embraces diversity, builds on trust, and requires a dying to self.[43]

Delegation develops ownership and responsibility. I often say that my job is sitting around drinking coffee and talking to people. That is not totally untrue! If I am doing my job right I only need to be available at critical points to provide relational support, discussion, or direction when the person who has accepted the delegation wants to talk. When team members accept our delegation they become leaders and we become resources that they manage as they carry out their delegated responsibility.

- **Ownership of results, not tasks**

Team members own the organizational outcomes, the results, not just their own job descriptions. When team members see something that needs to be done in order to accomplish their team goals, they do it, whether or not it is their job. A good team takes pride in the results

---

43. Max De Pree, *Leadership Jazz* (New York: Doubleday, 1992), 157.

of their unit as well as their individual contributions. They look for ways to support one another, to fill in the cracks, to do whatever is needed to achieve the results the team is seeking. A good team always keeps the larger picture in view and measures its success by results.

I will come back to this element when I look at vision and planning. In times of change, leadership is increasingly going to require us to focus on results rather than tasks or strategies. Yet it is so easy for our organizations to lock into the way we do things—the tasks or the strategies—as though the strategy is the mission. I will argue that organizations, like effective teams, must focus on a vision of results and be willing to change their strategies as necessary to fulfill their mission.

- **Equality of status**

Each member of the team is important. Each person has an area for which he or she is responsible. People need to know they are valued. Even though members are paid at different rates, for a variety of reasons, each person expects to be treated as equally important to the team—and this includes the leader.

- **Freedom to make mistakes—once**

This element is found in Peters' and Austin's list of characteristics. Mistakes are going to happen, no matter how hard we try to prevent them. Effective leaders do not allow the team to become paranoid about making mistakes. You cannot prevent them all. The principle is to try not to make the same mistake twice! Learn from mistakes. If people are not making mistakes, they are not trying new things. If they are making the same mistake twice, they are not learning new things! A good team knows that it can take the risk to try, to fail, and to learn from its mistakes.

- **Ownership is more important than hours worked**

Again, the focus of a team is on results. If the goals or results are owned, they will get done. If the hours clocked are a priority, you may not get the results you need. While team members identified this as an

Bob Ford on skiing —
"If you don't fall now + then, you're not learning to ski better."

important principle, it is actually implicit in the other points. The focus should be on the ownership of results, not on tasks or hours. As flexible hours and telecommuting are changing the way we work, it is increasingly important that the focus is on the results of the team efforts.

- **Commitment to a team approach**

Fitting into the team becomes an important qualification for a position. Alongside skills and experience, the team fit becomes an important element in the hiring process. I have often told new employees that their evaluation will be based on their ability to work as a member of the team as much as it will be on their individual competencies. All members of the team need to know that they belong; they need to feel valued and believe that they have an important contribution to make to the team's success.

These are the elements that one team identified as important to their success.

During the past thirty-four years I have also been one of seven men who have climbed mountains and explored backcountry wilderness together. All of us are engaged in leadership in business, academic, or nonprofit organizations. Paralleling our leadership journeys, we rope up to one another and climb onto high-mountain glaciers. On the mountain we are visibly and physically a team, as the rope ties us together and reveals our interdependence. Reflecting on these decades together we realize that we have learned some important truths about team building—truths that can be applied to our work as leaders. I have written elsewhere about these lessons from the rope.[44] But let me summarize briefly here. The overlap with management teams will be obvious.

---

44. Walter C. Wright, *Don't Step on the Rope! Reflections on Leadership, Relationships, and Teamwork* (Milton Keynes, UK: Paternoster, 2005).

• **A team pursues a shared vision or objective.**

By definition a team has an objective. People come together to accomplish something important to each person, something they know they can achieve better together than alone. The relationships that bind the team are grounded in the shared vision, the purpose or objective that gathers everyone's focus. Every member of the team is there because he or she wants to achieve the mission that defines the team. Team membership starts with shared vision.

• **A team reinforces shared values.**

Shared purpose keeps the team focused, but shared values hold it together. Not everyone belongs on every team. Relationships sustain the vitality of a team, and those relationships are grounded in shared values. Each person joins the team with a unique personality, personal history, belief system, and attitude toward life, wilderness, relationships, time, space, learning, growth, responsibility, authority, and achievement. We learned early on that the intensity of the shared vision or the desired objective impacted the amount of diversity we could accept in shared values. The shared values of the team determine its success as much as the shared vision.

• **A team nurtures results *and* relationships.**

Shared vision and shared values keep the team focused on results *and* relationships. Both are necessary for an effective team. Progress toward the vision, the mission that forms us, is measured by the results we achieve together. The values that unite us are measured by the health of the relationships among members. Both are essential. Without a vision, the group is little more than a social fellowship lacking the passion to ignite a team. Without nurtured relationships, the team is mechanical and sterile and will eventually succumb to entropy.

• **A team engenders trust.**

An effective team focused on results and relationships is powered by trust. Trust is the lifeblood of relationships and thus the fuel of teams. Trust is essential for cohesion and community. It is both given and earned. Through competence and behavior, others earn our trust. But the risk of relationship—the commitment to another—requires us to give trust before it is completely earned. In many ways trust is an act of faith. Joining a team requires high trust, since the outcomes are dependent upon others.

- **A team encourages growth and achievement.**

A good team is more than just its corporate presence. It is also a community of people. While individual agendas are subordinated to the group objective, an effective team provides opportunity and encouragement for its members to stretch themselves, to learn, and to grow. And it celebrates everyone's achievement.

- **A team communicates well.**

Good communication is critical to the effectiveness of a team. It is at the heart of relationships. Communicating is the bloodstream of trust. Everyone takes care of his or her own contribution and everyone is watching out for the group, doing whatever needs to be done when it needs to be done.

It is also important for the team to know how its members are feeling. The team is a network of relationships. Relationships need nurture and care. And the care of relationships requires honest communication of feelings and appropriate feedback. Communicating on a team is a matter of success or failure.

- **A team prizes community over individual performance.**

A team prizes its community of relationships as highly as its shared objective. An effective team acknowledges the contribution and growth of individual members but allows members to find their fulfillment in the accomplishment of the team. A good team is not a collection of star achievers. The team is the star achiever. Its success is dependent upon every member's contribution and mutual interdependence.

- **A team distributes leadership.**

Leadership is an act of service to the team, delegated by the team for a specific purpose. I think shared leadership is one of the defining characteristics of a true team. Servant leaders and coaches thrive in team settings. And teams need servant leaders. Every person may have assigned duties for the team's mission, but at any given time one person needs to be assigned the responsibility to see that the team makes the necessary decisions required by its vision and values.

In 1976 a team of climbers from the United States was organized to climb Nanda Devi in the Indian Himalayas. One of the organizers was Willi Unsoeld, a former Everest climber living in Seattle. He arranged the climb to celebrate the twenty-first birthday of his daughter, Nanda Devi, who would accompany the team to the summit of the 25,645-foot peak after which she had been named. The team was made up of highly skilled climbers, selected because of friendships and extended relationship links. Because they were all friends, and because they were all experienced and gifted climbers, no one person was designated as the expedition leader. Senior climbers shared the leadership, carefully deferring to one another in recognition of the community of gifts and abilities present.

Was it a successful expedition? Yes, if success is measured in the accomplishment of their objective. On September 1, 1976, the team placed three climbers on the summit of Nanda Devi. But at what price? As the climbing became more difficult, tempers grew shorter and decisions needed to be made to conserve resources and energy. Yet no one had been assigned the responsibility of seeing that decisions were made and implemented. Shared leadership broke down into disagreement and stalemates. Critical decisions were delayed. Most tragic of all was the case of Nanda Devi Unsoeld, the young woman for whom the trip was organized. When she became ill at a high-altitude camp, there was no one to tell her she could not continue the climb, that she had to go back down and recuperate. No individual decision, no group decision.

Everyone was nice to Nanda Devi. But she died on the mountain, a victim of a leaderless team of gifted people.

The trip ended on a tragic note. Fingers were pointed. Blame was passed around. Climbers belatedly suggested, "I should have stepped forward and pushed for a decision." Everyone was taking care of themselves. No one was taking care of the group. No one was helping the team make the decisions necessary for the accomplishment of its goal and the care of its members.[45] I doubt that any of those climbers ever joined another expedition unless it was clear who was taking responsibility for the care of the group, who had authority to enforce the implementation of the team's decision processes.

A gifted team is not enough. A gifted leader is also needed to *serve* the team: to see that the mission is pursued, the people are cared for, and the decisions are made. Effective leaders build and motivate teams of people who choose to take ownership for the team's results and participate in the decisions that affect their work together.

Conclusion: "If today you will be a servant . . ."

To close this chapter, we turn again to a biblical model. In 1 Kings 12 we see Rehoboam newly crowned as the king of Israel after the death of his father Solomon. The people were burdened by the harsh rule of Solomon in his later years and sent Jeroboam to plead their case with the new king. Rehoboam told Jeroboam that he would consider the petition and decide in three days. During that time he consulted the senior advisors who had served with Solomon. These elders advised him, "If today you will be a servant to these people and serve them and give them a favorable answer, they will always be your servants" (1 Kings 12:7).

---

45. The story is told poignantly in John Roskelly's *Nanda Devi* (Harrisburg, PA: Stackpole Books, 1987).

But this was not the answer that Rehoboam wanted, so he sought the advice of the young men who had grown up with him. Their counsel was to show himself stronger than his father, to use his kind of power to control and rule the people. Rehoboam followed the advice of his young counselors. He chose to rule rather than to serve. And it cost him his leadership. Within weeks he had lost most of his kingdom to Jeroboam. Rehoboam's decision to be a strong leader decimated the scope of his leadership.

> "If today you will be a servant to these people and serve them ... they will always be your servants."

As Emilie Griffin writes in *The Reflective Executive*, leaders hold something very fragile in their hands: the hopes and dreams and ideas and contributions of their people. These must be held gently with respect, not crushed in the fist of power.[46]

---

46. Emilie Griffin, *The Reflective Executive* (New York: Crossroad, 1993), 53.

Influencing with Vision

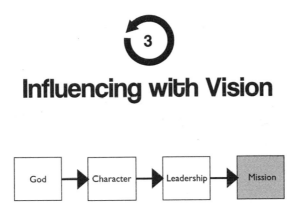

Clouds: Delivering Vision

"Clouds without rain, blown along by the wind." Again we return to Jude's challenging of the leadership of those who claimed to be leaders in his community. In his powerful metaphor of the cloud—promising rain and refreshment to a parched land but delivering only wind—we again see two contrasting pictures of a biblical leader.

The picture Jude paints of these toxic leaders shows them holding out hope but having nothing to offer. They promise leadership but care only for themselves. It is not hard to envision them in their pulpits, on their pedestals, gesturing with energy and passion but without content. They offer no lasting vision, no hope. They have no concept of a future that binds the community together. Rather they divide and polarize the people. These toxic leaders do not point to the power of God's presence in Christ but only to their own piety and personal spiritual pilgrimage.

On the other hand, we see Jude, the servant leader, pointing away from himself to God in Christ, serving his people by lifting up a compelling vision to give them hope. Listen again to the hope-filled words of his benediction:

> To him who is able to keep you from stumbling and to present you before his glorious presence without fault and with great joy—to the only God our Savior be glory, majesty, power and authority, through Jesus Christ our Lord, before all ages, now and forevermore! Amen.
>
> Jude 24–25

That is a vision to stir the heart. Jude sees the future—and it is God's!

Leadership is about vision that empowers.

Now let's look again at the Colossian drama and see what difference vision makes. This time put yourself in Philemon's place.

Philemon: Implementing Vision

How would you feel? You are a recognized leader in your church, a person respected for the care and commitment you shower on others in your congregation. You actively participate in and support the development of community in your church fellowship. People are refreshed in their faith because of your leadership and the depth of your relationship with Christ.

But you've had some problems lately. A member of your personal staff has betrayed you. A person you trusted has stolen from you and left town. Which hurts worse: the loss of a good worker, the theft of your property, or the betrayal by someone to whom you gave your trust? This event has not affected your vision or your leadership in the church, but it has hurt you personally. Perhaps you still carry a little anger—maybe a lot of anger! You were betrayed. Now you understand a little of what Jesus felt when Judas turned against him.

Judas was part of Jesus' inner circle: a disciple of the Lord, a person chosen by Jesus in answer to his prayer to God for twelve disciples. Jesus trusted Judas. Jesus loved Judas. And Judas betrayed Jesus. He violated that relationship of trust and turned on the one who loved him. You feel some of what Jesus must have felt when the person he had chosen, the person he trusted, turned on him. What are you going to do about these feelings?

Then one morning you look up and see two men coming toward you. One is the thief. What emotions do you feel? What thoughts run through your mind? Revenge? Repayment? Justice? Your fist clenches. Your stomach tightens. Your heart speeds up. Finally you can take care of this matter that has been eating at you, this hurt and anger that you have been carrying around.

But who is this other guy? Isn't that someone you've seen with Paul? Isn't his name Tychicus? What's he doing here? Perhaps he found out about that scoundrel and has dragged him back here to see justice done. And yet something seems wrong here as Tychicus greets you on behalf of himself and Paul. Your runaway staff member is watching you with a strange look in his eyes—a mixture of love and sadness. But not fear. Why not? You could have his head for what he did to you.

And then Tychicus hands you the letter—a personal letter from Paul who is in prison in Ephesus.

> Paul, a prisoner of Christ Jesus, and Timothy our brother,
>
> To Philemon our dear friend and fellow worker—also to Apphia our sister and Archippus our fellow soldier—and to the church that meets in your home:
>
> Grace and peace to you from God our Father and the Lord Jesus Christ.
>
> I always thank my God as I remember you in my prayers, because I hear about your love for all his people and

your faith in the Lord Jesus. I pray that your partnership with us in the faith[1] may be effective in deepening your understanding of every good thing we share for the sake of Christ. Your love has given me great joy and encouragement, because you, brother, have refreshed the hearts of the Lord's people.

Therefore, although in Christ I could be bold and order you to do what you ought to do, yet I prefer to appeal to you on the basis of love. It is as none other than Paul—an old man and now also a prisoner of Christ Jesus—that I appeal to you for my son Onesimus, who became my son while I was in chains. Formerly he was useless to you, but now he has become useful both to you and to me.

I am sending him—who is my very heart—back to you. I would have liked to keep him with me so that he could take your place in helping me while I am in chains for the gospel. But I did not want to do anything without your consent, so that any favor you do would not seem forced but would be voluntary. Perhaps the reason he was separated from you for a little while was that you might have him back forever—no longer as a slave, but better than a slave, as a dear brother. He is very dear to me but even dearer to you, both as a fellow man and as a brother in the Lord.

So if you consider me a partner, welcome him as you would welcome me. If he has done you any wrong or owes you anything, charge it to me. I, Paul, am writing this with my own hand. I will pay it back—not to mention that you owe me your very self. I do wish, brother, that I may

---

1. See N. T. Wright, *The Epistles of Paul to the Colossians and to Philemon: An Introduction and Commentary*, Tyndale New Testament Commentaries, vol. 12 (Grand Rapids: Eerdmans, 1988), for this alternative translation of verse 6 of Philemon.

have some benefit from you in the Lord; refresh my heart in Christ. Confident of your obedience, I write to you, knowing that you will do even more than I ask.

And one thing more: Prepare a guest room for me, because I hope to be restored to you in answer to your prayers.

Philemon 1–22

Subtly, lovingly, but clearly, Paul is sending you a message. Things have changed with Onesimus your runaway slave. He is now a Christian brother. Everything that you have been teaching and preaching at church and sharing with your friends at work is suddenly being put to the test. Participation in the fellowship of *koinonia* is no longer a lofty personal vision. It is no longer a theoretical theological concept of our common fellowship in Christ. It is now a demanding expectation of your faith. What you have been teaching as a commitment of your faith and an expression of your vision you are now being asked to demonstrate in relationship to a person who has betrayed your trust.

It's as though Paul is saying, "OK, Philemon, let's see if you really believe what you have been talking about. Your vision should make a difference in your life. Now is the time to see if that works. Reinstate Onesimus, not just as a member of your staff but also as a Christian brother. This is your chance to model what you believe!"

With a masterful stroke of his pen, Paul has confronted Philemon with the implications of his vision and stated commitments. The Christian love for which he is so well known all comes down now to how he will deal with Onesimus. Paul expects the gospel to make a difference. He is confident that Philemon will be able to transcend his sense of offense, his personal loss, and his pain at betrayal and embrace Onesimus as a changed person and a Christian companion, reinstating him to his staff and taking the risk of trusting him again.

Philemon knew his faith. He had a vision of what it means to live for Christ, what it means to be part of the body of Christ. He had a reputation for goodness and piety. But Paul wanted more. Paul had a theological vision for an eschatological community in Christ that shaped everything he did. He wanted Philemon's vision to make a difference, to permeate his total being in such a way that it changed the way he lived. It's one thing to have a vision for Christian community; it's another to see Jesus in the eyes of the person who has betrayed your trust and hurt you personally. For Paul, one leads to the other. A biblical vision, according to Paul, results in changed lives in everyday living. Everything that Philemon taught about his faith was now on the line in the way he responded to Onesimus.

The same holds true for each of us. Vision is seeing tomorrow so powerfully that it shapes today. Our vision of God in Christ at work in the communities and organizations that we lead will be put to the test every day in the way we live, the way we do business, the way we parent, the way we walk with friends or relate to strangers. An empowering vision of community means meeting God in the context of a community united in Christ.

In his carefully worded letter to Philemon, Paul tells us at least three things about his vision of community that we should note as we seek to be servant leaders.

Christian community includes all kinds of people

For Philemon, this was a dramatic revelation. A person who was once his slave he must now see as a Christian brother in the community. What will this mean? How does an upper-middle-class church leader relate to an uneducated runaway slave? But this is the essence of Christian community. We are a diverse fellowship of uniquely gifted people. Together we become the body of Christ pointing people to God.

This diversity will take different forms in various communities. At Regent College we welcomed students, faculty, and staff from over thirty-two different countries and cultures, seventy-five different church or denominational backgrounds, a variety of vocations, a mixture of ages and experience, and different levels of social-economic opportunity. This is diversity.

In his book *Leadership Is an Art*, Max De Pree calls this the "inclusive perspective" of leadership. If we believe "that every person brings an offering to a group, it requires us to include as many people as possible."[2] Leaders are *inclusive*, looking for ways to promote diversity and create space for people to develop their unique contribution.

I believe that diversity is an essential ingredient in Christian community. But diversity means differences, and differences produce conflict. And that brings me to the second point I find in Paul's vision and another reason why I find the Colossian story so compelling.

② *Christian community can handle conflict*

It is in community that conflict is reconciled. Paul has certain expectations for Philemon and the Colossian church in relationship to

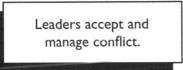

the conflict that Philemon has with Onesimus. His vision of community does not avoid conflict. He addresses it head on in the context of a caring relationship. In fact, I believe Paul's letter to Philemon outlines a very powerful approach to conflict resolution. Leaders accept and manage conflict. I will explore conflict in community a little more when we look at values.

③ *Christian community takes precedence over personal agendas*

The expectation that community will take precedence over personal agendas is the third element I see in Paul's vision for community. We began this chapter by looking at Philemon's feelings—his emotional responses. He has a debt to settle with Onesimus, a personal agenda to

---

2. Max De Pree, *Leadership Is an Art* (East Lansing, MI: Michigan State University Press, 1987), 61.

accomplish. Yet Paul is calling him back to his vision of community. Paul reminds Philemon of his reputation for investing himself in the network of relationships that form his community and for encouraging its members; Paul reminds him of his faith, his love, and his generous support for the community at Colosse. Now Paul sends Onesimus back as a member of that community—and expects Philemon's vision of community to take precedence over his own hurt, his own need for personal satisfaction.

Organizations are communities of diversity. They are filled with individuals with their own issues. Regent College is a community of over five hundred personal agendas. Early in my tenure at Regent I heard a professor comment that what made Regent different from other schools where he had taught was the willingness of faculty members to submit their strong personal agendas to the community agenda of the college. I pray that will always be true at Regent. It should be true for any organization that holds up a vision of Christian community.

Max De Pree would go further and apply these same principles to Herman Miller. He writes, "In a group like Herman Miller, we have both personal diversity and corporate diversity. When we think of *corporate* diversity, we think about the gifts and talents and commitment that each of us as individuals brings to the group effort. Channeled correctly and integrated properly, our diversity can be our greatest strength. But there is always the temptation to use these gifts for our personal benefit rather than dedicating them to the best interest of the group."[3]

Leadership, De Pree would argue, articulates a vision for the organization or community that is inclusive—creating space for individual gifts and talent and creating the context that allows these individual offerings to be integrated for the good of the group and its mission together.

---

3. Ibid., 82, italics in original.

> Leaders have visions that make a difference, empowering visions that offer hope for tomorrow and shape behaviors today.

Paul has such a vision. His vision for Christian community in Colosse embraces diversity, deals with conflict, and supersedes individual agendas. He expects that vision to make a difference in the immediate day-to-day relationships of living. That is the vision to which he calls Philemon. And that is the vision by which he would critique all of our plans for the future.

The Responsibilities of Leadership

Max De Pree says that the two primary responsibilities of a leader are to point the direction, or define reality, and to say thank you.[4] For De Pree, leaders articulate the vision—that is, they point the direction and define the reality which shapes both the leadership relationship and the followers' contributions to the organization. He immediately recognizes, however, that the vision articulated by the leader will only be accomplished with the contributions of those followers. Thus he sees the second responsibility of leadership as saying thank you: acknowledging our dependence upon and appreciation for the followers and their personal investment in the vision.

This, of course, returns us to the connections charted in chapter 1. Belief precedes behavior. Theology shapes character, which fuels leadership, which influences vision—direction or reality—and relationships—dependence upon followers. Visions and relationships: both are the product of leadership.

Whenever I am asked what my job is, I like to elaborate on De Pree's primary responsibilities by responding with four things which, I believe, defined my leadership role at Regent College and now at the

---

4. Ibid., 11.

De Pree Center. I am responsible for articulating the vision, reinforcing the values, empowering the people, and saying thanks. Obviously the first and last are taken directly from De Pree. The middle two are also consistent with his writing in all three of his leadership books.

In this chapter I am focusing on articulating the vision—the strategic responsibility of leadership—articulating an *empowering vision* that shapes the way we organize our corporate life together around a mission. In the next chapter I will pick up the second responsibility and discuss the crucial role of the leader in creating and reinforcing the *empowering values* that, when embedded in our organizational cultures, shape the way we live our community life together. In chapter 5 I will focus on the *empowering relationships* in which we contextualize the contributions of our people in terms of our mission and, as De Pree would say, "abandon ourselves to their giftedness."[5] Chapters 4 and 5 will unpack the relational-empowering task of leadership. In Chapter 6 I will conclude with a review of *empowering accountability*, which includes the dependent accountability of leaders to their followers—the men and women who, with the leader, share a compelling vision that shapes their relationships together, producing accomplishment and meaning.

Planning: Visions of Hope

Planning is the management process of lifting up visions of hope in times of change. Planning is the process of articulating a strategic vision or picture of the future in a way that compels others to take ownership for that future and understand why their contribution is important. One critical component of our role as leaders is to keep our organizations thinking strategically about who we are and what we want to accomplish before God. This strategic thinking or planning shapes the daily life and work of our organizations and directs

---

5. Ibid., 82–83.

the energies of our people. It shapes the direction and character of the organization in such a way that people are empowered to make their contribution and valued for that contribution. Planning articulates purpose, meaning, and hope in the living of a shared vision.

Defining strategic planning

We need to start this discussion with some definitions. Every planning text uses terms like purpose, mission, goals, objectives, actions, strategies, budgets, and controls. If you choose two texts, however, chances are that you will get different definitions for these terms. "Purpose" and "mission" are frequently interchanged. "Goals" and "objectives" are either used synonymously or one term is defined as the broader target with the other as the specific measurable benchmark.

"Strategic planning" tends to be the current label for what used to be called "long-range planning." Some authors try to distinguish between the two, but without much success. Generally speaking, long-range planning focuses on the time frame involved, something increasingly difficult to control in our changing times, while strategic planning focuses on the issues at stake. Margaret Wheatley prefers "strategic thinking," recognizing that change is occurring so fast that leadership is more about adapting on the move than planning in advance.[6] Knowing who we are and what is important prepares leaders to make future-shaping decisions as they work.

I like to define strategic planning as *a process initiated by the top leadership of an organization to review and monitor the purpose, the mission, the values (or culture), and the strategies of the organization.* Strategic planning is concerned about the health of the connections between leadership and productivity or outcomes—both strategic and relational. Let's look at the components of this definition.

---

6. Margaret J. Wheatley, *Leadership and the New Science*, 2nd ed. (San Francisco: Berrett-Koehler Publishers, 1999), 38.

Purpose is the primary role of the organization as defined by society and shared with other organizations. Regent College and Fuller Seminary share a similar purpose. First Baptist Church and Fairview Presbyterian Church share a similar purpose. Apple and Dell share a similar purpose.

Mission, on the other hand, refers to the unique calling or distinctive of each organization that defines that organization by geography, values, beliefs, services, resources, size, people served, etc. It is what makes you different from every other similar organization with the same purpose. Your mission is what gives you a right to exist and to utilize resources. It answers the question, What would be lost if we ceased to exist?

By *values*, or *culture*, I am referring to the stated or assumed beliefs, commitments, ethos, and qualities that govern everything that the organization does: the character of the organization, if you will—the manifestation of its soul, its faith and beliefs. This is the part that gets left out of most planning processes. Since I believe that values are as much a part of vision as mission, I will come back to this unique responsibility of leadership in detail in the next chapter.

I define *strategies* as unified sets of goals, including objectives and actions that move us toward the accomplishment of the organizational mission and values given our current and projected resources, opportunities, and threats. I choose here to avoid talking about specific goals, objectives, and actions in order to keep us looking at the packages we put together to implement our mission and values.

During my tenure at Regent College, every September began with a roar. The streets of Vancouver were blocked off, and the sounds of powerful engines filled the city. The Molson Indy pitted world-class racing teams against one another as their cars raced through downtown corridors. Drivers and crews were on the news and were the topic of most conversations during that long weekend. Each team was working out and discussing its strategies to finish first on race day.

They were talking about much more than goals and objectives. When these elements are unified in a way that controls our actions we have a strategy.

Race drivers don't take with them a list of key objectives to check off after each lap. Rather they live and drive their strategy. In today's fast-paced world, we lead like race car drivers. We don't have a strategy for achieving our mission until we have melded the various steps together into a way of life for the organization over the next few years.

There are two additional key components in this definition of strategic planning. Strategic planning is a *process*. The involvement of people is as important as the production of a plan. The plan shows that something was accomplished, and it also becomes the control document with which to evaluate the organization's progress. The process, though, involves people and creates ownership. It translates the shared vision into the commitments and actions of the members of the organization. This very strength of planning is why planning is so difficult. The process involves people—people with their own ideas, dreams, and plans. Planning for one person is relatively easy. As soon as you add a second person it becomes difficult, though absolutely essential if you want ownership of the vision and the strategies. The more people you involve in the planning process the longer it will take and the harder it will be. But it is critical to the ownership and motivation of the people.

I should note here that I am not talking about a democratic process. In strategic planning we need participation to advise the decision makers and develop ownership. Participants in the planning process, however, do not necessarily have an equal vote in shaping the future (that depends on the particular culture of your organization), but they do participate and contribute to the decisions that the leadership is responsible for making. The process is both the problem and the foundational principle of planning.

Finally, *the top leadership of an organization* must be the ones to initiate strategic planning. You will hear arguments for both top-down planning and bottom-up planning. The middle manager does not want to waste time planning until the president shares her vision, since "That's what we are going to do anyway." The president does not want to form her vision before hearing the ideas of the middle management. In either case, the leadership must be involved. The top leadership is responsible for the decisions that move the organization into the future: the allocation of resources and the delegation of authority to make things happen. If the president or pastor does not own the planning process, it is a waste of everyone's time!

Strategic planning, then, is a process initiated by the leadership that clarifies the organization's mission, within its basic purpose; that identifies the values that will govern the way the organization or church lives out its mission; that translates the mission and values into vision statements or scenarios for the future; and develops strategies to turn those scenarios into reality, including goals, objectives, actions, and budgets. Mission—values—strategies: these are the key components of strategic planning, the vital issues that leaders must constantly keep before their organizations in times of change.

Planning in times of change

Before we look at a planning model and the development of empowering vision statements, let's look briefly at the context of change in which we must lead.

I like to read Charles Handy. His two books on organizational change, *The Age of Unreason* and *The Age of Paradox*, stimulate me to think with fresh perspective, to think outside the lines.[7] Handy contends that we have moved into a time of discontinuous change. Change

---

7. Charles Handy, *The Age of Unreason* (Boston: Harvard Business School Press, 1989); *The Age of Paradox* (Boston: Harvard Business School Press, 1994).

comes so fast from so many directions that we cannot extrapolate into the future with any certainty. Apart from the foundation of our faith, the only constant Handy will allow us to take into the future is that it will change.[8]

In the world of tomorrow, "Built to last now means built to change."[9] Handy argues, as did Tom Peters in *Thriving on Chaos*, that with all this change bombarding individuals and organizations we have to plan within a context we experience as chaos.[10] It has become more critical than ever, claims Russ Chandler, for Christians to know who they are and with whom they are entering this chaotic future.[11]

Trajectories we set for ourselves as youths are no longer valid for many of us, not to mention those established by our children, or by our students, employees, or congregations. The one thing everyone agrees on is that things are changing and that the speed of change is increasing. The past is no longer the best predictor of the future. Things change; information circulates the globe instantly, determined more by relational connections than geographic distance. The Internet has distributed knowledge. Everyone knows; if they don't they can find out with a few keystrokes. The future is unpredictable.

The problem with planning—with any planning model, including the one below—is that it hints at the possibility that we might have control, that we can decide now the kind of future we will have. We do shape the future, but the decisions we make today are only a small piece of the process.

In his provocative book *The Black Swan*, Nassim Nicholas Taleb, a professor of risk and probability, argues persuasively that the major

---

8. Handy, *The Age of Unreason*, 5–9.
9. See Stan Davis and Christopher Meyer, *Blur: The Speed of Change in a Connected Economy* (Reading, MA: Addison-Wesley, 1998), 13.
10. Tom Peters, *Thriving on Chaos: Handbook for a Management Revolution* (New York: Alfred Knopf, 1987).
11. Russell Chandler, *Racing Toward 2001* (Grand Rapids: Zondervan, 1992), 314.

events that will shape our future have not yet happened, the technology that will change radically the way we do things has not even been invented yet. He demonstrates that the things that will most powerfully change our future are the unpredictable ones, or the ones we predict that do not happen.[12] Look at the events of September 11, 2001. Few of us imagined the horror of passenger jets deliberately flying into the World Trade Center, and yet that event—that "Black Swan"—has changed the way we think about travel, security, and life. As I write this chapter the world's stock markets appear to be in free fall as the credit crisis spreads around the globe. This possibility was foreseen by some, but not enough for leaders to take action to prevent the spiraling decline. Planning does not discover or eliminate these "Black Swans." Rather it prepares us for the reality that the future may be very different from anything that we can imagine.

Not only will the future be shaped by the unpredictable, it will be created by our presence. Studies in quantum physics show that we are not neutral observers in an unfolding world. Everything is in relationship. In her book *Leadership and the New Science*, Margaret Wheatley observes, "We live in a universe where relationships are primary. Nothing happens in the quantum world without something encountering something else. Nothing exists independent of its relationships. We are constantly creating the world—evoking it from many potentials—as we participate in all its many interactions. This is a world of process, the process of connecting, where 'things' come into temporary existence because of relationship."[13]

The future is not determined; it will be shaped by our participation in it. Quantum theory suggests that the very observation of an object changes it. The future is known by God, but it will take its shape as we engage it. We are part of the process. Having a vision does not

---

12. Nassim Nicholas Taleb, *The Black Swan: The Impact of the Highly Improbable* (New York: Random House, 2007), 49,135–36.

13. Wheatley, *Leadership and the New Science*, 69.

define a future or determine a destination; it creates a power—a force for change, the most serious implications of which we probably cannot predict.[14]

Planning is an ongoing cycle of envisioning, learning, and responding. It is never finished. Planning, at best, is knowing who we are and what we believe and value and envisioning possible futures that we anticipate will change as we engage. It is less about preparing for a specific tomorrow than about knowing ourselves well enough that, expecting the unpredictable and the unknown, we can move forward prepared to adapt. This, of course, is very uncomfortable space. We naturally resist change and attempt to reduce risk. Leadership seeks to create the participation and relational safety that influence others to envision a changing future.

Recent research in neuroscience is instructive in understanding the resistance to change within organizations. Change is painful—literally. The brain processes most of our habitual activity near its core with little energy required; we operate "without thinking." New experiences—changes—are handled by the working memory, a smaller energy-intensive part of the brain. Working memory compares new information with old and works to understand it and organize it into a habit that requires less energy. When the working memory space is activated it causes discomfort. Change confronts the working memory of our brain and requires more effort mentally and physically.[15]

Studies suggest that leaders involve followers in the development and articulation of new vision or strategy. When people solve a problem themselves the brain releases a rush of neurotransmitters that work like adrenalin. Engaging people in solving problems and developing vision may compensate for some of the energy drain they experience. Vision is owned much more quickly when it emerges within the follower.

---

14. Ibid., 55.

15. David Rock and Jeffrey Schwartz, "The Neuroscience of Leadership," *Strategy+Business*, reprint 06207 (Summer 2006), 3–4.

Questions that allow followers to experience their own insights into a vision or strategy go further than instruction or direction. Brain research also underlines the power of focus. That which gets attention gets owned. The more we focus on a positive vision the more we expect it, and that process creates ownership and changes the way we think and act.[16] A participative planning process with an engaging vision is the best antidote to resistance to change.

The pain of change is also cushioned by relationships. Ronald Heifetz notes that leaders nurture change by creating a "holding environment"—the space formed by a network of trusted relationships.[17] We seek to create a community with enough relational strength to offset the discomfort of change.

Especially through the leadership relationship, but also through peer relationships within the organization, trust can be generated to encourage us to risk the uncertainty of change. Here again the emotional-relational side of leadership steps to the fore, attending to the person while keeping the vision in focus. Leadership seeks to manage the tolerance for change with clear shared vision and strong relationships.

Planning is about living the vision

Articulating the vision may be a leader's single most important responsibility. The leader keeps the vision—the mission, the reason the church or organization was formed—before the people, continually asking what we need to do today and tomorrow to live out that vision.

People today are afraid. They see the economy offering little security to their future. They see violence increasing. They see an alienated youth culture with increasing openness to suicide. They see morality floundering rootless. They need hope! This is the role of

---

16. Ibid., 7–8.

17. Ronald Heifetz, *Leadership on the Line* (Boston: Harvard Business School Press, 2002), 102.

vision, of planning, in the context of our corporations, churches, and organizations.

Planning, management, and technology cannot bring about the future and may not even ensure a better future. At our best, we will fall short of the ideal. But planning can help us understand who we are and what is important to us. It can lift our attention up from our feet to the horizon and help us see a vision of a world in which God is at work: perhaps still a world that seems to be falling apart when measured by what we are used to, but a world in which God is still working—and a world in which we are still called to live out the loving presence of Christ in our midst.

German theologian Jürgen Moltmann said that planning offers hope, that planning is our attempt to shape history in a godward direction.[18] I am not sure how much we can shape history, but I do think we are called to live what we believe, being true to who we are—or even better, being true to who God is in the midst of the changing world. Belief precedes behavior; theology shapes leadership.

We need a renewed vision for our leadership that offers hope that shapes character, providing direction and declaring worth to the people we seek to influence. This is true regardless of the kind of organization we lead.

A Planning Model

One of the key responsibilities of leadership is the articulation of vision: pointing people to a future that compels them forward toward tomorrow and shapes their living today. Let me suggest a practical model for strategic planning that focuses particularly on the development of a vision statement or scenario.

---

18. Jürgen Moltmann, *Hope and Planning* (New York: Harper & Row, 1971), 184–90; see also Ray S. Anderson, *Minding God's Business* (Grand Rapids: Eerdmans, 1986), 139–40.

The planning model that shapes my thinking is a simple list of ten questions, which if wrestled with and owned by an organization will create both a vision and a process for the implementation of that vision. The ten steps to the vision are:

1. Who are we?
2. What is important to us?
3. Where in the world are we?
4. Where do we want to be?
5. What can we do?
6. How should we do it?
7. When will we do it?
8. Who will do it?
9. How are we doing?
10. Is God pleased?

The first four questions, I believe, are the questions of strategic planning. The next four are the questions of operational planning or management. And the last two are the questions of review and evaluation. The ten questions are sequential and cyclical, so that the data received from questions 9 and 10 bring us back again to questions 1, 2, and 3. Let's walk through these ten steps.

Who are we? (strategic planning)

The first task of leadership is to articulate the vision of the organization, and that starts with the mission. What is your mission? The mission is the unique calling or distinctive of the organization that defines it by geography or locations, by values, by beliefs, by services offered, by resources accumulated, by constituencies served, etc. The mission is that which makes you different from every other organization like you, that explains why you utilize the resources you do.

1. What is a mission statement?

A mission statement is a concise description of your organization that identifies your primary goals and distinctives. It answers the fundamental questions, Who are we? What do we do? What do we want to do? It may even answer the question, How do we do it? It is the final measure or standard against which all organizational decisions and activities are measured. It is a statement of your reason to exist.

Can you articulate your distinctives? Can you write a one-paragraph mission statement today for your organization or church that would distinguish you from everyone else? A mission statement that gives *you* hope and excites you to ministry? One that the people of your organization would recognize as a statement of their mission too?

2. Why have a mission statement?

First, *it clarifies who we are.* It is the charter or mandate around which the church or organization organizes itself. It tells how the organization or church, as a unique community, fits into the greater scheme of things. Edgar Schein, author of *Organizational Culture and Leadership*, suggests that the mission statement addresses the ultimate survival problem of organizations. It identifies that which is critical to our existence, the loss of which we could not accept.[19] We would rather go out of business than give this up.

The mission statement identifies our competitive arena and gives a confidence in our identity that allows cooperation with other organizations and churches. I am frequently concerned by the fear Christians have of cooperation with other institutions of the kingdom who believe differently in matters of faith, lifestyle, or social application. A strong sense of mission identity allows an organization to participate in cooperative diversity without fear of losing its distinctive.

---

19. Edgar H. Schein, *Organizational Culture and Leadership*, 2nd ed. (San Francisco: Jossey-Bass, 1992), 53.

Second, the mission statement is *the final goal or standard by which all organizational decisions, all budget and staffing allocations, are evaluated.* All planning spins off from the mission. It is the core of all strategy development. If I give you five hundred thousand dollars to start something new, how will you decide how to use the money? The mission statement guides the planning and implementation processes. It guides decisions regarding size and shape. It tells us which opportunities or threats must be addressed. It should answer the question, How do you measure your success or faithfulness: by identifiable results or by survival?

Third, the mission statement *gives meaning to those who serve in the organization.* It gives value or purpose to their work. It gives direction to their activities, a sense of fit or belonging. It becomes the core of the culture that forms as the organization matures. It answers the question, What will be accomplished if I invest myself in your mission?

Fourth, the mission statement *communicates to those outside the organization.* It reveals who you are to those who utilize your services and participate in your ministries, to those organizations with whom you work, to those who fund your programs and services.

Organizationally, the mission statement is the foundation of the vision. Leaders hold up a vision of the mission shaped by the organization's values and wrapped in results that make a difference.

3. What makes a good mission statement?

It should be concise, readable and understandable, and less than one page. It should not be etched in stone. While it will not be changed continuously, the statement needs to be reviewed regularly and changed when appropriate. It should answer some basic questions about the organization: Why do we exist? What need do we address? What "business" are we in?

We tend to focus on what we do rather than the results we want to accomplish. Management books have long critiqued railroad companies at this point, noting that they believed they were in the train business when they should have been in the transportation business. Japanese auto companies clearly have transportation as their mission. Some have 250-year strategic plans, with groups talking now about travel between planets. Or closer to home: Is your church a preaching station or an equipping center?

We also have a tendency to keep doing what we have done well without asking if it still meets a need. Are you in the business of making buggy whips or starters for moving vehicles? A good mission statement will keep pointing us to the need we are addressing and enable us to resist the temptation to focus on what we are doing now as our mission.

At the same time, the statement *should* answer the question, *What do we do?* This may well be your distinctive. But if what you do is make buggy whips, you will have a shrinking opportunity for service! What is our most important product or service? Education? Worship? Caring? Evangelism? Social concern? Equipping? Preaching? Widgets? What is our driving force? What are our other services? What else might we want to do? Is there something else we should be doing?

Who are we serving? Who are our customers? Churches struggle with this one. Do we serve the denomination, the members of the congregation, the clergy, or those in the broader community who are not in relationship with God? Where are our customers? Who participates in our programs? Who do we *want* to participate? Why do people come to us? It is quite fashionable for churches and seminaries to pride themselves on not being "market driven," claiming that they are focused on being "faithful" rather than "successful." That is fine if it is not simply a cover-up for the reality that we are in fact being driven by a different market (in schools, the faculty; in churches, the pastoral staff or a core of the congregation). It is wrong if we are using faithfulness as an excuse to keep on doing what we want to do rather than critically examining everything in terms of the mission.

What are the unique strengths of this organization? What special resources do we have? Why us? How do we differ from other organizations like us? Is how we do what we do unique and integral to our mission? What are our limits? What would be lost if we ceased to exist? If we went out of business today, who would miss us? How would our "customers" be served? These are some of the questions that a good mission statement might address.

The mission statement might also include theological distinctives, ethnic or cultural distinctives, organizational beliefs or values (although I will argue for a separate statement here), and any philosophy or character traits of importance.

There is no single "correct" form for a mission statement. There is not just one model. Mission statements are tools for the organization; they should take a form that works. What you want is a document that sets out the mission you believe in, that your leadership team owns, that your members want to carry out, and that your constituencies understand and support.

We must understand who we are before we can evaluate what we are doing. This is an issue of stewardship and accountability. Do you have a vision for your organization that gives you hope, that compels you into tomorrow? Are you articulating that vision in everything you do? Are you offering hope to your people? When speaking at Regent College I usually underlined both our mission to provide theological education to the whole people of God and the reality that God is visibly at work in our midst, transforming the lives of students.

Focusing on the vision keeps us asking critical questions about who we are. We do not simply want to maintain what we have always done. Take the church, for example. What does the church need to be to point the men and women of the twenty-first century to God? I once heard a researcher say that 60 percent of Canadians believe in God, in Christ, in the resurrection, and the Bible, and yet only 2–4 percent have anything to do with the existing church. Perhaps we need a new vision for the Canadian church, with new models to equip the

56 percent of the population—the unchurched Christians—to live for Christ in this world.

Vision keeps asking questions of renewal! Leadership is all about getting yourself and your people excited about what God will do through you in the years ahead.

What is important to us? (strategic planning)

The second question in our ten steps to the vision focuses our attention on a much-neglected aspect of the planning process: the role of organizational culture in shaping the life and future of the organization. I will develop a response to this question in detail in the next chapter when I look at influencing with values. For now, let me note in summary that every organization has a hidden set of cultural assumptions that reflect the true beliefs of the organization and are manifested in the behaviors of the organization. As Max De Pree reminds us, "Belief precedes behavior." Our theology determines the cultural values that shape our organizational action. They may or may not be expressed in the organization's official statement of values.

One of the most important roles of the leader is to teach, model, and reinforce a stated set of values in such a way that they become the shared values of the organization and are embedded in the organizational culture. These values wedded together with the mission give body and soul to the vision we offer. This is an area of personal passion for me. We will come back to it.

Where in the world are we? (strategic planning)

This is the research question. It is often called the situational analysis. It is the point when the planning process brings every aspect of the organization under the spotlight of the mission and the values of the organization and assesses the organization's strengths and weaknesses, its opportunities and challenges. In answering this question the organization usually conducts an environmental or external audit as well as an organizational or internal audit.

1. The environmental audit

In the environmental audit, we look at *social trends and demographic information* that might be important to the implementation of our strategies. What is going on in the world today? What has changed since we last reviewed our situation? How might things be different in the next decade? How might changes in our environment affect us? What "impossible" event might change what we do?

We look closely at those we seek to serve, our clients or "customers." What are they "buying"? What could cause this to change? Why do they participate in our programs? What is the exchange? When do they participate? How do they make decisions to participate? Where do they participate? How do they perceive us? Similarly, we look at our primary sources of support and ask the same questions.

This is a time to list all other publics or constituencies whose attitudes and behaviors have an impact on the implementation of our strategies. Which publics are most influential? Why do they have an impact on the organization? What are their objectives and the reasons for their concern with our organization? What could cause this to change? How do they perceive us?

The environmental audit also looks at competitors. We do not like to use this language in Christian circles, but I am talking about all other organizations who are providing similar services for our intended "customers" or participants. Who are our major competitors? How do they compete? What are their strengths and weaknesses?

And finally, this part of the audit looks also at the way changing technologies might affect the mission of the organization, the needs the organization addresses, the services the organization offers, and the strategies used by the organization. What "Black Swan" might surprise us?

2. The organizational audit

The organizational or internal audit focuses on *programs and services*. Every program, service, and activity of the organization should be listed. How central is this activity to the organizational mission? Will the need being addressed by this activity still be significant in five years? Is the level at which the need is being met a good return on the organization's investment of its resources? In an organizational audit every department and, ideally, every position in the organization is reviewed in terms of its contribution to the mission and the values. Is this a good return for the mission that calls us together?

From these two audits the leadership and planning team identify the *critical issues* that must be addressed by the organization as it moves into its future. They may be issues of direction, resources, personnel, or facilities. They are identified, often with alternatives, as issues that must be included in the ongoing planning effort.

The environmental and organizational audits are often the most time-consuming aspects of the planning process. But they are important. They keep us from letting planning become simply an uncritical extension of the present into the future. They ask the questions that keep us open to an unpredictable future. And they provide the backdrop of reality for the vision. For a vision to offer hope it must emerge realistically from the situation in which we find ourselves today. Only then can it transcend the present and point us to tomorrow.

Where do we want to be? (strategic planning)

With this stage of the planning process, the vision begins to take shape. This is the fun part. Using a management tool called a scenario, a vision is drafted and debated. After a brief look at the rest of the ten steps, I will return to the development of the scenario, the vision statement, in the rest of this chapter. It is a vision of a future that excites you, a future in which the mission and the values of your church or organization are being lived out with excellence, a future that addresses

the needs and concerns of today and sees a difference being made by
your organization.

What can we do? (operational planning)

With the creation and organizational ownership of the scenario or
vision, the strategic planning process is completed. Here I would argue
that the leadership team should take over and translate that vision into
an organizational plan for the next five years.

The first question the leadership team wrestles with is, Given this
vision of our future, what can we actually do in the next five years? At
this point the leadership team sits down and balances the goals of the
scenario and the critical issues of the audit with the reality of fiscal
and physical projections and makes decisions about what will in fact
be done over the next five years to move us toward that scenario, to
address those issues.

At Regent College we called this the Five-Year Financial Plan. We
projected a realistic budget alongside the strategies we would like to
develop for the short term, allowing the vision of the strategies to
stretch the budget and letting the constraints of the budget speak realism to the selection of strategies. This is a key responsibility for which
leaders are paid. Here the hard decisions are made to determine what
we likely can accomplish over each of the next five years to keep us
moving toward the shared vision of the future with fiscal responsibility.

How should we do it? (operational planning)

Drawing up a five-year financial plan results in a selected set of
strategies, unified goals, objectives, and actions that we want to shape
the way we live out our mission and values each of the next few years.
Regent, for example, in support of its missional commitment to equip
the laity, might select a specific strategy for implementation in the next
year. Selecting a strategy has financial ramifications. We may need to

postpone other strategies for a few years. This is the kind of decision that is made at this leadership decision point.

When will we do it? (operational planning)

At the decision point, selected strategies are identified for the time frame of the five-year financial plan. These strategies should be defined in terms of key objectives for each year, forming the annual plan that finds its quantitative expression in the annual budget.

You have probably read a dozen definitions of objectives, but let me repeat the definition one more time. Objectives are stated levels of performance or effectiveness representing realistic steps toward fulfilling the mission and values of the organization. They should be specific results-oriented statements. Their accomplishment should be measurable so that we can know when they have been attained. Finally, objectives should be connected to the reward system. Recognition (thanks) or rewards should be directly related to the successful completion of the assigned objectives because the key objectives establish the time line that keeps the process moving strategically in line with the scenario—the shared vision.

Who will get us there? (operational planning)

Delegation. Most plans fail precisely at this point. We do not have a working plan until each objective has been owned by someone who accepts responsibility to see that it is initiated and completed. This person assumes ownership of the results identified by the objective and has flexibility to modify the actions that are needed to produce those results. This is delegation, the point at which the plan moves from a shared vision to owned actions.

How are we doing? (review and evaluation)

Accountability. The ninth step to the vision is actually review and evaluation. This is the feedback loop that tells us whether or not the actions of the organization are in fact moving us toward our vision. In a world of rapid change with unpredictable "Black Swans" lurking on the horizon, continuous feedback is necessary. As we engage the future according to plan, we alter that future and need constant assessment and communication to respond to the new situation we have helped create.

The feedback comes through two loops. Information on the progress and effectiveness of the strategies returns to the leadership team and is taken into account in the operational planning when we decide what we can do for the next five years. The missional implications of the feedback—Are we, in fact, fulfilling our mission by using these strategies?—are taken into account by the planning leadership in the strategic planning when we look again at the mission: where we are and where we want to be.

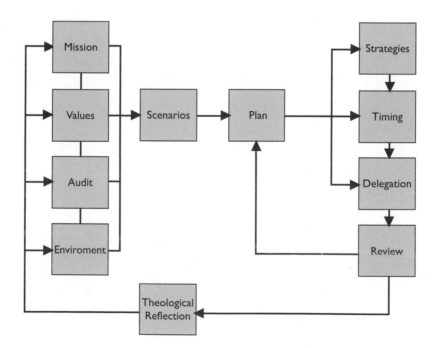

Is God pleased? (review and evaluation)

The final question is ultimate and strategic. It, too, is evaluative and brings us back to our vision—to our mission and values. Are we fulfilling the mission to which God has called us? Are we doing it in a manner that reflects our value commitments before God? Has living out of our vision pointed people to God? Have they seen the presence of Christ in our midst?

Our planning processes can be effective and keep our organizations and churches alive and active. But if our vision is not inspired by God, if our values are not shaped by the presence of Christ, if our strategies do not point people to God, then we have failed and probably should go out of business. Planning is a way to bring vision to reality. It is a way to involve others in a shared vision. It is also a time to listen to God, to see what God is doing in our midst, and to allow our vision to be shaped by his Spirit.

The Scenario: A Vision for Hope

As I noted earlier, the vision statement or scenario is a picture of what an organization might look like if the mission and values are incarnated in the future. This is the fun part of the planning process. It is also one of the most important components. I tend to think of it as the highlight of the planning process. Given an organization's mission, history, values, resources, and environment, this is where possible futures are created, where change can take place.

A scenario is a narrative picture of your community or organization in the future. It is a presentation of one way your future could look. A scenario is an understandable and positive description of your future, including ministries, programs, services, and products in place and the results of these activities. It is a planning tool designed to try on possible alternative futures, to clarify options for the future, and to move the organization or community toward consensus and ownership of that future.[20] A scenario is a statement of faith—a vision of how we see God working in our tomorrow.

When the planning team or leadership has reviewed and committed itself to the mission, affirmed its basic cultural assumptions and institutional values, assessed the strengths and weaknesses of its internal resources, critically evaluated its external environment, including the trends impacting its ministry, and identified the critical issues needing resolution, then this information needs to be translated into some pictures of the future. These pictures or scenarios assist the planning committee and leadership in selecting the directions (goals) they want to pursue, given the constraints of the mission, values, resources, and environment.

What is the purpose of a scenario?

Why take the time to construct a scenario? There are five reasons.

1. Scenarios clarify directions for the organization.

They help the decision makers see more clearly what their choices are. They feature the results of decisions that are being made today in a variety of alternative futures.

2. Scenarios become the basis of goals for organizational energies.

Once a scenario or vision statement has been adopted and owned as a direction toward which the community is committed it is translated into goals and objectives to allocate the organization's resources and energies. If Regent College's vision for the twenty-first century is to be an international graduate school serving the Pacific Rim, that direction will channel funding and energy away from increasing involvement in Europe and Africa and toward expanded service and programs in Asia.

---

20. James M. Kouzes and Barry Z. Posner, eds., *Christian Reflections on the Leadership Challenge* (San Francisco: Jossey-Bass, 2004), 17.

3. Scenarios are excellent tools for communication, motivation, and consensus-building.

It is much easier to get excited about a good scenario than about a list of goals and objectives. The goals and objectives set out in our planning end up on shelves, except for their important role in the control functions of leadership. Yet the scenarios, the statements of vision that capture the imagination and stir the spirit, continue to be vital living documents communicating our vision clearly to people inside and outside our organization. Because they are stories, scenarios allow people to imagine the role they will play. They let people know where we are going. Because a scenario communicates enthusiasm, it motivates people within the organization to move on to implementation, and it encourages people outside to provide the support and to participate in the programs and services. Again, it is easier to build a consensus around an exciting vision than around specific goals and objectives.

4. Scenarios can prevent uncritical extension of present trends.

Peter Drucker points out that it is all too easy for planners to write goals that simply extend current trends. He argues that leaders must avoid allocating resources to the defense of yesterday.[21] Scenarios can leapfrog over present trends into the future and raise necessary questions about the long-range validity of some trends.

5. Scenarios make change easier to introduce.

Because they are looking into the distance, scenarios are safe and nonthreatening. People can deal with the issues raised academically and theoretically, without feeling the pain of change now. I like to focus my scenarios ten to fifteen years in the future. That way people who might worry about a proposed change if they thought it would affect them today will not be threatened by something that will happen after they are gone! Since fifteen years from now is not too threatening to

---

21. Peter F. Drucker, *Managing in Turbulent Times* (New York: Harper & Row, 1980), 45.

most people, they can talk dispassionately about the issues involved. Interestingly, once they have taken ownership for the vision "out there," they will start to make things happen immediately. It changes one's perspective.

One year I served as the planning consultant for the West Coast region of an American denomination. As we used this scenario technique people who usually avoided planning meetings began to get excited. They started talking about things that up to that point had been taboo. Each board and committee developed and shared scenarios, and the combined leadership began to get excited about the future and the ways they could work together to make that future happen. If you can get people to talk about results in the future, they become much less defensive about strategies in the present. Remember that participation in solving problems reduces the neurological pain of change.

Who presents scenarios?

Who writes vision statements? It really depends on the organization and its current situation. Perhaps only the president or the pastor will be involved. Maybe all the members of the leadership team will be included. Or the process might be extended to the chairs of individual boards or departments.

When I was at Regent College I liked all of our cabinet officers to present scenarios to the planning committee, picturing their vision for the future of Regent through the eyes of their departments. From their combined vision, I prepared a college-wide scenario that was discussed and debated by the committee, the faculty, and the board. At the De Pree Center, where we have a much smaller team, everyone presents a scenario. The new ideas generated by the diversity of visions increases our enthusiasm. The alternatives visualized enable us to focus on what is fundamentally important and, we trust, equip us to adapt to an unpredictable future.

My approach is greatly shaped by Peter Block, who argues in *The Empowered Manager* that every manager within any organization should regularly be drafting a vision statement—a statement of how their piece of the organization might perform with excellence. Block notes that every manager is working from some vision anyway. The leader's job is to elicit that vision and allow it to contribute to the organization's vision of tomorrow.[22]

In one church I attended the vision statement was normally drafted initially by the pastor and then modified from the various levels of discussion. As I noted earlier, when I worked with the denominational group each board developed its scenario; one member was assigned to write it and present it to the combined boards. It is important that all the people we want to own the outcome of the planning process feel they are represented in the scenarios. Not all of them need a chance to develop and present a scenario, but they all need to know that they have been heard and that they have a place in the picture of the future.

I personally believe this is the most renewing part of the leadership task. You are given the opportunity to look ahead and project how God might use you and your organization over the next decade.

The more I write and share scenarios, the more excited I get about the future—which brings me to an important point for leaders: *If you cannot get enthusiastic about a scenario for the future of your church or organization, maybe it is time to change jobs!* This is a time to test your faith, your vision. When you look at the needs your organization addresses, when you review its mission and values, are you compelled to live out those values in your life and work? Does that mission still draw you to invest your life and energy? Can you envision a picture of your organization ten years from now making such a difference in this world that you want to be part of making it happen? It is difficult to

---

22. Peter Block, *The Empowered Manager* (San Francisco: Jossey-Bass, 1987), 107,123.

lead others if we are not led by our own vision of what God wants to accomplish through us.

To whom are scenarios presented?

Again, this depends on the organizational structure. Scenarios can be presented to the board, to the congregation, or to a strategic planning committee. Normally the strategic planning committee is the sounding board for the initial scenarios. My preference is to have the key leadership people of the organization prepare a ten-to-fifteen-minute scenario to share with the committee. Out of that discussion someone should be assigned the responsibility of drafting an organization-wide scenario that will be presented, discussed, and modified until ownership is achieved.

The broader the participation, the deeper the ownership. This takes time, but it is fun and it is important. Once a future is owned, the rest of the planning process falls into line. Everything else is simply looking for the most effective, efficient, and adaptable strategies to bring about that future.

But remember, a scenario is a faith statement; it is not an absolute statement of future reality. We prepare scenarios together, in community, but always on our knees before God. The process is important and can lead to important decisions for our organization. But the process— the scenario, the plan—does not necessarily declare the will of God. Leaders do their best to draw the wisest scenario out of the community that they lead, understanding that it is God's plan with which they are seeking to align their organization's resources and energies.

What makes a good scenario?

I have found eight elements to be important in creating a good scenario.

1. The scenario should articulate the mission and values.

Any statement of vision for an organization should be a reinforcement and articulation of the existing mission and value commitments—unless the scenario is being used explicitly to change the mission.

2. The scenario should sketch a picture of what the future will look like.

At this stage do not worry about how to get there—the strategies and resources. Work for the ideal as you see it completed ten to fifteen years from now in an imagined future. Sometimes this takes a little leadership effort because institutions have a tendency to want to talk about today's strategies rather than tomorrow's results. A good scenario, however, will keep focused on the future.

3. The scenario should look ten to fifteen years ahead.

This is far enough in the future not to be an immediate change threat. As I noted previously, everyone can talk comfortably about the far-off future. But if we start threatening what is being done today, the scenario will be resisted. Ten to fifteen years ahead keeps discussion at the level of theory and principles and avoids the personalized affective dimension. Your scenario needs to be far enough in the future for people to feel safe.

4. The scenario should be anchored in the present.

A scenario cannot be unrealistic. It needs to reflect a logical future, given what we know about today and who we are. A good scenario will also not be destructive of anyone's future. Again, a scenario will be resisted if it attacks the present too strongly. It must not challenge the present but rather hold up an exciting future that can be owned without having to sacrifice people's beliefs today. You can stretch people's thinking with a scenario, but it will be shot down if it attacks their strongly held personal commitments today.

I ran into this during one of Regent's planning processes. I presented a scenario for the future that emphasized a picture of Regent as a network of interrelated learning communities around the world. While the scenario attempted to affirm the present commitments to the Vancouver campus, it showed the most exciting developments and growth off campus. Unfortunately, a large segment of the planning committee had committed themselves primarily to the campus program. They read into the scenario a destruction of the Vancouver program for the sake of extended programming. Though this was not my intent, it was in fact the way the scenario was heard and read. Consequently it was not approved, and I had to prepare a revised scenario to underline my continued commitment to the Vancouver campus programming for the laity. (When I work with academic institutions now, extended education is no longer the concern. Now faculties are adjusting to a world that expects to learn online! And change keeps coming.)

5. The scenario should have a dream side.

Scenarios should have a faith component that stretches people's thinking. What might God do with your church or organization? What would we really like to do to fulfill our mission, even if it seems just out of reach? Sometimes the visualization of a scenario can actually generate the resources or opportunities that make that dream happen—remember quantum theory. If the planning process is appropriately integrated with prayer, the scenario may include a vision of what we think God wants us to be, even though we do not now see how it would be possible. A good scenario is practical and realistic and a risk taken in faith.

6. The scenario should include results as well as programs.

I have been alluding to this all along. Don't just say you will provide a program to feed the homeless. Tell how many homeless people will be fed and housed, along with recounting what has happened to those you have already served. What difference will your program make in people's lives? Think "stories"—a topic we will explore in the next chapter. It is too easy for us to describe our future in terms of programs, services, and staffing. A scenario is much more exciting when it talks in terms of impact and results. What difference will your church or organization be making in your community, with your constituencies, in 2020? It is that difference that captures people's imagination, not your programs.

7. The scenario should be flexible.

Though its dream side stretches us, a scenario should be feasible, integrating faith and realism. It also needs to have room for adjusting to new realities. Scenarios are never fixed, never set in concrete. They must always be open to change as new information surfaces. In a rapidly changing world our pictures of a decade ahead are tenuous at best. Scenarios are always open to discussion and modification. They are tools to open discussion about the future; they are not the future.

8. The scenario should describe a future you could own!

A scenario should generate enthusiasm in you and in everyone with whom you share it. It should be exciting, rallying, something you want to get behind. The scenario or vision statement takes the mission and values of your church or organization and creates an energizing picture of the future that compels you and your people to want to work toward it. Try pretending you are a reporter for the local newspaper or magazine and are looking at your organization in the year 2020. Write a story that describes what you see: the programs in place, the people involved, the impact the programs and services have. Can you get energized by the vision?

For several years I taught a strategic planning seminar. On the Friday of the week-long intensive course, each participant would present a brief, seven-minute version of a scenario for their church or organization. It was always the highlight of the week. Presenters would get excited, and their excitement would sweep through the group. Leaders would find renewal in a renewed vision as they shared that vision with others. It was a very emotional time. The scenario is a powerful tool for leadership.

Articulating the vision is one of the primary responsibilities of leadership. Servant leaders, in relationship with those for whom they are responsible, lift up a possible vision of God's future—a future in which we want to participate. This shared vision controls our leadership and motivates our people as they own it and it becomes theirs.

Conclusion: A Compelling Vision

To end this section on empowering vision, it is appropriate to read a vision statement written by the apostle John:

> Then I saw "a new heaven and a new earth," for the first heaven and the first earth had passed away, and there was no longer any sea. I saw the Holy City, the new Jerusalem, coming down out of heaven from God, prepared as a bride beautifully dressed for her husband. And I heard a loud voice from the throne saying, "Look! God's dwelling place is now among the people, and he will dwell with them. They will be his people, and God himself will be with them and be their God. 'He will wipe every tear from their eyes. There will be no more death' or mourning or crying or pain, for the old order of things has passed away." . . .
>
> I did not see a temple in the city, because the Lord God Almighty and the Lamb are its temple. The city does not need the sun or the moon to shine on it, for the glory of God gives it light, and the Lamb is its lamp. The nations will walk by its light, and the kings of the earth will bring their splendor into it. On no day will its gates ever be shut, for there will be no night there. The glory and honor of the nations will be brought into it. Nothing impure will ever enter it, nor will anyone who does what is shameful

or deceitful, but only those whose names are written in the Lamb's book of life.

Then the angel showed me the river of the water of life, as clear as crystal, flowing from the throne of God and of the Lamb down the middle of the great street of the city. On each side of the river stood the tree of life, bearing twelve crops of fruit, yielding its fruit every month. And the leaves of the tree are for the healing of the nations. No longer will there be any curse. The throne of God and of the Lamb will be in the city, and his servants will serve him. They will see his face, and his name will be on their foreheads. There will be no more night. They will not need the light of a lamp or the light of the sun, for the Lord God will give them light. And they will reign for ever and ever.

Revelation 21:1–4; 21:22—22:5

Now that is a vision to follow!

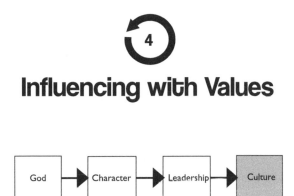

Influencing with Values

Fruit: Character and Values

Again we turn to our guide, Jude, to set our direction. "They are . . . autumn trees, without fruit and uprooted—twice dead" (verse 12). As we noted in chapter one, trees without roots produce no fruit. The toxic leaders Jude is opposing have nothing to offer the people of his community. Their character has no credibility, and consequently they have no values worth embedding in the culture of their community. Their leadership is not rooted in the love of God for his people. They love only themselves. They are doubly useless—not grounded in a relationship empowered by God and, therefore, not producing any growth in their community.

Belief precedes behavior; theology matters. The God we follow shapes who we are—the character revealed in our values. When leadership focuses on the leader, the leader becomes the god in whose service character emerges, producing selfish, toxic values. The biblical leader, on the other hand, reveals a character shaped in relationship to

God that spills over into all relationships. The "fruit" of this relationship with God is expressed in both our stated values—what we say is important—and more so in our lived out values—our actions. Biblical leaders live and model the kind of values that they hope to see expressed in the way the organization or community conducts its corporate life.

The character of biblical leadership produces value-laden fruit. Jude expects leaders who find their identity in their relationship with God to nurture organizations that care for people as persons loved by God. Leaders who find their security in their walk with Christ will nourish communities where diversity is comfortably embraced and where wounded relationships

> Leadership is a relationship of trust where commitments flow from character.

are reconciled and healed. Leaders who place their hope in God will be persons who respect commitments, who keep promises, who encourage trust.

In his book *Mr. Ives' Christmas*, Pulitzer Prize-winning author Oscar Hijuelos introduces us to Ives, a deeply spiritual man who, despite his beginnings in an orphanage, has made an enviable life for himself.[1] A successful Madison Avenue advertising illustrator, Ives is married to a vivacious, artistic woman, Annie, who shares his aesthetic passions and strong Christian beliefs. They live in New York City, where they raise their children, Robert and Caroline, with remarkable fair-mindedness and moral judgment. Ives gets promoted to vice-president at the advertising agency and lives comfortably with a community of friends. Seventeen-year-old Robert plans to enter seminary after high school to prepare for ordination as a Catholic priest.

Ives' perfect world is shattered, however, when Robert is gunned down by a teenage mugger at Christmas. Overwhelmed by grief, Ives

---

1. Oscar Hijuelos, *Mr. Ives' Christmas* (New York: HarperCollins, 1995).

struggles with doubts about the very values that have shaped his life and faith. His theology is severely tested.

The novel follows Ives through the next twenty-five years of his life as he searches for peace and understanding. In the end, his personal integrity, his character, and the values and faith that he taught his children compel him to reconcile with and forgive his son's murderer. Only then can he return to the core of who he is and reengage the life around him. To his friends he is a man of character: a person who navigates his life and work with deeply held values that shape his behavior and influence the lives of those around him. Ives' leadership at work and conduct at home were constrained and empowered by his character and commitments, his faith and values.

Who are you? And who cares? It starts with theology. The God whom you follow defines the core of your identity—your character. Leadership flows from character, from who you are. And leaders add value to all the relationships in which they are engaged; that is why people care about leadership. Leadership is about adding value to an organization and its people out of the strength of the character and values of the leader, character and values rooted in the love of God.

The Colossian Church: A Community of Character

Let's turn again to the Colossian community and see what values shaped their life together. This time imagine yourself in a meeting of the Colossian church shortly after Tychicus and Onesimus arrived with Paul's letters to Philemon and to the Colossians. The church has assembled in the home of one of the elders. Some people are sitting on chairs, some are sitting on the floor, some are standing. A new letter has been received from the apostle Paul.

In a day without Bibles, this is a major event. A word from God is going to be received as Paul's letter, written from prison, is read. There is an air of excitement and anticipation throughout the congregation. But there is also a ripple of anxiety and discomfort. You can feel the tension. Sitting in the room are Philemon and Onesimus. Philemon, one of the leaders of this church, was betrayed last year by one of his slaves, who stole from him and ran away. Philemon had been very upset about the experience and had shared it with the congregation.

And now here sits Onesimus, the runaway slave—sent back as a believer by Paul himself. We know that Philemon also received a personal letter from Paul; that must account for his willingness to have Onesimus here in the same room with him. Perhaps he will share Paul's letter with us.

How are we supposed to deal with this? Onesimus is a slave! Should he be here? Yet he seems to be a genuinely converted believer—and he has Paul's blessing. Should we let Christian slaves into our church? What about his crime? He stole from Philemon and ran away. That is punishable by death. Do we ignore that? Apparently Paul wants Philemon to take Onesimus back into his house, reinstate him as a member of his staff, and accept him as a Christian brother.

What's our role in this? We are the Christian community in Colosse. We are supposed to be the body of Christ. We know that Philemon is an important and active member of this community. And now we need to embrace Onesimus. How do we do this? How do we deal with the conflict that is obviously going on in many minds in this room? Can this really be of God if it is causing all this conflict for us?

It's not hard to imagine this scene on the Sunday after Tychicus and Onesimus arrived. Put yourself in their place and listen to parts of the letter to the Colossians, keeping in mind that Philemon and Onesimus are sitting here listening as well.

> So then, just as you received Christ Jesus as Lord, continue to live your lives in him, rooted and built up in him, strengthened in the faith as you were taught, and overflowing with thankfulness. . . .
>
> Since, then, you have been raised with Christ, set your hearts on things above, where Christ is seated at the right

hand of God. Set your minds on things above, not on earthly things. For you died, and your life is now hidden with Christ in God. When Christ, who is your life, appears, then you also will appear with him in glory.

Put to death, therefore, whatever belongs to your earthly nature: sexual immorality, impurity, lust, evil desires and greed, which is idolatry. Because of these, the wrath of God is coming. You used to walk in these ways, in the life you once lived. But now you must also rid yourselves of all such things as these: anger, rage, malice, slander, and filthy language from your lips. Do not lie to each other, since you have taken off your old self with its practices and have put on the new self, which is being renewed in knowledge in the image of its Creator. Here there is no Gentile or Jew, circumcised or uncircumcised, barbarian, Scythian, slave or free, but Christ is all, and is in all.

Therefore, as God's chosen people, holy and dearly loved, clothe yourselves with compassion, kindness, humility, gentleness and patience. Bear with each other and forgive one another if any of you has a grievance against someone. Forgive as the Lord forgave you. And over all these virtues put on love, which binds them all together in perfect unity.

Let the peace of Christ rule in your hearts, since as members of one body you were called to peace. And be thankful. Let the message of Christ dwell among you richly as you teach and admonish one another with all wisdom through psalms, hymns and songs from the Spirit, singing to God with gratitude in your hearts. And whatever you do, whether in word or deed, do it all in the name of the Lord Jesus, giving thanks to God the Father through him.

Wives, submit yourselves to your husbands, as is fitting in the Lord.

> Husbands, love your wives and do not be harsh with them.
>
> Children, obey your parents in everything, for this pleases the Lord.
>
> Fathers, do not embitter your children, or they will become discouraged.
>
> Slaves, obey your earthly masters in everything; and do it, not only when their eye is on you and to curry their favor, but with sincerity of heart and reverence for the Lord. Whatever you do, work at it with all your heart, as working for the Lord, not for human masters, since you know that you will receive an inheritance from the Lord as a reward. It is the Lord Christ you are serving. Those who do wrong will be repaid for their wrongs, and there is no favoritism.
>
> Masters, provide your slaves with what is right and fair, because you know that you also have a Master in heaven.
>
> Colossians 2:6–7; 3:1—4:1

Powerful words for a church struggling with conflict. But what does this have to do with us nearly two thousand years later? Do we ever have conflict in our communities?!

For recreation I often go mountain climbing or white-water canoeing. My friend Don and I have been roped together or shared a canoe now for over thirty years. We have grown close, learning to trust each other and to care deeply about each other's lives.

Do we ever experience conflict? Only every time the canoe heads over rapids with me in the front! Don and I are both opinionated, controlling people with very definite ideas how to get through the water and rocks alive. Since I sit in the front I am the first to taste the rapids; and when my paddle goes into the water I have a major effect on the control of the canoe, whether Don agrees or not. Don and I have debated procedures before, during, and after both successful runs and total disasters. We have experienced many conflicts; but we have many shared values. We care for each other and have linked our survival by roping up on a mountain glacier or sharing a canoe on the river. We both have a vested interest in the best outcome and are willing to confront each other on our behaviors and procedures and listen to the other person carefully. Failure to listen usually ends up with one or both of us swimming downstream!

Close community includes conflict. But caring relationships work for the resolution of conflict and the growth of community.

I would like to reflect on conflict, confrontation, character, and accountability, and see if we can learn something about values from the way Paul approached this situation in Colosse.

Should there be conflict in a Christian community?

What is conflict? Conflict, psychologists tell us, is not something that happens between two people. It is something that happens in us as individuals when we encounter differences, something that does not fit our understanding of a situation.

Conflict is probably a required corollary of community. The very definition of Christian community includes an acceptance of diversity—witness Philemon and Onesimus—and diversity means differences: differences of approach, of values, of perspective, of opinions, of expectations, of hopes, of commitments. And differences cause conflict.

Conflict not only is possible in Christian community, it may be a necessary byproduct of community that is an important catalyst for growth as we learn to adjust to the differences caused by the diversity of community. No conflict may suggest no diversity, and possibly no growth. Both Philemon and Onesimus experienced conflict before and during their reconciliation, and their presence together in the church probably produced conflict in many of the members of the Colossian church. On this side of heaven, I believe there will always be conflict in Christian community as we struggle to learn to live like the body of Christ in this world. And it is precisely this conflict that shapes character.

If conflict is inevitable, how do we handle it?

Here I think Paul gives us a good model, a model I would call caring confrontation and accountability over against criticism and gossip. In the passage we read earlier, Paul discards anger, rage, malice, and slander as appropriate characteristics for a Christian community. He affirms compassion, kindness, humility, gentleness, patience, forgiveness, and love as the marks of Christian character. It is clear that Paul sees a caring attitude of love dominating all community relationships. Yet he goes on to encourage the Colossians to engage one another in teaching and instruction or confrontation that emerges from their study of God's Word.

I believe Paul expects confrontation, but he expects it to be conducted in the context of a caring relationship, a relationship in which both parties are genuinely concerned about the growth and development of each other in the community. And as a leader that is exactly what Paul sets out to accomplish.

Let me distinguish between caring confrontation and criticism. I believe that confrontation addresses a person's behaviors or attitudes in light of that person's stated values or commitments, not my values or beliefs. Confrontation holds people accountable to live what they teach or claim to be important. It is a call for integrity. It does not assess their progress by standards that I hold up for myself. If confrontation is to be effective or constructive, a caring relationship must surround it. Within the context of a caring relationship you can hold me accountable to my own values and beliefs because I know you care and want to see me grow in my faith.

On the other hand, criticism attacks the other person's values without the supportive context of a caring relationship. Criticism may address a person's failure to live up to his or her commitments or beliefs but with little genuine interest in the person's growth and development. Often, however, criticism reflects my internal conflict. When your values and behaviors do not align with my beliefs and values, the difference creates a dissonance—a conflict within me. Because I am in conflict, I want you to change—not because I care about you, but because I am focusing on me. Criticism may be voiced to the person who is causing my conflict, but it is often directed to someone else about that person. I call that gossip.

Caring confrontation is concerned about the other person's growth and emerges within a relationship of trust; criticism emerges from our own conflict and usually destroys trust. Confrontation wants to see positive growth; criticism wants to express hurt and conflict. Confrontation usually seeks resolution; criticism usually seeks removal of my conflict.

These distinctions are important in an organizational context. Leaders are there to hold people accountable to the shared vision of the community and to the standards they have agreed to achieve. This happens in a caring relationship of influence. Leaders hold followers accountable to the shared vision, mission, and values of the organization, *not* to the vision, values, or opinions of the leader. Confrontation occurs in a relationship in which the leader cares about the follower and the vision they share. Confrontation measures progress against a shared organizational mission *owned by the follower*. Criticism usually occurs when the leader is self-focused and progress is measured by the leader's standards or mission.

I think this is the genius of Paul's confrontation with Philemon. Read his letter again and watch how Paul underlines his deep love for Philemon—the caring relationship—and holds Philemon accountable to act according to Philemon's commitments to a vision they share. The relational-emotional-values side of leadership provides the holding space where conflict surfaced by competing visions and expectations is resolved.

In the context of a deep and caring relationship, Paul has confronted Philemon with the implications of his commitments. Philemon is known for his encouragement of fellow believers and for his participation in and support of community, and to this Paul appeals. He does not attack the institution of slavery. He does not hold Philemon accountable for a value system that we in this century think he should have understood. Rather, he stays within the values and culture of Philemon and the Colossian church; but he lovingly points out to Philemon that his commitment to community might require him to take a second look at his relationship with Onesimus. I think we can learn five things about Paul's values and about the requirements for caring confrontation and accountability from the way he writes to Philemon.

1. A caring relationship

First, Paul clearly establishes the context of a caring relationship. There can be no question that Paul and Philemon are integrally bound together by mutual respect and love. It is the strength of this relationship that allows Paul to hope to influence Philemon.

2. Identification with the conflict of the other person

Paul brings Onesimus directly into that relationship by underlining his own deeply personal and spiritual relationship with the converted slave. Philemon can no longer deal with Onesimus as one who has offended him personally or as a subhuman slave. Now he must deal with his relationship with Paul. He must see Paul when he looks at Onesimus.

3. Acceptance of the person's stated values and commitments as the starting point

Paul confronts Philemon with his own commitments. The opening prayer gives thanks for Philemon's contributions as a member of the

Colossian community, his investment in the members of the church. The refreshment and encouragement for which Philemon is known Paul now asks for himself and through him for Onesimus.

> Note that while there is strong expectation running throughout Paul's letter there is no indication that the relationship with Philemon would be terminated if Philemon doesn't comply. Paul resists using his authority, at least directly, and leaves it up to Philemon to decide how far he will go in his acceptance of Onesimus.

4. A personal investment in the resolution

Paul takes the cost of the confrontation upon himself. He assumes Onesimus' debt and offers to cover all costs due to Philemon. Effective confrontation asks the question, What can I do to help you succeed in living up to your values? In this case Paul is willing to cover all of the debt that Onesimus owes Philemon.

5. A commitment to long-term accountability and growth

Paul builds accountability into the confrontation. He states that he will be visiting soon to see how things are going. Philemon knows that this person who cares about him will be checking in to see how he has responded to his confrontation. Part of accountability is the willingness to have our progress monitored. People who care enough to confront you with your own values are marvelous friends to have. People who follow up and care enough to hold you accountable for your growth are wonderful gifts from God.

It is not hard to see the Christ-motif in Paul's approach. Two people are to be reconciled through Paul, who bears the cost of that reconciliation personally. Now there is a model for relational leadership—for servant leadership!

Conflict is inevitable in a Christian community. Yet conflict can be resolved through caring confrontation that invests itself in the growth and development of the other person. Confrontation and accountability, I believe, are values deeply embedded in the concept of community and must be embraced by leaders.

Leadership Is Being Oneself for Others

We have been looking at leadership as a relationship. Leadership is a relationship in which one person makes an investment in another to influence the behaviors, vision, values, beliefs, or attitudes of that other person. This influence has two major purposes: the growth of the follower (and the leader) and the accomplishment of a mission shared by both. As we saw earlier, the leadership relationship exists only when others choose to accept our influence and allow us to lead them.

Research by James Kouzes and Barry Posner has underlined the fact that people follow leaders who are credible, who have integrity of character. By integrity of character they mean three things: personal values or beliefs—that is, a credo of what is right; capabilities or competence—that is, the ability to turn your words into actions; and trust or confidence in your ability to do what you believe.[2] Character is more than stated beliefs and values. Character is something that emerges from within; it comes from the soul. It represents those deeply held beliefs or value commitments—the theology—that shape who you are, that control all that you do. Character is revealed in action.

I am making a distinction here between character and stated values. Stated values are the commitments that we affirm, such as the Spirit-shaped characteristics we read about in Colossians. Character, however, reflects those deeply held beliefs out of which our behavior and attitudes actually emerge. If someone watches our actions they will see our true character, regardless of the values we espouse. Everyone

---

2. James M. Kouzes and Barry Z. Posner, *Credibility* (San Francisco: Jossey-Bass, 1993), 59.

has character; everyone has values. We all live out of a set of values that find expression in our behavior. Ideally, with the help of the Spirit of God, our affirmations and our actions will be consistent—will demonstrate integrity. That at least is our calling, I believe.

Kouzes and Posner argue that leadership starts with the leader, with a person whose character is worth following.[3] Great leaders, Warren Bennis claims, are people who are "being themselves" with character and integrity.[4] You become an effective leader by living out of the strength of your character, by living what you believe. That kind of character—that kind of integrity—produces credibility, and people follow people who are credible. We began this chapter with the accusation of Jude. Lack of integrity is precisely Jude's concern. The toxic leaders in his community had no roots. There was no God-shaped character to give content to their leadership. They were not believable as leaders. Biblical leadership starts in the soul with a desire to live out our calling in Christ as Spirit-shaped people. Only in the strength of this relationship with God in Christ are we in any position to offer leadership.

Six disciplines for maintaining credibility

In their book *Credibility*, Kouzes and Posner outline six disciplines that leaders continually should work at to maintain their integrity and credibility.[5] When it comes to building character, none of these are substitutes for spending time with God, but they are helpful reminders about important components of the leadership relationship.

> ➤ **Discover yourself.** Take time to think through what you believe, looking at your life and actions to see what kind of values are reflected by your behaviors and attitudes. What are the important value commitments that you bring to the

---

3. Ibid., 32.

4. Warren Bennis, *On Becoming a Leader* (Reading, MA: Addison-Wesley, 1989), 40, 51.

5. Kouzes and Posner, *Credibility*, 51–56.

table—that you want to model and to which you are prepared to allow others to hold you accountable?

➤ **Appreciate your constituents.** Focus your attention on your people; understand them as they are. Value the diversity they represent and confront the conflict that emerges with differences. Kouzes and Posner want to shift the focus as quickly as possible from the self to others, so that trust can be built by listening and caring about those for whom we are responsible.

➤ **Affirm *shared* values.** Community is built upon shared vision and shared values. Leaders are responsible for articulating, modeling, and reinforcing both vision and values in the life of the communities they seek to lead. We will look at this in more detail later.

➤ **Develop capacity.** Make an investment in followers that increases their ability to contribute. Following the model of Paul Hersey and Kenneth Blanchard that we looked at in chapter two, Kouzes and Posner want to see everyone growing into levels of maturity that allow them to lead out of deeply embedded values and compelling visions.

➤ **Serve a purpose.** For Kouzes and Posner, leadership is service. It focuses on the shared vision and empowers people to make a contribution to that vision. Again, leadership flows from character reaching outward to serve the vision and the people.

➤ **Sustain hope.** As people of vision and people of character, leaders keep hope alive. They have the courage to live out their vision and to strive to live out their values, and they encourage others to do the same. Christian character, in the final analysis, is based on a vision of God at work in this world and the renewing presence of the Spirit within us.

Character is life lived in relationship with God. It is about being the person whom God intends you to be for the sake of the people whom God brings across your path. People of character become leaders whether or not they hold a position of leadership. They are people whose integrity and credibility earn trust. People listen and follow. In the context of Christian communities, we look for Christ-shaped character in our leaders, since leaders have a significant responsibility in shaping the character of our churches and organizations.

Character, Culture, and Values

The first responsibility of leadership is to articulate the vision, to keep the mission and values before the church or organization. Effective leaders offer a compelling picture of the future that motivates people to get involved. The second responsibility of leadership, I believe, is to reinforce the culture. This is the point in our communities where the intersection of leadership and spirituality is most visible.

Character

The character of the community and the character of individual members of that community are what the leadership literature calls *organizational culture.* Current studies are repeatedly underlining the leader's responsibility for reinforcing the culture of the organization with intentional, personally held values.

This is an area of particular interest to me as I seek to bring my faith to bear on my leadership responsibilities. This is where I try to work out my own spirituality in the context of my positional responsibilities as a leader. I have a strong concern, almost a passion, for healthy organizations being both effective and efficient and at the same time manifesting the fruit of the Spirit.

I want to see organizations and churches run effectively and accountably with the best of leadership and stewardship. I also want to see them living out their corporate lives together in a way that reflects the presence of the Spirit of God in their midst. The fruit of the Spirit should be manifest in the way they do business together. I do not believe these are mutually exclusive. In fact, I believe that a Christian organization must by definition be both an effective organization and a vital Christian community. Now I do not know many places where this is true yet, which is why I prefer to avoid using the phrase "Christian organization." It is something we worked on consciously and intentionally at Regent College, and we knew that we still had a long way to go. But I believe strongly that we must keep working at it if we are to be leaders who reflect the presence of Christ in our communities.

Those of us leading organizations as followers of Christ talk a lot about community, love, values, and the fruit of the Spirit, and yet we frequently live and lead our organizations with actions that do not match our words. Max De Pree, my friend and mentor, captures the link between actions and words in a story recounted in his book *Leadership Jazz*:

> Esther, my wife, and I have a granddaughter named Zoe, the Greek word for "life." She was born prematurely and weighed one pound, seven ounces, so small that my wedding ring could slide up her arm to her shoulder. The neonatologist who first examined her told us that she had a 5 to 10 percent chance of living three days. When Esther and I scrubbed up for our first visit and saw Zoe in her isolette in the neonatal intensive care unit, she had two IVs in her navel, one in her foot, a monitor on each side of her chest, and a respirator tube and a feeding tube in her mouth.
>
> To complicate matters, Zoe's biological father had jumped ship the month before Zoe was born. Realizing

this, a wise and caring nurse named Ruth gave me my instructions: "For the next several months, at least, you're the surrogate father. I want you to come to the hospital every day to visit Zoe, and when you come, I would like you to rub her body and her legs and arms with the tip of your finger. While you're caressing her, you should tell her over and over how much you love her, because she has to be able to connect your voice to your touch."

Ruth was doing exactly the right thing on Zoe's behalf (and, of course, on my behalf as well), and without realizing it she was giving me one of the best possible descriptions of the work of a leader. At the core of becoming a leader is the need always to connect one's voice and one's touch.[6]

Max De Pree is calling us to practice what we preach: to live out our values in our organizational life, our community life together. He expects our character to be reflected in the way we lead within our organizations. Our behaviors are to be in sync with our sermons. Our voice should be seen in our touch.

Public television often has superb presentations about leadership. One series of *Classic Theater* focused on the story of the Borgias, Rodrigo Borgia (who became Pope Alexander VI) and his son Cesare, the Duke of Romagna. If there was ever an example of the clash between stated values and personal character, the Borgias must be supreme. In the name of the Christian church and all the values it stands for, Rodrigo, Cesare, and Lucrezia Borgia (Rodrigo's daughter) ruled with a self-serving wickedness that later became the model for Niccolò Machiavelli's *The Prince*, often seen as the prototypical description of an evil leader. They lied, cheated, and used their power to play their friends and their enemies against one another. They spoke the language of the holy church, but their actions were those of evil incarnate.

---

6. Max De Pree, *Leadership Jazz* (New York: Doubleday, 1992), 1–3. Used by permission.

Their true identity was not in their words but in their touch—in their behavior.

Culture

When I am teaching about leadership I often use a simple exercise with Tinkertoys. I break the class into small groups and give each group a can of Tinkertoys. Each group gets sixty seconds to build, without talking, the tallest possible self-standing structure. At the end of the sixty seconds I measure each structure and we analyze why the groups did not perform better. Why are the structures so small and often disjointed? Most groups initially conclude that they didn't have enough time. So we do the exercise again. Only this time I give them three minutes to talk together and plan how to use their sixty seconds of Tinkertoy construction. After the planning time, I again ask for silence and the exercise is repeated with the same rules. This time, however, skyscrapers fill the room! Nearly every group improves significantly when they have a plan for the use of their limited resources (time and supplies) and a role for each to play. Time is not the issue. Planning and delegation are key. Constraints actually allow creativity to flourish.

At the end of this second exercise, however, I usually ask the second- or third-place groups, "If the objective was to have the tallest structure in the room, why didn't you knock down the other towers or take their materials?'

Most groups, particularly in Christian communities, are shocked at the suggestion and usually respond that it would not be right or fair or something like that, at which time I point out that they have a hidden value system or culture that is constraining their choice of strategies to achieve their objective. Their behavior is being shaped by their values without any conscious awareness on their part.

This is a simplistic example, but it is exactly what is going on in all of our organizations and churches. Every organization has a hidden culture that has developed over the years and controls what is actually done regardless of the values we espouse. The problem is that, when the stated values of the church or the organization are not in sync with the cultural beliefs and assumptions, organizational dissonance is created and people get caught in the middle.

I believe you can learn more about the culture of an organization by observing the behaviors and actions of the people than by reading the statement of organizational values. In organizations, people tend to live out the values of the culture they have been part of rather than the values that are articulated by the leadership. If we want to create community in our organizations or churches as an intentional value, we need to start with an understanding of the cultural values we are already reinforcing.

Over the last couple of decades the importance of organizational culture and organizational value systems has been emerging in the leadership literature. Books like *Corporate Cultures, In Search of Excellence, Creating Excellence, A Passion for Excellence, Thriving on Chaos, Leadership Jazz, Credibility, Above the Bottom Line, Leading Change, Good to Great,* and *In Good Company* have recognized that all organizations have deeply rooted beliefs and assumptions that shape the way those within the organizations live and work together—and that the relationship between the leader and the organization is a key variable in the reinforcement or change of these beliefs.[7]

---

7. Terrence E. Deal and Allen A. Kennedy, *Corporate Cultures* (Reading, MA: Addison-Wesley, 1982); Thomas J. Peters and Robert H. Waterman Jr., *In Search of Excellence* (New York: Harper & Row, 1982); Craig R. Hickman and Michael A. Silva, *Creating Excellence* (New York: New American Library, 1984); Tom Peters and Nancy Austin, *A Passion for Excellence* (New York: Warner Books, 1989); Tom Peters, *Thriving on Chaos* (New York: Alfred Knopf, 1987); Max De Pree, *Leadership Jazz*; James Kouzes and Barry Posner, *Credibility*; J. Michael Fuller, *Above the Bottom Line* (Toronto: Macmillan Canada, 1993); James O'Toole, *Leading Change* (San Francisco: Jossey-Bass, 1995); Jim Collins, *Good to Great* (New York: HarperCollins, 2001); Don Cohen and Laurence Prusak, *In Good Company* (Boston, MA: Harvard Business School Press, 2001).

Edgar Schein, a distinguished professor at MIT's Sloan School of Management, goes so far as to suggest that perhaps the only thing of unique importance that leaders do is to create and manage culture.[8] In his excellent book *Organizational Culture and Leadership*, Schein points out that our values are the observed manifestations of our organizational culture. He uses *values* here as the visible actions and publicly stated affirmations of what is important to us. Michael Henderson and Dougal Thompson see the lived values of an organization as the tip of the iceberg of beliefs.[9] Our actions are value statements as much as our affirmations. Hopefully they match. By *culture*, Schein refers to the basic assumptions and beliefs that are shared by members of the organization and operate unconsciously,[10] defining the organization's view of itself. The elements of an organization's culture cannot be seen and are seldom talked about. But they are at work as deeply and powerfully as the beliefs that kept the class from knocking down the Tinkertoy towers.

Every organization has this hidden culture. It is the character of the organization, formed out of the shared history and experiences of the organization as it develops and survives. The founding leadership of our churches and organizations implant the first seeds of the culture. Then, over time, the community living together develops some unconscious ways of doing things. "The way things are done here" becomes automatic, reinforced over the years by what is valued and what is opposed.

Tradition becomes strong and deeply rooted. Most of us can easily come up with illustrations from our church experience. Tradition is strong in churches and difficult to change. In North America, most

---

8. Edgar H. Schein, *Organizational Culture and Leadership*, 2nd ed. (San Francisco: Jossey-Bass, 1992), 2.

9. Michael Henderson and Dougal Thompson, *Values at Work* (Auckland, New Zealand: HarperCollins, 2003), 16.

10. Schein, *Organizational Culture and Leadership*, 12.

churches still meet at eleven o'clock on Sunday mornings to accom-
modate the milking of the cows—in spite of the fact that very few
church members own cows anymore! And music—every church has
horror stories about the traditions involved in the music of the church!
The organizational culture is that set of traditions, assumptions, and
beliefs that are taken for granted and operate unconsciously in all of
our organizations.

Schein's research demonstrates that every organization has a hidden culture. Interestingly, he goes on to argue that most organizational
cultures take shape around a similar pattern. The culture is formed
as an unconscious institutional response to six basic issues: how the
organization understands truth, time, space, human nature, human
activity, and human relationships.[11] Theological issues!

By *truth*, Schein refers to the "shared assumptions that define what
is real and what is not . . . how truth is ultimately to be determined, and
whether truth is revealed or discovered." By *time*, he is referring to the
shared assumptions that define time, how time is measured, "how many
kinds of time there are, and the importance of time in the culture." In
terms of *space*, he sees organizations as having "shared assumptions
about space and its distribution, how space is allocated and owned,
the symbolic meaning of space around the person," the role of space in
defining intimacy, privacy, or importance.[12]

His issues concerning *human nature, activity, and relationships*
touch the core of our work in the church and in theological education.
They include the shared assumptions about what it means to be human.
Is human nature good, evil, or neutral? Are human beings perfectible
or not? What is the right way for people to relate to their environment?
What is the appropriate balance between activity and initiative and
passivity and reaction? What is work? What is play? How are power

---

11. Ibid., 95.
12. Ibid., 95–96.

and love distributed in human relationships? "Is life cooperative or competitive; individualistic, group collaborative, or communal?"[13] How are conflicts resolved and decisions made?

> Culture is as important as vision. The vision of leadership articulates the mission and defines the organization. The relationships of leadership pass on the values and create the culture that determines how, and often if, the mission will be lived out. Both shape the expectations for activity within the church or organization.

Schein would argue that, without thinking about it, every organization forms assumptions about these six dimensions that become the context for all of its corporate life. These assumptions form a hidden pattern or worldview, which he calls *culture*. That culture shapes the actions, decisions, policies, and procedures of the organization in the formation of the values that govern all that the organization does.

Values

While we should understand the cultural assumptions operating in our organization, the role of leaders is targeted primarily at the values level. As we noted previously, values are the visible expressions of the organization's culture—the stated affirmations that communicate how we intend to work together and the operational assumptions that actually determine our behaviors.

Michael Henderson and Dougal Thompson, who refer to themselves as "organizational anthropologists," work directly with organizations to clarify and align corporate and personal values, recognizing that values are key to organizational success. In their excellent book

---

13. Ibid., 96.

Values at Work, they identify nine principles that have emerged from their work with leaders seeking to build healthy organizational cultures.

1. Values are the priorities and preferences of individuals and groups, which reflect what is important to them.

> Values are the visible demonstration of character—personal character and corporate character or culture. They reveal what is important as they shape decisions and actions. Values reflect a prioritizing of perceived worth. And of course organizational and personal values must be prioritized, since leadership decisions so often are made in the face of competing values.

2. Unprioritized values create conflict.

> A perceived difference in values produces conflict within us. Clarifying and prioritizing values reduces ambiguity and facilitates the interaction of relationships. It also facilitates the decision-making process as we choose from alternatives before us. Among the given choices, each of which often reflects an important value, what is most important? Without that sense of priority, leadership struggles.

3. An organization's values are its real leader.

> While the values of leaders are embedded in organizations over time, it is the culture of an organization that sustains and constrains the day-to-day life of the community. Decisions are made throughout the day on the basis of the organization's culture. We often act without reflection, living out a set of values that shape our visions, our relationships, our decisions, and our actions. Personal and corporate values are highly influential in organizational life. Leadership flows from personal values; personal and

corporate values shape organizational behavior. We lead with values.

4. Values are the DNA of all organizations' culture.

Values run in the bloodstream of an organization. They give life to the community, determining what happens and why. Every organization or church operates from a set of values deeply embedded within its culture. Effective leaders understand this and work to surface and reinforce the culture they seek to create, aligning corporate values and personal values for the sake of the mission and the growth of the people.

5. Organizations do not put their values into practice, people do.

Values are incarnated in people—most visibly in the leaders, but powerfully in the followers. The values that control behavior shape the organization. Leaders and followers make value decisions throughout the day.

6. Values drive performance.

Research tells us that values are critical to the productivity of the organization. They shape the behavior leading to the success or failure of the mission. For this reason alone leadership needs to give more attention to the alignment of values. If the personal values of followers are complementary with the corporate values of the church or organization, the people will thrive in the pursuit of the mission. If they are not aligned, the values of the follower will undermine the corporate culture or the follower will choose to leave. Successful achievement of the mission is directly tied to the values of the people.

7. Decisions are based more on values than rational analysis.

As studies on emotional intelligence have revealed, decisions are shaped more by emotional response than reasoned logic. We choose on the basis of our values and priorities and then look for reasons to support our decision.

8. Values determine quality.

Values determine value; we commit ourselves to that which we believe has worth, and that attention and focus promote quality. Quality is a value. Max De Pree often says that his father, D. J. De Pree, the founder of the Herman Miller Corporation, defined quality as truth, linking it back to a core value for all relationships.

9. The values at work within an organization influence behavior.

The values that take root in a church or organization shape the environment or community experienced by those who work and serve there. They guide decisions, channel actions, and ultimately influence outcomes. The culture of the organization enhances or distracts from the accomplishment of the mission.[14]

I would add a tenth principle to this list:

10. Leaders create and reinforce culture.

As Goleman, Boyatzis, and McKee remind us, leaders are the most-watched individuals in any group of people. Every word and action is observed and assessed as followers seek

---

14. Henderson and Thompson, *Values at Work*, 18–19.

to understand how they might thrive in the organization.[15] Jean Lipman-Blumen raises the bar another notch. She argues that every person is seeking to understand how to live life in the face of impending death. On that journey we look to those we have identified as leaders to see what they believe is important. Every action of those leaders is evaluated and related to our own emerging philosophy of life. The influence of a leader's values extends beyond the work relationship; it speaks into the human quest for meaning in life.[16] Thus Schein concludes that the unique contribution of leaders is the creation, articulation, modeling, and reinforcement of the values that form the controlling culture of the organization. The influence of leadership resides deeply in the values of the leader.

Leaders must consciously work to reinforce the values that they affirm by every action and word. If the culture produces values that are not consistent with the affirmations we make, leaders must slowly and patiently continue to reinforce the stated values until they are embedded in the culture deep enough to last. The culture shapes the behaviors of the people in the organization.

Leaders create and sustain culture in everything they do. If we want to make a difference in our organizations and churches, we need to be aware of this reality and be intentional with our actions, recognizing that we are working on cultural assumptions even as we articulate and implement vision. This may well be the place where leadership has the most significant long-range impact on the life and mission of the organization. The culture a leader creates is a legacy that contributes to the health of the organization long after the leader's tenure. Or stated

---

15. Daniel Goleman, Richard Boyatzis, and Annie McKee, *Primal Leadership: Realizing the Power of Emotional Intelligence* (Boston: Harvard Business School Press, 2002), 8.
16. Jean Lipman-Blumen, *Connective Leadership: Managing in a Changing World* (Oxford: Oxford University Press, 1996), 22.

in reverse, the health of the organization after the leader has left is a measure of the culture that was established and reinforced by the leader.

This brings us back to the discussion of planning. Previously we focused on the mission of the organization in response to the critical question, Who are we? What Schein underlines for us is the significance of the second question in our earlier planning model: What is important to us? I believe that a complete vision includes both mission and values. It creates a picture of a future that captures who we are—both what we do and the values that we communicate in the doing of it. As we saw in the connections of leadership (chapter one), there are two systems involved in our organizational planning and leadership.

Let me illustrate with a simple story. One evening I met with a prestigious professor at a regional college, seeking to recruit him to teach in a continuing education program. We met in the evening because that was the only time available in both of our schedules. During our discussion, the door of his office opened and a young student janitor walked in, pushing a vacuum cleaner. It was Thursday night, the night the professor's office was scheduled for cleaning. She proceeded to vacuum the floor, asking us to lift our feet when she needed to vacuum under our chairs. We finally had to stop talking because we couldn't hear over the roar of the sweeper. When she finished her task she left; we smiled and went on with the negotiations.

Now, was this young woman doing her job? Yes and no. Yes, according to the purpose system of her objectives for the evening. No, according to the values system of what is important in the mission of her job. According to the traditional purpose system, she was doing precisely what she was supposed to do. Her piece of the organizational mission called for her to keep professors' offices clean, and her objective for Thursday night was to clean this professor's office. She was doing her job, and progress could be measured against the mission, at least according to the purpose system.

The values system, however, asks a different set of questions that also impact the mission. What are we about? What is important here? Under the values system, her job was not to keep the professor's office clean but to provide an environment that facilitated or made possible the professor's ministry. Her role was to support the professor's ministry and so further the mission of the organization. Had she been operating consciously under both systems she would have noted that the professor had a guest, recognized that the best support she could provide at that moment was *not* to clean the office, and revised her work schedule so she could clean that office later.

Even in this illustration, we are dealing with assumed values. My critique of the janitor was based on my stated value that she was there to support the professor's ministry. On the other hand, she behaved differently, most likely acting out of the cultural values of her organization. She had learned that she would be rewarded for cleaning this office on Thursdays, not for exercising judgment and switching days. She was acting under a values system. Her actions, however, suggested that the governing value system preferred conformity to creativity.

There are two systems involved in the planning process, flowing from the two core responsibilities for leadership: vision and relationship. The purpose system (see the diagram below) is a pyramid of goals, objectives, and actions descending from the organizational mission. The values system is a pyramid of values, norms or policies, and actions ascending from the beliefs or culture of the organization. Both are important to the planning process of any organization. Both will impact the selection of strategies and the implementation of operational plans.

Traditionally, planning has focused on the purpose system: setting goals and measurable objectives. Schein believes it is absolutely essential that leaders examine the organizational culture and values system because culture constrains strategy.[17] It is difficult to plan beyond the boundaries of the culture, both the intentional value commitments and the unintentional, unconscious culture or tradition that has developed over the organization's history.

Two Systems of Strategic Planning

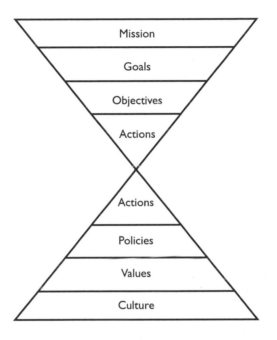

When I was serving as a denominational planning consultant, we experienced a classic example of the tension between the two systems. The denomination operated three campgrounds on the West Coast. Two of them barely broke even financially. One was so far in debt that the interest on the outstanding loans was greater than the property was worth! My suggestion to consider selling one or more of the camp-grounds was met with great resistance. The idea was quite painful

---

17. Schein, *Organizational Culture and Leadership*, 12.

because the culture of the churches wanted to protect something that was important to their past. As one person said, "But that's where my dad found the Lord!"

That is culture at work—deep-seated beliefs and assumptions, traditions that control the way we do things: an affective response that was strong enough to hold fiscal reality at bay for years. It took some time for us to surface what was happening and bring the group to the realization that they were holding on to tradition and good feelings that were actually hurting their ability to provide current ministry. They did, nevertheless, eventually sell the campground.

Organizational culture is a powerful force in all of our churches and organizations. While both strategy and culture are essential for organizational success, research suggests that culture is significantly more critical. Henderson and Thompson report that an eleven-year study of organizations demonstrates that values-based organizations outperform other organizations. "Their growth was four times faster, job creation seven times higher, and stock prices grew twelve times faster; profitability was on average 750 times higher than non-value-based organizations."[18] On their website they cite additional research revealing "that a company's culture is eight times more influential on performance variance than a company's strategy or business plan."[19] Culture is a force that leaders must understand and address, because leaders create and reinforce organizational culture.

Leaders Create and Reinforce Culture

These two broad areas of organizational culture and leadership values have been an interest of mine for years. While completing my doctoral studies in New Testament I financed my education by working

---

18. Henderson and Thompson, *Values at Work*, 35.
19. "An Introduction to Values AT Work," 2006, 2, available at http://www.valuesatwork.org/IntroBrochure.pdf.

as an administrator. I was painfully surprised to see very little crossover between the two arenas. Theologians who handled the Word of God all day would enter the halls of governance in the seminary with a style and behavior that seemed rather different from the fruit of the Spirit that I had been studying with them earlier. I don't want to single out any one school here; I find this paradox in Christian education everywhere. Nor is the church exempt. Pastors often treat their staff and volunteers with a different set of values than they proclaim on Sunday morning. And the problem goes both ways. Businesspeople who understand leadership and management and organizational culture will walk into a church board meeting and act as though they have left their gifts and skills at home. All of their experience and education is discarded as not being "spiritual" enough for a good organizational decision in the context of the church.

By now you should realize that I do not agree with the dualism, the dichotomy, between organization and community. When a group of men and women gather to accomplish a mission we are by definition an organization. But we are more—much more. When we gather in the name of Christ we are also a taste of the kingdom of God on earth. We are a community of the Spirit. We are a community whose organization is shaped both by its mission and by the gifting presence of the Spirit.

I do not want to accept anything less than both effective organizational life and vital Christian community life. They are not mutually exclusive; they are essentially complementary. I realize that I am holding up an ideal—one that I cannot live up to fully. But I want to hold up a vision of what we should be—what, with God's help, we can be. At the very least, I want us to articulate how we think we should live and to be prepared to be held accountable for how we live up to our values and beliefs, like Philemon was held accountable by Paul.

I think this principle holds true also for leaders who are living out their calling in business or corporate organizational settings. Relational leadership—servant leadership, leadership from character—is even more important when it is exercised in a community without the foundational assumptions of Christian faith. The leader is still the primary person to identify, instill, and reinforce the values that will shape the way the organization lives and does its business in the years ahead. This alone is sufficient reason for followers of Jesus to seek leadership positions in our public and private corporations, locally and internationally.

Leaders add value. Ideally, biblical leaders incarnate the spiritual values articulated by Paul, with a strong commitment to respect for individuals and the interdependence of relationships. They know the value of community as a natural expression of human relationships grounded in the creative love of God. Biblical leaders bring identity, hope, and character to their leadership relationships. They have a wonderful opportunity—the organization indeed expects it of them—to add value to the organization in a way that communicates worth, purpose, and hope and that nurtures people's development and their growth in the ability to participate in and contribute to the mission of the organization. And, as we learn from Goleman and Lipman-Blumen, the impact of leaders' values reaches far beyond the workplace, touching lives and families and extended relationships. Leadership is a relationship of character that shapes culture. Leaders have a responsibility to their organizational mission and to the people for whose development they are accountable.

Most organizations I work with have strongly stated values regarding the importance, care, and development of their people. This is especially true of Christian communities. Yet many "Christian" organizations pursue their mission with such passion that they burn up their human resources, expecting them to sacrifice themselves for the sake of the mission. Our organizations and churches are filled with victims, people who are trapped between the articulated values of their community and the cultural realities of how they are treated. Sometimes this is because the organization is operating in a manner different from its stated values. Sometimes it is because the members of the church or organization have a different understanding of the stated values than does the organization. In both cases there is conflict to be resolved.

Several years ago we released a person at Regent because he was not able to do the job for which he was hired. We released him after extended probation, special training, and coaching. He was not able to complete the assignment we needed done. When we finally gave him notice, he and many of his friends at the college felt we were violating biblical values. They claimed that the responsibility of Christian community meant keeping him when he could not fulfill his assignment. We spent considerable time underlining that community is an important and critical value and may require the "second mile," but it does not supplant the mission that brings us together in the first place.

Community, for me, is a very highly regarded value; for Regent, it is a deeply entrenched cultural assumption. Culture may in fact constrain the implementation of the mission, but it is not the mission. Who are we?—The mission is still the driving force, the organizing principle that unifies people and resources. What is important to us?—The culture and values shape the way that people live together and utilize their resources in pursuit of the mission.

Schein argues that it is the responsibility of the leader to identify, reinforce, or change the culture.[20] For me this responsibility goes beyond simple organizational strategy. I believe we are called to model in our organizational and community life the very fruit of the Spirit that we teach and preach from our faith. Our touch must match our voice.

This is something I worked on at Regent College for twelve years and now at the De Pree Center for eight years. I would like to believe that both institutions have made progress, but I confess immediately that both have been far from an organization that lives what it believes.

---

20. Schein, *Organizational Culture and Leadership*, xiv, 2.

We have tried. We have failed. We have forgiven. And we have kept trying. I pray that we will always keep trying to be who we say we are.

When I first arrived at Regent, I called a meeting of the total college staff. I articulated my vision of the college as a community, invited comment, and sought to encourage dialogue and constructive criticism—caring confrontation. Committed to a relational model of leadership, I encouraged staff members to give direct feedback and suggestions to me and the other managers. This was the way I had always worked.

They couldn't do it. No one would speak up. No one would criticize anything. No one offered any constructive ideas for anything. When I pushed further, I was told that staff members had learned over the years that it was not appropriate to critique the administration. According to one staff person, "It is not appreciated and is considered a violation of community. It might even cost you your job." Earlier administrations would deny this was ever their policy or value. In fact, they were hurt to hear this opinion. But whether or not it was their intent, the cultural beliefs that controlled the employees said very loudly, *Keep quiet; don't rock the boat!* Regardless of how much I stated that things had changed, that speaking out was a sign of ownership and community accountability and was valued highly, the staff would not give feedback or constructive criticism. The culture had such a strong grip that they would not believe my stated values as the new president.

We experienced a breakthrough several months later when we hired a new person who did not yet know the culture. She believed my stated values and proceeded to speak out and even to argue when invited to her first staff meeting. She pointed out all kinds of problems facing the staff that were not being addressed. The longtime staff members were shocked and apologized to me for her impertinence! But she gave me the opportunity to praise her publicly for her commitment and ownership and, in that act, to reinforce the new culture. We acted on the problems she raised and in this way reinforced the stated values as accurately reflecting the new culture.

Over the first year most of the staff came to the point where they would confront me with issues and proposed solutions. They were willing to accept ownership and look for solutions rather than only see problems. Interestingly, the culture changed first around me. During the first year the staff would only risk sharing critiques related to me. They didn't really believe that their managers who had been part of the old culture would live with the new values. During the second year we were able to move more of the feedback and participation into the leadership relationships between the staff and their managers. Eventually everyone started speaking out! And that was good. We increasingly came to have a community of owners who took responsibility for the mission and the community.

Another example of culture in our organizations forms around power and the making of decisions. At Regent, academic decisions typically were made by consensus, reflecting the religious tradition in which the college was founded. Consensus was affirmed as a sign of community. Governance, however, remained officially (according to the by-laws) in the hands of the administration and the board. I was used to a model in which academic staff also participated in the governance of the college. I was very enthusiastic about introducing this model, but I was not willing to live with a consensus model for decision making. Too often consensus-style decision making leaves the power in the hands of the negative voice, not in hands of the community. I wanted a majority vote model that put the power in the hands of the academic staff as a group if they were going to participate as a group in governance.

This was an issue of participation and community accountability. This was an issue of culture. Using Schein's terms, it dealt with the nature of reality and truth and how decisions are made. Before I could involve the academic staff in governance, a basic cultural assumption had to be changed. We had to move to a belief in the appropriateness of arriving at "truth," at a decision, by vote—which legitimized a person's right to vote no and still support the group's decision. In many ways, it was a redistribution of power. We were taking the power away from a few strong individuals and giving it to the broader community.

It was interesting to watch the slow shift to a new cultural assumption. The decision to move to the new model was made by majority vote; but since no one voted against the change, it was in fact decided by consensus! The first real test came when two members voted against a motion that was supported by the majority of the academic staff. Several people wanted to reopen the discussion until the two holdouts could be won over. The old culture still had a grip. The group was still resistant to deciding by majority. I intervened and encouraged the academic staff to give their colleagues the space to express their convictions and still support the decision. Both the individuals affirmed their support for the decision, and there was a corporate sigh of relief. I think every decision we made after that was decided by split vote! And it was not unusual for an issue that I believed in to be defeated in the corporate governing process. Power was distributed. And yet you could still feel the grip of the old culture. It is hard to move forward when conflicting views have been championed at a meeting.

Here's one more story from my Regent days, which not only underlines what I am talking about but suggests that we made progress.

Like most organizations, we had a receptionist. He or she tended to be an entry-level person on the staff. Seemingly, no manager wanted to take responsibility for this position. And yet this person was Regent's first voice and face. She or he was the first line in establishing the values. How the receptionist treats you when you call or walk in begins to form your relationship with the school. That person can greatly affect your attitude and interests before you ever get to the president's office. It is a key role.

When I started at Regent, I moved the receptionist position into the president's office—not physically, but in terms of accountability. The receptionist was considered a member of my staff. I spent time with her, keeping her included and informed about events and activities and the college's plans. I tried to articulate and model the kind of culture that was important to us and what I wanted her to communicate to people when they called or walked in.

Later, even though I no longer supervised that staff member, I did occasionally participate in the interview process; and I tried to communicate regularly with the receptionist about the importance of the position. This position, perhaps more than any other, demonstrates the culture and values of the college. Receptionists need to understand this. And they did. We had a string of very good receptionists over the years, and I regularly used them as illustrations of what I meant by modeling our values.

One time I was talking about culture to a group of people and the receptionist was in the room. As usual, I referred to the importance of her position and the critical role she played in establishing Regent's culture. Afterwards, however, she came to my office and asked to see me. She said, "I wish you wouldn't keep talking about the importance of my position when you speak!"

I responded in surprise, "Why not? It *is* important! You are the voice and face of Regent for many people."

Her response: "That's not the issue. You tell everyone else how important I am to Regent, but you don't come down very often and tell me!"

Well, she was right. I wouldn't stop using the receptionist as an illustration, but I was clearly confronted by someone who cared and who showed me that I was not living up to my stated values. My behavior had to change. I needed to tell the receptionist how important she was to the community as often as I told others.

But note, while it wasn't very comfortable for me to hear that I wasn't fully living my values, it was encouraging to realize that the culture was taking hold. The very fact that she came to the president's office to share her concerns and feelings suggests a level of trust and ownership that I was pleased to see.

Articulating Personal Values

Each of us brings a set of personal values to our role in the organization and each of us in a leadership role reinforces an institutional culture—the values or the character of the organization—with each action, decision, or policy. It is a worthwhile exercise to try to write out some of the values that you think you bring to your community. What is important to you? To what are you prepared to be held accountable in your leadership role? How do those values shape the way you want to live out your leadership?

I experienced a good illustration of personal values at work one time when my car was towed away. It was a cold and stormy morning in Vancouver; but I had an important meeting, so I bundled up and walked out to my car. It was gone! The construction crew working across the street had it ticketed by the police and towed away—even more irritating.

I had come home from another important meeting late the night before. I thought I had parked outside the temporary tow-away zone. I had not; in fact, I parked right under the sign! As you might imagine, this did not start my day well. I was rather irritated, to put it mildly. This was a major inconvenience. I needed to be at an important meeting on the future of theological education, but my car had been towed.

When I learned the name of the towing company, I called to find out where my car was. My Christian character was not obvious in my conversation! Yet when I hung up, I had to smile. The woman on the phone had handled me very well. I realized that the situation was my fault and that I couldn't blame her. She had managed to keep the conversation positive, light, and even humorous.

When I arrived at the large, dirty parking lot, with a wooden shack for an office, I had to wait in line for the woman to take care of other disgruntled individuals whose cars were now in her possession. She managed them well also. When I reached the window, I told her that I thought she had handled me well earlier on the phone. She replied, "Thank you. Everyone who calls me or comes to this window is angry. My job is to see that it doesn't ruin their day!"

Rather profound words on organizational culture and personal values from a clerk in a towing company shack! She was reflecting personal character with more integrity than the president of a theological school who stood at her window. And she was articulating a marvelous understanding of organizational culture or character as she focused on the people-building results of her work rather than the mechanics of her job. She saw value in her work and lived it well.

Everything the leader does reinforces the culture. As president of Regent I was watched to see if I reinforced the organization's stated values. Did I live up to what I taught? How I behaved was seen much more as institutional policy than what I said, and it reinforced the culture. Was I friendly or distant? Was I a workaholic or reasonably paced? Did I have presidential perks, such as a reserved parking space? Did I talk or listen? Did I keep my promises?

For five years I was a visiting lecturer at the University of Calgary's Executive Management Program. I was brought in to talk about vision and values in today's organizations. One year a participant asked me what values I brought to Regent, to my leadership. Intrigued by this question, that evening I drafted a list of seventeen values in my first attempt to write out my personal values for leadership.

The seventeen values I listed that night related to people, work, and relationships. Here is my list.[21]

---

21. This list was published in J. Michael Fuller, *Above the Bottom Line* (Toronto: Macmillan Canada, 1993), 164.

People

1. People have intrinsic worth.

We need to value who they are as well as what they do. We have to communicate dignity and worth. We need to stop to say "thank you," to acknowledge our dependence upon others.

2. Everyone should make a commitment to the mission.

Again, I see the mission as the unifying force in an organization. We come together around the mission, and all members of the organizational community should make a commitment and contribution to that mission.

3. People who work with us should grow.

We should be making an investment in the people who invest in our mission. In a small organization like Regent we had very few layers. There was very little opportunity for promotion and growth in scope of responsibility. I believe that turnover is a good thing in this kind of organization. I would rather invest in good people who move on than in poor workers who stay. But I want those who do move on to move on better equipped at what they do, better prepared to serve wherever God takes them.

4. No one should take himself or herself too seriously.

I regularly turn to Romans 12 for a reminder that we are all in this together. Paul lists leadership as one of the gifts given to the church, but it is not first. It falls between giving money and showing mercy. Thus, if I can paraphrase Romans 12:3, "Don't take yourself too seriously."

5. All people should be treated as contributing peers regardless of their scope of responsibility.

While people may get paid at different levels because of competence, experience, or responsibility, every member of the organization has something to offer and deserves to be valued for his or her contribution and humanness.

6. Leadership should be empowering.

This is what this book is about. Leadership is the process of giving power away, not collecting it. It is moving the power to influence into the hands of the people we are leading so that they can pursue the mission.

Work

7. The mission of the organization normally takes precedence over individual purposes.

By this I do not intend to demean individual purposes or objectives. But I do want to remind us again that it is the mission that brings us together, and in the context of the organization personal agendas are always subordinated to the community agenda or mission.

8. Participation produces ownership of results.

I commented on this in chapter two when I looked at team building. It will show up again in the next chapter when we look at motivating people. I have found from experience what research underlines continuously: when people are involved, they take ownership for the results. Participation is the best form of motivation.

9. The workplace should provide community.

In today's world, the workplace and the church are the primary arenas for social relationships. As a leader, I believe I should encourage this—the development of relationships that enable people to care for and learn from one another. As I noted previously, community implies diversity and requires us to be inclusive in our thinking and our employment.

10. People should have fun and find joy in their work.

Not all work is fun, but the community in which we work should be a place we enjoy. While a specific task may not be pleasant, people should be able to find joy in the mission to which they are contributing. I want people to look forward to Monday, not Friday! I want them to look forward to seeing their friends and experiencing a sense of belonging and contributing.

11. We should always provide professional service in a friendly environment.

We are in existence to serve. The needs of our constituents should be our first priority, and we should serve them well. We should give them our best and do it with quality. And in line with the previous value, we should be such a friendly place that visitors want to come back, even if just to say "hello."

Relationships

12. Truth is found in relationship.

I do not have all the truth and I doubt if you do either. Together we can listen and learn. Personally, I put a very high value on relationship. It is in relationship that God reveals himself. It is in relationship that I learn how to interpret the truth around me. I do not assume that I have the truth. I seek to learn it in dialogue in relationship.

13. Information is friendly.

No surprises. Openness. Everyone should know where I am going. Not everyone will agree with what I am doing, but people can't say that they don't know what I believe and where I am trying to lead the organization. I share everything. I believe that the more people know, the more they become partners.

14. Confrontation is a sign of caring.

As already mentioned, community includes diversity and diversity means conflict. Confrontation addresses conflict by caring enough for the other person to engage him or her in a relationship in which both parties are held accountable to their stated values. If I really care about you, I will give you feedback on what I see and how I respond to it.

15. Criticism without constructive action is destructive gossip.

We noted this in the Colossian case. Criticism usually holds you accountable to my values rather than your own. And gossip occurs, I would argue, any time criticism is taken outside of the relationship. My definition of gossip is pretty strong. Anytime anything negative is said about someone to a third party without the permission of the person being talked about, that is gossip. And I think it is inexcusable, even when it happens in the context of prayer. I have great difficulty with people who need to give me a prayer request for someone else. That to me is a form of gossip. If I genuinely care about someone, I take the negative or critical comment to that person directly. That is the only way the relationship can be healed and grow.

16. Honesty, integrity, and trust are essential in everything we do.

This is what followers look for in leaders. It is also what God expects from his people. We can hold ourselves to no lower standard than honesty and integrity. Only then will people give us their trust.

17. Forgiveness should characterize our life together.

I listed this one last, but it is not the least important. There can be no leadership without forgiveness. Leadership involves the risk of making decisions when we really do not know what is best. This risk of leadership requires the context of forgiveness. Further, forgiveness is a prerequisite to empowerment. I am convinced that there is a direct correlation between forgiveness and empowerment. No one can be empowered without the freedom to fail. Forgiveness is freeing. It implies trust. It encourages risk, growth, leadership. I'm not talking about freedom from consequences, but freedom to learn from failure and then being encouraged to try again. A culture of forgiveness encourages the risk of leadership. But even further, leaders need to be able to forgive themselves. We have a tendency to carry our mistakes around with us, as well as our uncertain decisions. We replay them in our minds, thinking of what we should have done differently. This paralyzes our ability to take the risk of deciding and limits our leadership. We must be prepared to live with consequences, but we have to be able to live with mistakes, to forgive ourselves, if we are going to lead.

Whenever I list these values I feel the need to make disclaimers. I do not consistently live up to this list, nor does Regent College nor the De Pree Center, but I am prepared to be held accountable to these values. I expect to fail. I expect to be confronted by someone who cares. I expect to be forgiven and encouraged to try again.

As leaders we do bring values to the community, perhaps articulated as I attempted to do, but definitely lived out in everything we do. Whether or not you take the time to write them out, you are in fact living out of your own list of deeply ingrained values.

In my leadership workshops I share my list and ask leaders to identify the values that shape their leadership. Initially I sent them off alone to draft a list the way I did. Later, after reading G. Ward Kingsley's *Letters of a Businessman to His Daughter*,[22] I altered the assignment. I now ask them to think of someone for whom they care deeply—like a daughter—and to imagine that this person has just been appointed to his or her first leadership or management position. I ask them to draft a letter telling that individual what he or she needs to know to thrive in this new leadership role. I underline the exercise as an opportunity to pass on values.

The second form of this exercise has been powerful. When we make a list we organize thoughts from our head. When we draft a letter we express the emotions of our heart. Writing the letter is a powerful emotional exercise for participants and is a more accurate reflection of the values that actually govern their leadership. Our credibility as leaders is directly tied to the congruence between our stated values and the values reflected in our living—our voice and our touch. To lead

---

22. G. Ward Kingsley, *Letters of a Businessman to His Daughter* (Toronto: McClelland & Steward, 1989).

an organization to live as a Spirit-shaped community we must be willing to be held accountable to live and lead as Spirit-shaped men and women of character.

Now, what might this look like when applied to an organization?

Articulating Corporate Culture: A Values Statement

The list of seventeen personal values I drafted for the Calgary executives was published in the June 1991 issue of the *Regent World*. That article drew more comment than anything else I have written, with letters from companies and organizations at scattered locations around the world telling me that my list had became the basis for a variety of values statements. The Regent College strategic planning committee also saw the list and asked me to draft a values statement parallel to the mission statement in our institutional publications. This was what I had been waiting for—a chance for the college to articulate a set of shared values that together we could reinforce and embed in the culture for decades to come.

So I tried my hand at writing what I called *The Character of a College*. It was a much more difficult process than I would have imagined. I should have remembered Max De Pree's words in *Leadership Jazz*: "The organization expects the leader to define and express both in writing and especially through behavior the beliefs and values of the institution. This may not be easy, but like many disciplines, it's essential. Writing down what an institution values makes everyone come clean. It can also make people uncomfortable. The safety of vaguely known beliefs will disappear pretty fast."[23]

I spent considerable time preparing a first draft. It is one thing to list seventeen values; it is quite another to flesh them out in a form that can stand the test of community scrutiny and accountability. When I finished, I had produced something that I believed in deeply.

---

23. De Pree, *Leadership Jazz*, 26.

In many ways it was an expression of my soul. When it was circulated, however, the common response was "Maybe in heaven!" What I found to be a compelling document, pulling me to live out a set of values, was seen by nearly everyone else as too complicated, too idealistic, or too threatening. No one wanted to vote against anything in the statement, but no one was prepared to put it in print as something to which we corporately should be held accountable. I tried to revise it but found myself personally committed to each point. I am prepared to be held accountable to each of these items, even though I expect to fail regularly.

After a year of discussion it was decided that we did need such a statement at Regent, but that it should be much simpler. And conventional wisdom about core values statements suggests that they should include no more than five values.[24] In the end we settled for four core values: personal spiritual growth and maturity; biblical scholarship; experienced Christian community; and vocational integration. These became the official stated values that we wanted to shape our mission and our corporate life together. That was as precise as our community was prepared to be during that round of planning.

The Character of a College still exists, however. It still represents the kind of community I want to be part of. I still distribute it, not as a Regent statement but as a statement of my personal commitments—a statement of what I am trying to model and an articulation of that to which I am still willing to be held accountable. Interestingly, people kept asking for copies, and I regularly saw behaviors modeling the commitments of the statement. Later, the chairman of the board suggested that I have a copy framed and hung in the president's office as a reminder to others of my vision for Regent. I did so, and it hung there unofficially for the rest of my tenure.

---

24. Henderson and Thompson, *Values at Work*, 110.

When I resigned from the college to move to the De Pree Center, the board invited me to sit in on the process to search for a successor. I was pleasantly surprised when, during a meeting in which the board was detailing their expectations for the new president, one member circulated copies of *The Character of a College* (see example on next page). The board read through the document and decided unanimously that was the kind of organization they wanted the new president to lead. Never approved—but clearly taking root in the culture!

This was my attempt to articulate a statement of values for Regent College. The influence of Paul's letter to the Colossians can be seen on my thinking. I encourage you to try to draft such a statement for your organization. It is the first step in the process of surfacing the cultural assumptions and beliefs that shape our actions as we attempt to put in writing those values to which we are committed.

Many "cultural" questions are raised when we try to understand the culture of our organizations. As we work through these questions and identify the shared value commitments present, we pave the way for a statement of values that captures our intentions and focuses our leadership. How is conflict resolved in your community? How are people valued and affirmed? How are people disciplined and released? What does kindness mean when you must release someone? What does love mean when someone has a different view? How is the receptionist perceived? How is the leader perceived? What is the culture of leadership: reactive or proactive, entrepreneurial or bureaucratic? Is community defined by inclusiveness or exclusiveness? Is the culture written or oral? How is information disseminated? Does conflict produce confrontation or criticism? What is expected from God?

Recently the Max De Pree Center for Leadership partnered with Cardus (formerly the Work Research Foundation) to examine how successful companies embed the values of leadership into the culture of the organization. Over a three-year period we studied five companies that were recognized as leaders in their industry and led by chief

The Character of a College

Regent College seeks to be a learning and nurturing community of faculty, staff, students, board, and senate, where the presence of God in Jesus Christ through his Holy Spirit is manifest in the human relationships, institutional policies, and organizational procedures of the community.

I. A Community of Thanksgiving
A. a place of prayer and thanksgiving, acknowledging our dependence upon God;
B. a place of joy, where we relax in the security of God's love;
C. a place where every organizational or community operation is an act of worship before God;
D. a place where we meet God, gaining a biblical perspective on our personal identity and calling;
E. a place where we acknowledge in gratitude those gifts entrusted to our stewardship.

II. A Community of Wisdom
A. a place where we seek wisdom to see this world from God's perspective;
B. a place where we seek truth with intellectual rigor and critical minds;
C. a place where we have space to think and grow;
D. a place where we are listened to;
E. a place where knowledge is informed by biblical spirituality;
F. a place where we bring together the varied pieces of our lives under the lordship of Christ.

III. A Community of Character
A. a place of love, where we learn the importance of interdependent community;
B. a place characterized by integrity, encouraging honesty and trust;
C. a place of peace, where we can explore ideas with strife-free critique;
D. a gentle place, where people and procedures nurture and encourage, where facilities and policies have compassion;
E. a kind place, where we care actively for one another in true humility;
F. a place of patience, where we are accepted as we are and encouraged to become what God intends us to be;
G. a place where we see Jesus when we see one another.

IV. A Community of Service
A. a place where we are empowered to develop our gifts in the service of others;
B. a place where we are encouraged to live for Christ, bringing love and justice into the world;
C. a place where we are equipped to make a difference in the marketplace and public forum;
D. a place that serves in partnership with the local church;
E. a place where cooperation is initiated;
F. a place where mercy takes service the second mile.

V. A Community of Forgiveness
A. a place of forgiveness and second chances;
B. a place of trust, of God, of others, and of ourselves;
C. a place where lives and relationships are healed;
D. a place where failure is never final;
E. a place of renewal and growth;
F. a place of mercy and hope.

VI. A Community of Commitment
A. a place where commitments are made and promises kept;
B. a place driven by vision rather than efficiency;
C. a place where the present is shaped by the future as well as the past;
D. a place of accountability where responsibility takes precedence over rights;
E. a place where stewardship replaces ownership;
F. a place where excellence requires continual renewal;
G. a place where the unity of community is continually reformed by the diversity of individual contributions;
H. a place preparing to stand before God.

executives with strongly held Christian values. We interviewed each CEO to ascertain the source and content of those values, then met with each of the key leaders on the senior management team. During an extended visit to each company's location we conducted focus groups with operational levels from senior management to the shop floor, often including customers, suppliers, and community leaders. Then we surveyed every employee of the company, asking them to evaluate the company by an instrument that measures servant leadership and by the company's stated core values.

The visits were fascinating. In each case the leadership team articulated strong, clear values based on the leader's deep biblical convictions. In each case the middle management affirmed the core values but acknowledged that they were not consistently applied. In nearly every case we found numbers of employees who were not clear about the values application to their work. As a result of our study, every company significantly increased the attention they paid to values training at all levels.

One company, Dacor, a manufacturer of high-end kitchen appliances, has developed a highly successful program of values education. Michael Joseph, president of Dacor, led a process to develop a set of core values:

> ### DACOR'S COMPANY VALUE
> To honor God in all that we do
> - by respecting others
> - by doing good work
> - by helping others
> - by forgiving others
> - by giving thanks
> - by celebrating our lives

These values are posted in every office and plant of the company, and they are printed on the front of all business cards. When sales representatives present their cards, they hand them values side up, stating that this is the company they work for and their contact information is on the back side. Dacor is a successful business with a diverse workforce, a competitive market, and a CEO who believes that he works out his calling among the people who work for his company.

When our research team visited Dacor the values had been developed and posted and a training program had been initiated. Listening to employees, we were able to convey to the management team a perception that values training had not yet reached all the production lines. Dacor quickly corrected that by implementing a sophisticated educational program company-wide. Every employee at Dacor receives a minimum of eight hours of values training from his or her supervisor, articulating the "company value" and what each value means for organizational behavior. Starting with the president, managers are responsible for educating, managing, and evaluating the application of Dacor's "company value" with the people for whose success they are responsible. Dacor has made this process a high value within the company and holds itself accountable. Every year every employee is surveyed and asked to rate the company on how well each value is being lived out in their community. The management team responds in word and action. It is not surprising that Dacor has a solid reputation for quality, service, and growth shaped by its culture.[25]

Creating and reinforcing the culture is a key responsibility of leadership. It is a long-term process that requires a long-range commitment by the leadership. Without an organizational crisis, I am not convinced that a leader can permanently embed values in less than ten years! It requires patiently walking with people, modeling and reinforc-

25. Ray Pennings, Joyce Avedisian, Gideon Strauss, and Walter Wright, *To Honor God: Dacor's Pursuit of Corporate Virtue* (Pasadena, CA: De Pree Leadership Center, 2004), 10.

ing the new culture. It requires visionary leaders who can see what God wants to accomplish with their organization and what their church or organization can look like with Christ present in its midst. It requires relational leaders who make themselves vulnerable by making an accountable commitment to a stated set of values. It requires servant leaders who have learned to depend upon God and who expect to see God at work in their organizations in the years ahead. Vision, values, and vulnerability—maybe that is what relational servant leadership is all about.

Reinforcing Corporate Culture: The Power of Stories

Everything that leaders do and say reinforces the values taking root in the organizational culture. This is true whether or not we are intentional. We live values—we demonstrate what is important—we teach theology—all day long. Servant leaders seek to build a healthy culture that honors God and nurtures people as it pursues the mission. A powerful strategy for communicating values is the telling of stories. Stories capture the imagination of people, reveal values at work, and create a context in which people can picture themselves.

At several points in this book I have related stories told by Max De Pree. If you read his books you will find them filled with stories. Whenever Max speaks he tells stories. Stories linger; they survive; they take root in our memory—which makes them wonderful vehicles for passing on values.

For the past three years I have been presenting values workshops to small groups of CEOs across the United States and Canada. Vistage International and TEC Canada have contracted with the De Pree Center for me to lead about two dozen events each year based on my book *Don't Step on the Rope!*[26] The popularity of the workshops seems

---

26. Walter C. Wright, *Don't Step on the Rope! Reflections on Leadership, Relationships, and Teamwork* (Milton Keynes, UK: Paternoster, 2005).

to be fueled in part by my use of mountain-climbing stories to illustrate the relationship between leaders and followers. The stories bring into dramatic focus realities that are taken for granted in everyday work life. They create new opportunities for self-assessment and strategic thinking. One of the chapters in the book, featured in the workshop, underlines the importance of stories for passing on values and shaping culture. We communicate what is important in the stories we choose to tell.

The title of the book comes from a climb several years ago of Mount Rainier, the beautiful volcano that dominates the horizon of Seattle. After making the climb with Rainier Mountaineering guides, I convinced several friends to join me in climbing the mountain again. We asked another friend, a backcountry ranger in Mount Rainier National Park, to lead us. He agreed, provided we would ascend the mountain up a route he had always wanted to try. We decided to climb the southwest side of the mountain and descend the northeast side, doing so over five days in August and spending at least one night on the summit.

We started with energy and enthusiasm, hiking in to Klapatche Park and roping up to climb the Puyallup Glacier. The climb was much harder than anything we had done to date. Those were the days before ultralight gear—our packs were heavy and the days seemed long. We had been climbing for sixteen hours on one particularly difficult day. We were tired and impatient to reach the place were we would camp. As we moved sluggishly up the glacier, Don, who was ahead of me, began to slow down, creating slack in the rope that connected us. Too tired to pay attention as I moved slowly up the mountain, I stepped on the rope—prompting a sharp rebuke as Don called out, "Don't step on the rope!"

And of course he was right. When I stepped on the rope, two things happened. Don, wearily trudging along, was jerked to a sudden stop and nearly pulled over backwards. This was not appreciated! But more important was the fact that since we were on a high-mountain glacier we were wearing crampons, sharp metal spikes that provide traction on snow and ice, on the bottom of our boots. When I stepped on the rope wearing crampons I risked damage to the link that connected us, the rope with which we would hold each other secure if we fell. I was tired and thinking about dinner. I should have been thinking about the connection—the lifeline—the relationship upon which we depended.

I tell that story in the workshops because the metaphor sticks in people's minds. Leaders and followers are tied together. The mountain-climbing rope makes visible the relationship that connects us, and that relationship is fundamental to leadership. It must be attended to and nurtured. It is of the highest value to climbers and essential to leadership. Saying the relationship is important is articulating a valuable truth. But creating a picture of that relationship as a rope critical to our survival gives it added meaning. People think in narrative. Narrative intelligence plays a foundational role in human behavior and communication. Stories are not just stories. They are narratives that make sense of listeners' lives as they perceive them—narratives weaving together the listeners' experiences and the new story envisioned by the leader.[27]

Stories mine learning from the past. We tell stories of past experiences to pass on what we have learned, both good and bad. In its retelling, the story creates opportunity to live the experience again and change it or reinforce it. We select the story in the first place because it surfaces something we wish to communicate. For ages this was the primary way that history was preserved. Tribal elders sat around the fire and told stories of "the old days," recreating the heroic events and the fearful tragedies that led to the present.[28]

---

27. Stephen Denning, *The Secret Language of Leadership: How Leaders Inspire Action Through Narrative* (San Francisco: John Wiley & Sons, 2007), 35, 114.

28. Richard J. Leider and David A. Shapiro, *Claiming Your Place at the Fire: Living the Second Half of Your Life on Purpose* (San Francisco: Berrett-Koehler, 2004), vii.

Stories reinforce shared values. We select stories to underline specific values. Stories are value-laden. They can help people see a new, different, and better future that they have not yet visualized. Or they can entrench a view that resists change.

A few years ago I was asked to lead a two-day retreat for a network of hospital executives. The head of the network wanted to build a strong leadership team that would reform the way health care was provided. Fifteen executives from hospitals, nursing associations, and government offices convened at a beautiful resort to build relationships and create a corporate culture. I used exercises and teaching designed to expand their knowledge of one another, increase their emotional connections, and envision a collaborative future. People engaged and had an enjoyable time. On the second day, however, one of the hospital presidents commented to the group, "This has been a great time together. We know each other better and have developed stronger relationships. But we all know that when we return to our offices tomorrow morning it will be business as usual. Nothing will change."

All the people in the room nodded their heads in agreement. At first I was distressed. *Am I wasting my time if all that happens is a warm social time together?* Then I realized that this participant had just told a story and everyone had accepted it: when we go away on retreats we have an emotional high that is replaced immediately by reality when we return to our work. That was the controlling story; and if we did not change it, that would be exactly what would happen the next day.

So I pointed out what we had just done—the story we had just affirmed—and suggested that we change the story. I asked all the participants to tell one story from their hospital that illustrated something they were proud of that reflected the values we had been discussing and that they would like to see protected in the year ahead. As we went around the room the stories became longer, more passionate, more exciting. By the time we had heard all fifteen stories a new picture was emerging—a new narrative was being crafted that they wanted to preserve. They left that retreat and launched a successful round of health reform for their network of hospitals. Stories reinforce shared values and create a future.

Stories rekindle relational intimacy. The retreat just described did in fact develop stronger relationships. The exercises allowed participants to tell their personal story as well as their organizational story. As we share our story and listen to others we connect at the emotional level of relationships. When we tell stories we show and share the emotions that drive us. This attracts attention. People respond to stories that are emotional and personalized. The emotional content gives stories more power because it causes them to stand out in our mind and be remembered longer.[29]

Once the emotional connection is made, the story can be reinforced with reasons that underline the purpose of the story. Stories that reveal your heart open a path to increased intimacy, to the emotional connection that defines relationship. Hollywood filmmaker Peter Guber, who is in the business of creating compelling stories, observes:

> Here is the challenge for the business storyteller: He must enter the hearts of his listeners, where their emotions live, even as the information he seeks to convey rents space in their brains. Our minds are relatively open, but we guard our hearts with zeal, knowing their power to move us. So although the mind may be part of your target, the heart is the bull's-eye. To reach it, the visionary manager crafting his story must first display his own open heart.[30]

Stories envision a new future. The power of stories to create a new future was evident to me at the retreat for hospital executives. But I

---

29. Denning, *Secret Language of Leadership*, 31, 33, 97.

30. Peter Guber, "The Four Truths of the Storyteller," *Harvard Business Review* (December 2007): 56.

should not have been surprised. This is the role that the scenario plays in our planning processes. The scenario is a story of tomorrow, a story that embeds the values that we want to govern our work together in the future. This gives immense power to the storyteller. The person who is telling the stories is the person who is shaping the values of the future. Leaders must be storytellers—or, as Max De Pree says, they must identify and elevate the tribal storytellers in the organization who will keep the past visible, the values illuminated, and the future alive.[31]

A few years ago I was asked to lead a values workshop for the headquarters staff of a construction company. After talking about values, relationships, and organizational culture, I had them break into small groups to share the stories that employees told about the company. While they were doing so the president stepped out to make a phone call. He returned just as the entire group was reconvening. When I asked them to tell me the stories that were being passed around their headquarters, the president's face drained of color. Looking panicked, he turned to his assistant and said, "This is not good; we have potential clients waiting for me around the corner and they will hear the stories."

I thought, *Wow! He doesn't know the stories being told in his company and he fears the worst. He is not telling the stories.*

As the stories were told, the man's color returned. Every story was about the company going the extra mile for an employee or a customer. They were great stories. But the president didn't know them. If the leader doesn't control the stories being told, the stories will control the leader. If stories shape the future of the organization, leaders should be storytellers. This is one way we can contribute to the formation of our future together.

---

31. Max De Pree, *Leadership Is an Art* (East Lansing, MI: Michigan State University Press, 1987), 81–92.

Effective stories ring true. Peter Guber claims that effective stories are always true. They are true at several levels. First, they are authentic—they are in touch with reality. Fabricated stories do not ring true and erode trust. Second, effective stories reflect the truth of the leader's story. If the story you tell is not an extension of the values you live, it will weaken your influence and cast doubt on your leadership. Third, the story must fit the narrative that listeners are currently living. It should identify the listeners' emotional needs and address them with integrity; otherwise they will not respond. And finally, the story must be true to the mission. Guber writes:

> A great storyteller is devoted to a cause beyond self. That mission is embodied in his stories, which capture and express values that he believes in and wants others to adopt as their own. Thus the story itself must offer a value proposition that is worthy of its audience. . . . Even in today's cynical, self-centered age, people are desperate to believe in something bigger than themselves. The storyteller plays a vital role by providing them with a mission they can believe in and devote themselves to. . . . A leader who wants to use the power of storytelling must remember this and begin with a cause that deserves devotion.[32]

Effective leaders articulate a vision—a mission worth investing in—and embed the values that flow through relationships of influence into the culture of the organization. They teach what is important through their words, actions, and policies. They tell stories that connect with human emotions, capture the imagination, reveal values at work, and create a future in which people can picture themselves. Effective leaders influence with values.

---

32. Guber, "Four Truths of the Storyteller," 58–59.

Conclusion: The Prayer of Forgiveness

The Bible is an inspired collection of stories: stories that ground our theology in the knowledge of God, stories that establish the measure for human character and illustrate the values of relational life, stories that reveal the expectations of biblical leadership and the frailty of human leaders.

We cannot talk about organizational culture and the leader's responsibility to articulate the corporate values of the community, model those values, and reinforce them in the fabric of the culture without coming back to the leader. The character of the leader is reflected when leadership seeks to influence the culture of the organization. If that were the end of it, we might all choose not to lead. As hard as we try, our character is flawed. We fail to live up to the calling that God places before us. We fail and must be forgiven. *Is that good enough? Can I hope to transform the culture of my organization with my biblical commitments when I struggle to live them out consistently in my own life?*

It is at this point that I take great comfort in David's anguished cry before God: "Have mercy on me, O God, according to your unfailing love" (Psalm 51:1). Without forgiveness, there is no hope for leadership. I am not referring only to the forgiveness of the people, of the organization, when our risk taking is wrong. That forgiveness is critical and is required for leadership to be effective, but what I am talking about here is more fundamental. It is the forgiveness of God that we need if we are to be audacious enough to stand up and lead the people of God when we know that we do not live up to the marks of character that we read about in Colossians.

David was a leader chosen and used by God. His escapades are described well in the Old Testament. And his failures are recorded for all time. The story of his failure with Bathsheba is well known. With a devastating lack of character David pursued her, resulting first in adultery and then in murder. The king had fallen. God's leader had failed. And yet, even as I reflect on this moral collapse, I am fascinated and encouraged by David's final poetic testimony, composed near the end of his life:

These are the last words of David:

> "The inspired utterance of David son of Jesse, the utterance of the man exalted by the Most High, the man anointed by the God of Jacob,the hero of Israel's songs:

> "The Spirit of the LORD spoke through me; his word was on my tongue. The God of Israel spoke, the Rock of Israel said to me: 'When one rules over people in righteousness, when he rules in the fear of God, he is like the light of morning at sunrise on a cloudless morning, like the brightness after rain that brings grass from the earth.'

> "If my house were not right with God, surely he would not have made with me an everlasting covenant, arranged and secured in every part; surely he would not bring to fruition my salvation and grant me my every desire."

> 2 Samuel 23:1–5

Powerful words from one who failed God so blatantly. In spite of all his struggles and acknowledging his weakness and failures, at the end of his life David can say, "I was chosen by God"; "God spoke through me"; "Because I was dependent upon God, people were empowered by my leadership"; and most poignantly, "I am forgiven—I trust in the covenant love of my God."

Only in dependence upon God and in recognition of our need for forgiveness can we dare to accept the responsibility to lead those to whom God sends us.

This recognition of David's failure and acknowledgment of God's forgiveness gives me hope—hope that takes me to my knees continually in prayer—prayer that regularly finds expression in Psalm 51. This prayer of David, coming shortly after Nathan's caring confrontation, provides a model for men and women in leadership who know they can survive only as long as God chooses to "create in [them] a new heart and renew a steadfast spirit within [them]."

It seems fitting to end this chapter on personal and organizational character with the powerful prayer of a very human leader:

> Have mercy on me, O God,
> according to your unfailing love;
> according to your great compassion
> blot out my transgressions.
> Wash away all my iniquity
> and cleanse me from my sin.
>
> For I know my transgressions,
> and my sin is always before me.
> Against you, you only, have I sinned
> and done what is evil in your sight;
> so you are right in your verdict
> and justified when you judge.
> Surely I was sinful at birth,
> sinful from the time my mother conceived me.
> Yet you desired faithfulness even in the womb;
> you taught me wisdom in that secret place.
> Cleanse me with hyssop, and I will be clean;
> wash me, and I will be whiter than snow.
> Let me hear joy and gladness;
> let the bones you have crushed rejoice.
> Hide your face from my sins
> and blot out all my iniquity.
>
> Create in me a pure heart, O God,
> and renew a steadfast spirit within me.
> Do not cast me from your presence

or take your Holy Spirit from me.
Restore to me the joy of your salvation
and grant me a willing spirit, to sustain me.

Then I will teach transgressors your ways,
and sinners will turn back to you.
Deliver me from bloodguilt, O God,
you who are God my Savior,
and my tongue will sing of your righteousness.
Open my lips, Lord,
and my mouth will declare your praise.
You do not delight in sacrifice, or I would bring it;
you do not take pleasure in burnt offerings.
My sacrifice, O God, isa a broken spirit;
a broken and contrite heart
you, God, will not despise.

May it please you to prosper Zion,
to build up the walls of Jerusalem.
Then you will delight in the sacrifices of the righteous,
in burnt offerings offered whole;
then bulls will be offered on your altar.

Psalm 51:1–19

5

Influencing through Relationships

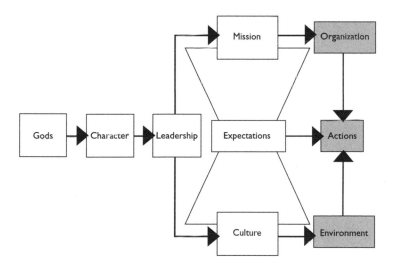

Waves: Power, Purpose, and Relationship

To launch us into a discussion about motivating and empowering people, we should remember Jude's fourth image: "wild waves of the sea, foaming up their shame." In this potent picture, Jude captures power and purpose and relationship. These self-appointed leaders were making a big splash, but they were not going anywhere. They were grabbing attention with the roar of pounding waves, but they left nothing of value behind. As the tides of their leadership receded, there was nothing but debris and destruction on the shorelines of their community.

These were persons who used their power and position to point to themselves, to further their own interests. They believed that leadership was about them and for them. As we have seen, leadership is a relationship—a relationship of influence. Leadership is the process of one person seeking to influence the vision, values, behaviors, or attitudes of another. Relationships of influence are power relationships. Power, as we noted, is the potential for influence. It is what followers see in a person that causes them to accept the influence and act or think in the manner suggested. Leaders have power when followers see a reason to accept the influence. Followers have power to choose whether or not to act.

Power exists at the heart of the leadership relationship, but power without direction—without purpose—becomes self-serving and toxic. Leadership within organizations has purpose. It influences with strategic vision flowing from purpose. Leadership without purpose focuses on the power broker, the one seeking to influence, the one desiring to be "leader"; and it fails to nurture the relationships necessary for leadership to have effect.

The so-called leaders in Jude's community lacked purpose. Consequently, their energy was not useful; it tore down and eroded like an unruly sea. They were basically concerned with themselves. They were not mobilizing the people. They saw leadership as a position of power to be celebrated rather than a relationship of influence to accomplish something. They were interested in themselves, not the mission nor the people whom that leadership should be serving. Because there was no purpose defining their leadership they had not invested themselves in relationships with the people who might have allowed their vision and energy to be channeled through others for the mission of the community. All they offered was relentless churning, without communal purpose or direction.

Leadership is powerful, but it is power with purpose exercised through relationships. Leadership exists to serve the mission and to serve the people in the pursuit of that mission. Vision and relationships: both are the responsibility of leadership in organizations.

> **Leadership is a relationship of dependency upon people.**

Biblical leadership is always about relationship—a long-term relationship modeled on God's patient outworking of his purpose in our lives. Leadership is a relationship that cares enough to walk patiently with people toward a shared purpose. Leadership is a relationship of dependency upon people. Leadership is not about leaders; it is about the people we lead.

Tychicus: Caring about Relationships

It is the people who make the Colossian story so compelling. We have been watching real people trying to work out their faith in their daily lives together. Now we will return to Colosse and look at the story through an unfamiliar set of eyes.

We see Paul writing with articulate theological persuasion, Onesimus beaming with newfound faith, and Philemon bristling with hostility. Into that mess walks Tychicus. Paul writes the letters and gives both letters and Onesimus to Tychicus with the assignment: "Now you go to Colosse and sort this out." Does that feel like a familiar situation?

Positionally, Tychicus is not the leader. At best he is a member of the team, a member of Paul's immediate circle of friends, a volunteer into whose hands Paul's vision is entrusted. It's all theory and plans until it gets into Tychicus' hands. He has to make it work. Tychicus represents for me the essence of followership. He is the employee, the staff member, the volunteer. He is the one empowered by Paul to carry the mission to its appropriate conclusion. If leadership is about empowering people to own and implement the mission, Tychicus is the classic example of the empowered follower—the purpose of the leadership relationship.

We don't know very much about Tychicus. In Colossians 4:7–8 Paul says:

> Tychicus will tell you all the news about me. He is a dear
> brother, a faithful minister and fellow servant in the Lord.
> I am sending him to you for the express purpose that
> you may know about our circumstances and that he may
> encourage your hearts.

In this brief description, Paul tells us five things about Tychicus. He is a dear brother, a faithful minister, a fellow servant, a trusted communicator, and an encourager of people. Not bad titles to have behind any of our names!

• *Tychicus is a dear brother.*
  He shared in the *koinonia*, the community of believers that made up the body of Christ. As we have seen, this is an important theme for Paul in both of these letters, as he appeals to Philemon and the Colossians to live out their participation in *koinonia*, their membership in the community. It is this bond that links Paul, Philemon, Onesimus, Tychicus, and the Colossians together. There are different roles to be played in the drama, but a common participation in the community of Christ.

• *Tychicus is a faithful minister.*
  He did his job well, and because of that Paul entrusts him with the life of Onesimus and, in a critical way, the spiritual growth of the Colossians. How Tychicus presents the letter and Onesimus, how he carries out Paul's instructions, will have a major role in shaping the response of Philemon and the Colossians. So, too, with every

person we seek to lead. How they respond to our influence and carry out their responsibilities determines the effectiveness of our leadership. This is also true for leaders. How leaders serve the people entrusted to them will have a significant impact on the people's growth and the accomplishment of the mission.

- *Tychicus is a fellow servant in the Lord.*
  The mission of the kingdom controlled all that he did. His life was given in service to God, to glorify God in Christ. All of his work was a reflection of that commitment. As one called to be a servant of the Lord, Tychicus was in fact a servant of the mission and a servant of the people. He accepted the purpose for which Paul wrote the letters, and he gave himself to this task. In service to Paul, he accepted this assignment and in so doing offered himself in service to Onesimus, Philemon, and the Colossian church. Nowhere is the leadership relationship more clearly modeled than in the unassuming, almost hidden, service of Tychicus.

  I remember interviewing two people for a faculty position. When we were through, the choice seemed clear. One person had introduced us to himself and his program; the other had introduced us to God, passing quickly over his own significant gifts and accomplishments. Who do people see when they walk into our offices? Who are we seen to be serving?

- *Tychicus is a trusted communicator.*
  Paul is in prison. He has no telephone or fax machine, no e-mail or text messaging, no way to communicate the details of his situation: the frustrations and the hopes, the challenges and the fears. But he has Tychicus. He has a close, trusting relationship with Tychicus. Paul trusts him with the letters, he trusts him with Onesimus, and he trusts him to represent his position accurately. Paul has invested in a relationship with Tychicus that enables the apostle to serve Philemon, Onesimus, and the Colossians—

through Tychicus. This is what the leadership relationship is all about. This connected web of relationships between Paul, Philemon, Onesimus, and the Colossian church—with Tychicus in the center—is the prototype for relational servant leadership. Who is the leader? Who is the follower? Who is the servant? Who is being served? Relational leadership is about leaders who are followers, followers who are leaders, servants who lead, and leaders who serve. Leadership is a relationship of mutual interdependency.

- *Tychicus is an encourager of people.*
  What other kind of person could Paul send into this situation? Tychicus cares for people and works to build them up—to encourage them in their faith, in their work, in their personal lives.

    Throughout this drama we have seen the importance of relationships for Paul. Paul appeals to his relationship with Philemon to persuade and encourage Philemon. Paul emphasizes his relationship with Onesimus to give Onesimus credibility. Paul expects Philemon and Onesimus to be reconciled because of their common faith, and he expects that reconciliation to be encouraged by the broader Colossian community. But think also of the relationship between Tychicus and Onesimus. Think of the trust that Onesimus must have in Tychicus, who in many ways holds Onesimus' life in his hands. If Tychicus does not take this seriously, Onesimus is the one who loses. But think also of the benefits of that trust. Onesimus must go back, but he does not go back alone. He has a friend going with him. Tychicus is there to support and encourage Onesimus as much as to challenge Philemon and the church. Paul has a vision. Tychicus implements that vision. That is what the leadership relationship is all about.

    Tychicus—a dear brother, a faithful minister, a fellow servant, a trusted communicator, and an encourager of people—a follower with a critical assignment in the drama of Paul and the Colossian church. Paul knew want he wanted to accomplish, but he was dependent upon Tychicus to make it happen.

Organization, Environment, and Action

Leadership starts with following; it begins with the God we choose to follow. That choice, with all the beliefs it contains, shapes the person we are—the character that others see in us. And it is character that finds expression in leadership, both in the vision we articulate and the values we live. Our vision gives shape to the mission; our values take root in the culture. Vision defines the structure of the organization as mission assignments are delegated to the followers. And leadership values, deeply rooted in the organizational culture, shape the work experience of the followers as they accept the assignments and take responsibility for the mission.

This is the practical heart of the leadership relationship. Leadership breaks the mission up into human-sized assignments and seeks to influence followers to accept responsibility for one piece of the mission. This delegation allows followers to take ownership for the mission and measure the accomplishment of their work. Leadership depends on followers accepting delegation, and the leader contextualizes the followers' contributions, showing how their work furthers the mission of the organization and celebrates their accomplishments.

> Followers will experience their work environment as much in terms of the relational values they encounter as the tasks and objectives they are assigned.

Job descriptions, performance reviews, and the recognition of achievement are important to the strategic success of the organization. How these tools are implemented in a particular community is shaped essentially by the values embedded within the culture of the organization. Here the emotional-relational dimension of leadership moves to the fore. Followers will experience their work environment as much in terms of the relational values they encounter as the tasks and objectives they are assigned. It is this experience that clarifies their expectations, constrains their behaviors, and gives meaning to their efforts. The values of leadership, embedded in the organizational culture, create the context in which people work and determine whether they will find meaning and achieve their potential.[1] Relational leadership cares about the people being influenced and seeks to grow them as together they pursue the mission of the organization.

The Care and Nurture of Paid and Unpaid Staff

Leadership is a relationship of dependency. Leaders articulate vision. Leaders reinforce values in all they do. But leaders are dependent upon other people to make it happen. In this chapter I'm looking at the leadership relationship in terms of the care and nurture of the people through whom we accomplish our vision and with whom we live out our values. This is the point where the relational character of servant leadership is most visible. In the interdependent relationship of leader and follower we hear the heartbeat of servant leadership most clearly.

I want to sketch the basic components of a human resource management system as developed by the corporate and nonprofit, or service, sectors. However, in order to underline the importance of relationship in leadership, I would like to look at a people development model primarily from the perspective of a volunteer. I choose this approach for several reasons. First, I believe that all human resource management principles and processes apply to unpaid workers or volunteers. Second, with the development of "portfolio" lifestyles and the emerging retirement of Baby Boomers, we will increasingly

---

1. Richard Boyatzis and Annie McKee, *Resonant Leadership* (Boston: Harvard Business School Press, 2005), 21.

find ourselves employing volunteers in our organizations as well as our churches.[2] Third, as leaders and followers we will find our own self-expression and ministry expanding in volunteer service. Finally, I agree with Max De Pree, who argues that nearly all employees today are essentially volunteers. They *choose* to stay in their current jobs; they are not bound to a particular position. De Pree argues that people stay with an organization because they believe that organization offers them a fair return on their invested time and effort. When they believe the contrary, they begin to look elsewhere for employment. In that sense all workers are volunteers.[3]

Think about it. Do you stay in your present position primarily for the money? Probably not. Do you remain in this position because you have no other options? Again, not likely. We *choose* to do what we do. We *choose* to stay in the position in which God has currently placed us. To that extent we are volunteers. Daily we *choose* to be where we are.

It is crucial that leaders recognize this choice. As the "Silent Generation"—those born between 1925 and 1942—settle into retirement with pensions, health care, and unprecedented affluence,[4] "Boomers" (1943–1960) will enter retirement with a different set of values, leaving a very different workforce of "Gen X" (1960s–1970s) and the "Millennial Generation" (1980s–1990s) to volunteer for work in our organizations. Warren Bennis and Robert Thomas underline the importance of this shift in their study of leaders, *Geeks and Geezers*, revealing how unique life experiences—the era, values, and defining

2. Charles Handy, *The Age of Unreason* (Boston: Harvard Business School Press, 1989), 82, sees more part-time and contracted services and volunteer activities being pieced together in a portfolio of commitments.
3. De Pree, *Leadership Is an Art*, 28; see also Max De Pree, *Leading Without Power* (San Francisco: Jossey-Bass, 1997).
4. Neil Howe and William Strauss, "The Next 20 Years," *Harvard Business Review* (July–August 2007): 4.

moments in each person's journey—form the choices that shape their leadership.[5]

Those who study generational differences envision Boomers leaving our organizations over the next decade or two, continuing their search for meaningful life and self-perfection. Boomers see themselves as protectors of the values of society, becoming elder statespersons focused on championing vision, values, and religion. Partly because of their numbers, they will enter old age with a splash, desiring to make it a meaningful time of life. Some will be reluctant to retire completely, seeking consulting roles with institutions. Boomers are expected to forge a new retirement ethic, looking for meaningful ways to invest their lives. By numbers, by health, and by inclination Boomers will become a strong pool of potential volunteers. But they will want choice; they will want control of their lives. They will struggle with the pragmatism of the Gen X leaders and seek to influence them as mentors and consultants.[6]

The Gen X leaders and followers who will carry the weight of our organizations reveal a different profile. Growing up with working mothers, they had to fend for themselves—often with too many choices. As a group, they tend to distrust institutions, including the family. They are seen as highly pragmatic, with less focus on moral authority than practicality. Having typically married late, Gen Xers want to build security for their family, becoming highly protective of their children, wanting to provide them a more secure and structured childhood and education than they remember. As leaders, they are seen as "getting it done." They make quick decisions, streamline the organization, downsize the bureaucracy, and remove any middlemen who do not add value. Their pragmatic, survival orientation makes them "the

---

5. Warren G. Bennis and Robert J. Thomas, *Geeks and Geezers: How Era, Values, and Defining Moments Shape Leaders* (Boston: Harvard Business School Press, 2002), 2–21.
6. Howe and Strauss, "Next 20 Years," 4–12.

greatest entrepreneurial generation ever."[7] They want to be free agents, negotiating their own deals, asking directly for special compensation incentives, and switching employers at a moment's notice. They want to be their own boss, and will quit and move on if they encounter a workplace problem. The work assignment has to make sense; they need freedom, control, and high-trust leadership. But they will get things done—as long as it is a good deal for them.[8]

The Millennial Generation is getting a lot of attention from leaders today. I often hear from CEOs and recruiters the same observations that emerge from the research. They are "upbeat, team oriented, close to their parents and confident about the future."[9] This is the pampered and protected "Baby on Board" generation, their busy lives structured in detail by their parents. They were babies when babies were cultur- ally "in." Their parents often began preparing for their enrollment in specific colleges before their birth and have run interference for them in regard to grades, admissions, selection for sports teams, and now even over job recruitment.

Job recruiters aren't surprised when they receive a call from a parent of a Millennial. And in one case when the young employee didn't show up for work the company called my friends—the parents! Millennials have been shaped in their formative years by terrorism, along with the rise of the hero (for example, the New York 9/11 first responders). Having been told all their lives that they are smart and winners, Millennials expect to be successful in the workplace. They have high expectations and are shocked if everything doesn't fall into place for them. Rather than biding their time waiting for a promotion, they expect to achieve today and be promoted tomorrow.

---

7. Ibid., 2.

8. Ibid., 6–12. See also Camille F. Bishop, *We're in This Boat Together: Leadership Succession Between the Generations* (Colorado Springs: Authentic, 2008), 44–45.

9. Ibid., 2.

Unlike Gen Xers, who want space to be their own leaders, Millennials prefer to be managed. They want clear rules, lines of authority, standards and goals, and immediate feedback. Well-connected to others, they desire to work together rather than alone. This is the Internet generation; they expect nonstop communication with peers, social networking, and virtual communities. They are so "proficient with e-mail, SMS messaging, Skype video calling, blogs, forums and virtual online workrooms, they don't see a need to be physically present in the same office to collaborate, solve problems or produce products."[10]

Millennials have a very different understanding of relationships than the Silent, Boomer, and Gen X generations.[11] They engage naturally online in ways that earlier generations could only understand face-to-face. This generation expects to succeed; they want to succeed. They want opportunities to learn, especially with friends. They want to have fun and work with flexible schedules. They want respect in the office, even if they are brand-new. They want to be challenged and work with positive people. They want honesty and integrity from their leaders. They want to learn in teams—through technology, games, and experiential activities. And they want to be paid appropriately for their investment in the organization, with benefits to maintain their lifestyle.[12]

Consultant and author Claire Raines gives advice for managing Millennials that I believe is appropriate for any generation:

> The key is to get to know each as an individual: find out what is important to him or her, why they're working, what they want to get out of their jobs. Get them to teach

---

10. Tim Shaver, "Understanding Generation X and Y Employees," Client Advocate Network online newsletter, http://www.clientadvocatenetwork.com/articles/people_2008-07_xandy.html.

11. Ibid., 107.

12. Claire Raines, "Managing Millennials," excerpt from *Connecting Generations: The Sourcebook* (2002), available at http://www.generationsatwork.com/articles_millenials.php.

you how to motivate them. Then ask them to do the task and sell them on the benefit to them of doing that task. It may also help to set goals with each of them for the next 60 days or so, with a reward at the end, so that when you assign tasks, they can see where accomplishing that task will take them.[13]

Though Boomers are leaving our organizations, they will stay close as consultants and volunteers—as they choose. Gen X workers bring energy and pragmatism to get things done, expecting strong leadership vision, limited management, and space to grow. With their loyalty being to themselves, they will stay with an organization only by choice. Millennials are arriving with confidence, expecting strong management and direction and opportunities to learn, grow, and take on responsibility. If they find this, they may choose to stay long-term.

More than ever before, leadership is about relationship—a relationship between leader and follower in which the leader delegates responsibility for accomplishment. This relationship nurtures growth toward potential and provides meaning and fulfillment for both leader and follower.

Management books and journals talk about paradigm shifts and the new information age. One of the paradigm shifts is that followers *choose* to follow. People no longer stay in a position (if they ever did) out of loyalty to a company or organization. Organizations no longer promise to take care of their people for the length of their careers. Things are changing so fast that no one can coast. Organizations cannot afford to keep people who simply do the job they used to do the way they used to do it. Organizations need people who are learning and growing and changing with the organization and its environment. At the same time, people can no longer learn a skill or gain a level of

---

13. Ibid. See also Howe and Strauss, "Next 20 Years," 6–11, for review of the specific traits of Millennials and other generations.

knowledge and ride it out for life. What we know and do today may well be obsolete tomorrow. We all must keep learning and growing in order to continue making a contribution in the changing context of our organizations.

Fast Company is a journal for the young workers of the information age. When I first started reading the magazine you could pick up any issue and see the headlines scream-

Followers choose to follow.

ing this new reality. "The Brand Called You," "Free Agent Nation," "You Decide," "The Talent Market," "The War for Talent," "Hire Today ... Gone Tomorrow."[14] Now, ten years later, the editorial emphasis has shifted to social networking and design, but the current issue still reveals "How to Monitor Your Brand 24/7"—with "brand" referring to the person as much as the product.[15] The initiative is with the follower. The choice belongs to the follower. To be employable—whether as a paid employee or as a volunteer—we must keep learning and growing. Those who do are the people for whom every organization is looking.

But this new paradigm, this new reality, puts a burden on both people and organizations. Organizations have to take active leadership in the recruitment and retention of their employees—their volunteers—their free-agent, temporary-contract service providers. Recruitment is never finished. It is an ongoing responsibility. At the same time, people must keep themselves renewed and growing in order to contribute to changing organizational environments and goals. They must take responsibility for their own learning and growth. Those who cannot keep up will find themselves marginalized. The opportunities for contribution and growth are escalating, but so is the probability of unemployment and economic despair.

---

14. *Fast Company: How Smart Business Works*, August 1998.
15. *Fast Company*, May 2009.

This presents a new challenge for leadership. Leadership, as I have said, serves both the mission and the people. These two "services" increasingly will be in tension. The mission is served by embracing gifted people who own the mission and continually renew their own ability to contribute as the mission is renewed. Leaders must focus first on the mission that defines the organization. At the same time, leaders must recruit good people and so invest themselves in the growth and development of these people that the team members both will be able to contribute over the long run and will find the organizational setting a place in which they want to invest themselves for the long run. Leadership is a relationship of service to people that continually renews them and reengages them in the life of the organization.

Another reason for looking at the topic of people development through the eyes of a volunteer is that this is the point where most organizations totally fail to develop their people. The best organizations take their paid human resources very seriously, seeking to develop them as individuals and as resources. Sadly, however, too many organizations do not care for their people well. In fact, religious organizations have a reputation for not taking their paid employees seriously and practically abusing their volunteers. Focusing on the leadership relationship from the perspective of the volunteer enables us to identify important issues that are key to the motivation and leadership of all members of our organizations.

Unfortunately, it is difficult to find good models of volunteer programs. I have encountered, over the years, a few organizations that take volunteers quite seriously. I have been particularly impressed with the way volunteers are developed at the Los Angeles Zoo, American Red Cross, Sierra Club, and the Huntington Memorial Hospital in Pasadena. Hospitals seem to have done a better job than most organizations in developing volunteer programs that attract and retain good people who find an outlet for their gifts and values. On the other hand, though churches utilize more volunteer resources than any other kind of organization, they are notorious for the lack of relational investment in their volunteers.

Everything we will explore in this chapter about managing human resources, about developing people, applies equally to volunteers and paid staff, profit and nonprofit organizations, and the local church. I will use the term *volunteer* to represent all team members—paid and unpaid—as a reminder that the follower *chooses* to follow.

Why people volunteer

Why do people volunteer? Why do they choose to spend their time and invest their talent with a particular organization? There are many reasons. People volunteer to gain love and acceptance, to belong to a community. They volunteer to gain recognition and status, to have power. Service on advisory boards, governing boards, and civic committees often provides prestigious affiliations. People might get involved because an organization gives them an opportunity to influence decisions that affect them. Serving with the Sierra Club, AARP, or a local homeowners association touches quality of life issues.

People volunteer to feel important. One time when I was leading a workshop in Washington, DC, I did the usual tourist things, like visiting the various monuments. In the tall Washington Monument I met Jerry, a volunteer elevator operator. He volunteers eight to ten hours per week. He is very pleased to be connected with this historic center in his country. He pointed to his "volunteer" cap with pride and told me that he had to be active at least ten hours each month to keep his status. How many people in your organization are worried about losing their volunteer status?

People volunteer to find self-fulfillment and growth. Sharon works as a volunteer in children's ministry in order to give meaning to her life in a way that she doesn't find in her paid work. Some volunteer for self-expression. Beverly volunteers as the gardener at a home for the physically challenged because she loves to garden and lives in a condominium without a garden of her own. People also volunteer to explore paid employment. Florence volunteers for the church library because she wants to go into library science when her children get older.

People volunteer to promote a cause they believe in, to make things happen, or because they want to "be where the action is"—part of something that is making a difference. Don organizes and serves food at an ecumenical shelter for the homeless because he believes churches should work together to alleviate human suffering. Matt volunteers for an organization that enables him to promote his political views. He also volunteers to teach in an inner city school—for pay—because he sees education as critical for hope. Jean volunteers as an assistant in a continuing education program because she wants to see educational resources made available to persons who cannot participate in traditional schooling. Elizabeth volunteered as director of alumni services at Regent because she wanted to change the fact that this area had been significantly underdeveloped.

People volunteer to "be with my kind of people." They volunteer as much for the social connectedness as for the actual task. Who they get to work with is very important to many who join our organizations. People also volunteer to serve others, to feel good about the investment they are making in other persons.

And finally, behind all of these reasons we hope that people are also investing in our organizations because they want to serve God. They see our organization—our community—as one place they can work out their calling before God.

I mention this reason last because it is the one that frequently sidetracks Christian leaders, especially pastors. I have heard many pastors articulate a belief that I should volunteer to serve God and accept the assignment they have in mind as an expression of my gratitude to God. I want to counter this argument by first noting that I am grateful to God and I do both work for pay and volunteer to serve God; I do believe that all that I do is an outworking of my calling as a follower of Jesus Christ. However, I do not believe that necessarily means I should work in your church in that assignment. Show me how the position for which you want me to volunteer will serve my goals as I seek to invest my limited hours in a way that fulfils my calling to serve God. There are many places a volunteer can invest gifts and time and still be serving God. The church is one.

Leaders need to take their relationships with volunteers seriously, serving the volunteer as they serve the mission. This is an important principle for the leading and motivating of people. There is an exchange that takes place in every volunteer relationship. Volunteers, paid and unpaid, have something to give. But there is also something that they want, a need that must be addressed. This is important. There is a reason why they are willing to give their time and their talent. Relational leadership takes that seriously.

In Canada, where social policies have led to less emphasis on volunteering than in the United States, organizations have come to realize that people give their time by choice. An article in the *Vancouver Sun* noted that people volunteer for a reason. They engage in the volunteer relationship for the exchange, not just to volunteer.[16] As the government has pulled back on services and the volunteer sector has begun to emerge, the exchange embedded in the volunteer relationship has also surfaced as an important focus for the leadership of volunteers. To the extent that we understand the exchange with our volunteers, we will be able to address their needs, motivate them, and nurture their contribution to our organizations.

The point I want to make here is that there is an exchange. Volunteers—all workers—want something out of the relationship. They cannot be taken for granted. Volunteers want a return on the investment of their time. And the exchange differs from generation to

---

16. *Vancouver Sun*, July 1, 1990.

generation, from person to person. This is a foundational principle for the management of people, paid or unpaid. Only when we recognize this truth can we begin to lead people in a way that grows them and accomplishes our shared vision and values.

The recruitment and orientation of volunteers

The leadership relationship begins with recruitment. Recruitment is first of all a planning and communications issue. It is only when we know the organization's needs that we can communicate those needs with specificity in a call for volunteers.

Remember that we are not in the business of employing volunteers. Creating work is important, but a byproduct. We are organized for a mission. We only want volunteers, therefore, who will assist the organization in carrying out its mission. Consequently, recruitment starts with planning. What are we trying to accomplish? What kind of staffing will it take to accomplish this? Specifically, what kind of person, what set of gifts and experience, does the organization need in order to accomplish this piece of our mission? The recruitment of volunteers is always mission-driven. The mission determines what needs to be done; what needs to be done determines our staffing needs. Volunteers are always recruited to achieve the mission.

The best source for volunteers is referral by other satisfied volunteers. We need to develop a reputation for being a good place to volunteer, a place that cares about the contribution and the growth of its people.

The recruitment process with both paid and unpaid volunteers should involve an honest presentation of the needs of the organization, as represented by the particular position for which the person is volunteering, as well as a careful review of the person's gifts, interests, experience, and abilities. I always ask, "Why do you want to work here?" I want to understand the exchange need and be sure that it is one we can and want to meet. And as a volunteer, I want to know that this service will use my gifts and allow me to grow. When I was invited to serve on an advisory board for international leadership development, I asked about the responsibilities and what the board members thought I could contribute. We choose how to invest our limited time.

Similarly, we must be willing to turn down volunteers who are not qualified and move them to other opportunities for which they are qualified or train them for the position for which they have applied. This is hard for those of us in Christian organizations to do. We are very reluctant to turn anyone down, especially for an unpaid position. We are also afraid that we won't find anyone else. Yet the experience of successful volunteer agencies is precisely the opposite. Tightening the screening for a position only increases the importance of the position—it does not make it harder to recruit!

Susan is a docent at the Los Angeles Zoo. She leads groups of children on tours of the zoo, introducing them to the various animals. In order to obtain this volunteer position Susan had to undertake ten weeks of study and pass a major qualifying examination, and now she is required to complete annual training and retesting. What does a person need to do to qualify to lead children in your church or to volunteer in your organization?

Sierra Club volunteer trip leaders must complete two rigorous training courses and keep their mountaineering skills up to date. If we want to keep people in our organizations, we must invest in their training regardless of their form of compensation. There is a myth lingering over unpaid employment: we are afraid that if we make the qualifications too high no one will volunteer. Not so. If the opportunity for service meets the exchange requirements of the volunteer, high qualifications only underscore the importance of the task. There is a waiting list for docents at the Los Angeles Zoo.

Recruitment is about finding the best person to contribute to the organization's mission. Understanding and presenting the position in light of the mission is critical. It is also important, however, for leaders to understand the exchange need of the volunteer. Even with high-salaried volunteers, the exchange need varies depending on where people are at in their own life, career, or ministry.

Salary is seldom the issue in recruitment. Hours may be a concern. Colleagues—those with whom a person will be working—are often a major issue in recruiting key individuals. Future potential is highly valued. My son left his established position as an attorney to join a financial consulting firm that offered him a stake in their future. Housing is a concern for organizations like Regent College that are located in areas where residential housing is quite expensive. Schooling for children, transportation, sabbatical leaves, and continuing education opportunities—are all issues that may need to be addressed in the recruitment process.

For many of us in Christian communities, this is new. Long-term employees talk about the sacrifices they made when they joined the organization. New recruits want to nail things down in advance and explore all of the exchange needs up front. I was surprised when my twenty-eight-year-old son agreed to change jobs but requested a paid vacation the first month. I was more surprised when they gave it to him! Two years later he considered another move, so his company offered him a car and a gasoline credit card for his commute. This is no longer unusual; it is the way the entrepreneurial generation of the twenty-first century thinks. The recruitment of people has become more complex in this changing "talent-scarce economy."[17]

When the right person is found for a position and the interdependent commitments of the exchange have been negotiated, the agreement of service should be spelled out in writing. Both the leader and the volunteer should have the same understanding of the terms of the appointment and of what is to be accomplished.

---

17. Scott Kirsner, "Hire Today . . . Gone Tomorrow," *Fast Company: How Smart Business Works* (August 1998): 138.

Once a volunteer has been added to the team, there is usually an orientation process to help the new member learn how things are done in this organization—an introduction to the culture. Every volunteer has the right to a clear understanding of the organization: its vision and values, its ministries, and its policies. This can be handled by a volunteer manual, an orientation program, or both. At this point I refer churches and other organizations that employ volunteers, especially in the United States, to their nearest hospital. Most major hospitals have developed very sophisticated volunteer programs, including a good volunteer manual and usually an effective volunteer-orientation program.

A good manual is a valuable tool for orienting volunteers. The manual might include a letter of greeting from the president, pastor, or chairperson of the board. It should have a description of the organization or church and its community and denominational relationships. It might include a brief description of programs and services and perhaps even an organizational chart that shows who is responsible for whose success. It might include the names and titles of board members and other staff, a current operating budget, policies and procedures for volunteers, volunteer job descriptions, the criteria for recognition as a volunteer, emergency procedures and phone numbers, and sample forms that will be used regularly. At Regent College we developed an extensive manual for our board that became a model requested by many theological schools across North America. The college, of course, also has the traditional handbooks for academic and administrative staff— paid and unpaid.

Once the need for a position has been established in the planning stage, a volunteer has been recruited to fill that position, and the orientation program has drawn the new staff member into the organization, then the leadership relationship moves to the fore. The focus now is on the motivation and nurture of the volunteer.

The CARE Plan

It is fitting now that we return to the heart of leadership: the relationship between the leader and the follower. It is in the context of this relationship that we are able to influence people in a way that empowers them to contribute to the shared mission of our organization and enables them to grow in their own competence and confidence.

I want to describe this leadership relationship using a simplified human resource development model that I call the CARE Plan. This model is built around four commonsense responsibilities of leadership: Clarify expectations; Agree on objectives; Review progress; and Equip for performance and growth.

Clarify expectations

Here we look at two things: job descriptions and performance standards.

1. Job descriptions

Everyone has a right to know what they should be doing! I realize this is a rather simplistic, commonsense statement, but it is often ignored. This is what job descriptions or position descriptions are all about: letting people know what their job is, what they are supposed to be doing. Even in the best of organizations job descriptions are often treated as a necessary evil—the paperwork of bureaucracy. In volunteer organizations, such as local churches, job descriptions are practically nonexistent. I would argue that job descriptions should be prepared for every position in a church or organization, whether full-time or part-time, paid or unpaid.

A job description is a written record of the duties, responsibilities, and requirements of the position. It answers the question, *What is my job?* It should describe the job carefully and identify the tasks the person is expected to perform. It should identify the limits of responsibility and authority. It should be specific and brief.

The amount of detail in a job description is directly related to the responsibility of the position. The more responsible the position, the more broadly responsibility and authority are assigned. The description does not spell out specific tasks, but defines the skills and abilities needed and leaves room for initiative in how tasks will be carried out. The less responsible the position, the more specifically the duties, time, and skills are spelled out—exactly what needs to be done and when.

The job description we wrote for the director of church relations at Regent College identified the need for relational skills, the ability to drive oneself around the greater Vancouver area, and the requirement to speak with a hundred pastors each year about the school's programs. It was a part-time position, and the volunteer was given significant latitude in regard to time and approach. When we needed an audio-visual assistant, however, we were not only precise about the skills needed but we were very specific about the hours to be worked and what needed to be accomplished at specific times—for example, running the sound system during chapel every Tuesday from 11:00 to 11:45 a.m.

When composing a job description, don't get too complicated. Something simple that works is best. This isn't about doing paperwork but about empowering the follower, the volunteer, to contribute to the mission. The job description is a tool designed to help both leader and follower understand what the organization requires of them. The objective is to produce a document that spells out, ideally in one page, what the leader and the follower understand as "the job."

Over the years, I have used a very simple form for getting started with job descriptions. We have used this form in a variety of churches and in a few organizations. It is a workable starting model. I do notice, however, that eventually, especially for more responsible positions, the description tends to become longer. Most of our senior positions at Regent had two- to three-page descriptions. I am not convinced this is necessary, particularly if we are preparing job descriptions in an organization where they have not traditionally been used.

The base model I start with, if the organization does not have another way of doing things, is a single page that looks like this:

POSITION DESCRIPTION

Job title:

Date established:

Department:

Supervisor:

Relationship to mission:

Duties, responsibilities, and authority:

Skills required:

Time required:

Training required and provided:

Job location:

---

(1) Job title. This is simply the designation within the organization. What do we call this person? Director of church relations? A-V assistant? President? It is a point of identification for the organization's records. I might note here that Tom Peters has commented on the power of titles in recognizing and motivating employees. Giving someone a title that accurately reflects a specific area of responsibility is more motivating than a generic title of "clerk."[18]

(2) Date established. This again is only for the organization's records. When was this position established?

(3) Department. This provides context. It identifies how the person fits into the larger community of the organization, how the person will be part of the team. At Regent, the director of church relations is part of the development office and the A-V assistant is part of the administration office. Similarly, an assistant Sunday school teacher may belong to the Christian education department.

(4) Supervisor. This one is important. Who is responsible for the success of this person? I will come back to this point later, but for now I would strongly assert that if you cannot identify the supervisor, no one should accept the job! Again using the Regent example, the vice-president for development is responsible for the success of the director of church relations, and the director of audio-visual services is responsible for the A-V assistant. But, again, we will come back to this one.

(5) Relationship to mission. What I look for here is a description of the responsibilities or contributions of this position in terms of the organization's mission. Why is this position important? How does it contribute to the larger mission of the organization? Completing this part of the job description is a reminder to both the leader and the follower that the position was established to serve the mission of the

---

18. Tom Peters and Nancy Austin, *A Passion for Excellence* (New York: Warner Books, 1989), 213–18.

church or organization. The position exists as an important part of the larger mission and strategies. It doesn't exist for the benefit of the leader or the follower, but rather for the mission. That may seem like an insignificant point, but it is important for the leadership relationship for both the leader and the follower to recognize that they are there to serve the mission. The follower is not there to serve the leader. In fact, as I will argue shortly, the leader is there to help the follower serve the mission. Defining the position and the leadership relationship in terms of the mission provides objectivity for the human dynamic within the relationship.

(6) Duties, responsibilities, and authority. This is where the specific tasks that are to be accomplished by this position are spelled out. What precisely do we want the volunteer to do? What is this person responsible for accomplishing? What authority does this person have to carry out these responsibilities? What decisions should this person make on his or her own? When does this person need approval before proceeding? As I noted earlier, the detail here will be inversely proportional to the level of responsibility. The more responsibility, the less specificity. What we want is a list of responsibilities that will allow anyone picking up this job description to quickly understand this person's exact responsibilities.

(7) Skills required. What does this person need to be able to do to fulfill the requirements of the position? Be comfortable with technology? Know a particular software program? Is a driver's license needed? Does the person need teaching experience? A certain level of education? These expectations need clarification before the leadership relationship begins.

(8) Time required. Here the follower deserves an honest assessment of the amount of time this assignment will require. This is especially important for unpaid volunteers who are giving the time and receive no overtime compensation. Clarifying this expectation is important

both ways. The follower and the leader need to know the organization's expectations for the amount of time as well as the use of time. And the leader needs to understand the follower's expectations regarding how much time he or she is willing to invest in this position.

(9) Training required and provided. This item assumes that the organization is interested in the growth of its people and is investing in their continued training. This is another clarification of expectations that is important both ways. The volunteer or employee should know exactly what kind of training will be provided to enable him or her to complete the assignment and grow into more responsibility. At the same time, the organization needs to make it clear if training will be provided in which the volunteer is expected to participate.

I frequently hear churches complaining about the poor attendance of Sunday school teachers at their teacher training workshops. Typically I hear three reasons for this. First, the workshops are scheduled at a time that volunteers have not committed—often Saturdays—and are reluctant to give up. Second, the quality of the workshops often leaves something to be desired. Third, there was no clearly stated expectation that taking on the responsibility of teaching also meant accepting responsibility for attending a set number of training workshops. If volunteers are expected to participate in training, clarify this expectation in the job description, schedule the training at a time designated by the participants, and make sure the workshops are of such quality that no one would want to miss them.

(10) Job location. This information is less critical but is included especially for unpaid volunteers. Where will the person work? Where do we expect him to carry out these responsibilities? Will she have an office? A classroom? Will he work out of his home? Will she use her own car? These are the kinds of things that are best clarified up front in any leadership relationship.

This particular outline is obviously not definitive. It is one I have used effectively for many years. If you have a model that works well for you and your organization, use it. If not, feel free to start with this basic plan.

Job descriptions are all about the clarification of expectations. I am not simply promoting more paperwork; I strongly believe that job descriptions are an important foundation for the leadership relationship. They make a difference. If the assignment we want someone to do is important enough to do, it is worth describing. If it is not worth taking the time to describe on one page, it is surely not worth anyone's time to do it.

If you find yourself in an organization or church without job descriptions, one way to start is to give everyone a blank job description form. Let them fill out the form based on their experience of the job. Then have them sit down with their supervisors to clarify what the church or organization needs to see in that job description. If they understand their jobs well, job descriptions will be written in that process. If they do not understand their jobs well, you obviously need to have these discussions! You need to clarify expectations.

While I was serving as the chair of the Christian education committee of our church we had a need for two teachers to supervise the toddlers during the main worship service. We were not yet using job descriptions in our church, but we announced the need and began to look for volunteers. No one volunteered. Finally a recommendation was brought to the committee that we should hire two individuals to cover this critical assignment. Job descriptions spelling out the expectations and compensation were written. Almost immediately three people *volunteered* for the position. When the church communicated that the responsibility was important enough to describe specifically and to pay for, three persons decided it was important enough that they would volunteer their time without pay. That was the beginning of job descriptions for all volunteer positions at our church.

For years Doug had struggled to recruit volunteers for his church's social services center. Looking for help, he registered for a workshop I was leading on the care and motivation of volunteers. He said that he spent so much of his time recruiting new volunteers to staff the center that he was not able to fulfill his responsibilities to the church. He still had two unfilled positions. If something didn't change, he would have to shut down the center. The center provided food, clothing, and shelter for the homeless and others in need; and he hated the thought of shutting it down. Doug completed the workshop and took the CARE Plan model back to the center. He wrote me nearly a year later to let me what happened. He immediately drafted job descriptions for every position in the social services center, and he posted the two openings. On the first Sunday after the postings were announced, he had eight new volunteers for the two positions. Now, one year later, he reported that volunteerism was up 35 percent over the past year. All positions were filled and he had a waiting list of volunteers. This plan works!

The Huntington Memorial Hospital in Pasadena, California, used to have a special program for infants who had to be in the hospital without their parents. Volunteers were recruited to spend one hour per week rocking babies. They simply held the little infants and rocked them, letting them feel the physical presence of love. My wife saw an article about the program in the newspaper and was immediately captured by the idea. The next day she went to the hospital to get a job description and sign up as a volunteer. Every position was filled, and 150 people were put on a waiting list!

Now think about that. How long is the waiting list to volunteer in the nursery of your church? Same job, but look at the difference. The hospital said, *This is an important service to babies and their families; come and be part of this important ministry.* Too often churches communicate, *Will someone help keep these babies quiet while we get on with the real ministry taking place in the sanctuary?*

Do you see the difference? The hospital gave dignity and value to the work. Too many churches and organizations fail to give dignity and worth to the task they ask people to undertake. Job descriptions are one simple and important way to underline the value of a job and give dignity to the assignment.

After attending a class on leadership and volunteers, Gary used the outline we just reviewed to design job descriptions for every position in his church. Next he had them approved by the church board. Then all of the job descriptions, from the part-time volunteer to his position as the senior pastor, were bound together in a simple booklet. The response amazed him. He saw people look at the booklet and comment to one another, "Look, here I am; I'm in the same booklet with the pastor!"

What seems like a small thing is in fact an important way to recognize the contributions of all the players on our ministry teams and reinforce their value to our mission.

2. Performance standards

The job description clarifies the basic expectations for the position. It addresses the strategic organization of the mission. The values embedded in the culture also define quality expectations or standards for the level of performance expected, and these should be clarified also. What do you expect? What do you expect to see accomplished, over what time period, and with what quality? How will you evaluate performance in this position? By what criteria will you know that the job is being done right? Performance standards focus on results, outcomes, and the way we work.

In Christian circles there is too often a tendency to resist standards, measurement, and accountability. As I noted earlier, however, a reading of Ezekiel 34 or Jude 12–13 should call us up short. God seems to have clear expectations for those of us in leadership. Accountability and evaluation accompany responsibility. We need to understand what is expected of us as leaders, and we owe the same clarification to the people we lead.

Several years ago a new manager told me that he wanted to fire one of his assistants. When I asked him if he had discussed the situation with her, he said no. I told him he could not release her until they had gone over the organization's expectations for the position and he had given her at least three months of closely reviewed time to help her succeed. He did this and reported back to me that no one had ever told her what was expected. She turned out to be his best employee once the expectations were understood.

Clarify expectations. Give value and dignity to the work. Set up the standards by which volunteers can measure their progress as they seek to make a contribution to the mission of the organization.

Agree on objectives

All employees have a right to know what is expected of them. This means that each volunteer, every member of the team, must have a *supervisor*—someone assigned to support and enable the person to carry out his or her responsibilities. This is important! This is the core of relational leadership, of servant leadership. We are talking about leadership as an empowering service to those for whom the leader is responsible—not vice versa.

Notice how I keep repeating the phrase "for whom the leader is responsible." The leader is responsible for the success of the follower, paid or volunteer. In the leadership relationship, I prefer to ask "For whose success are you responsible?" rather than the traditional "Who reports to you?" It keeps the flow of power moving in the right direction: from the organization, through the leader, to the follower, for the accomplishment of the mission.

Leaders are responsible for the success of their followers. This, for me, is a fundamental principle of leadership. Early in his tenure as president of Fuller Seminary, David Hubbard found himself in conflict with members of his board. Max De Pree, then a young member of the board, took Hubbard aside and told him, "I am on your side in this matter, and I will commit myself to your success as president of this school." Many believe Hubbard's long and successful tenure at Fuller was because of the fact that he had De Pree in his corner for those thirty years. David Hubbard would have agreed. Would that everyone could have a leader, a supervisor, committed to his or her success.

The supervisor or leader can be a paid member of the team or an unpaid volunteer. Salary does not make one a leader. I should note in fact that *any position can be filled by an unpaid volunteer as well as a paid volunteer.* I know unpaid volunteers who are chief executive officers, chief financial officers, chief administrative officers, consultants, teachers, directors of marketing, directors of development, etc. There is no position that cannot be filled by a competent qualified volunteer, paid or unpaid, who has a good job description and a leader responsible for his or her success.

Having no supervisor communicates to a volunteer: *No one cares what you do.* The supervisor and the volunteer together need to work out the specific objectives for the volunteer's assignment. What, precisely, do we want this person to do? These objectives should be spelled out—preferably on one page—clearly enough that anyone would know exactly what the volunteer is expected to accomplish in the specified time frame. This becomes the standard by which the volunteer's progress and performance will be measured.

While I was president of Regent College, all employees, paid and unpaid, presented a draft of their objectives for the year at the time of their performance review. In discussion with their supervisor, these objectives were revised, as necessary, based on the needs of the college. They then became the standard against which employees evaluated their own progress at the next review. Each year the senior management team prepared a draft of the key objectives for their departments to review with me and the management cabinet. I then compiled these objectives into the "president's annual plan," which was presented to the board along with the annual budget. In the fall, each senior manager submitted an evaluation of his or her department compared to the previous year's annual objectives. I compiled this information into the "president's annual report" for review at the annual meeting of the board of governors.

In the leadership relationship, the leader or supervisor connects the follower—the volunteer—to the organizational mission. The leader is responsible for seeing that the volunteer succeeds in contributing to the mission. Through the establishment and review of objectives, the leader keeps the follower growing in that contribution.

Review progress

The third principle of this people development model focuses on evaluation. In human resource management this is called *performance review*. This is the area of people management about which I have the strongest feelings. Unfortunately, it is the most misunderstood and abused component. Conducting such a review is thought to be judgmental and critical, destructive to motivation. And it frequently is!

Performance reviews are intended to keep the organization's goals in focus. They are designed to assist the leader in developing employees or volunteers in their own growth toward leadership. The intent is to enable people to do their jobs to the best of their ability.

A performance review is a tool for development and growth—not a time for judging and criticizing, not a time to give an annual grade. Leaders need training to do these reviews well. Unfortunately, the typical performance review does not involve caring confrontation. Instead, it is a mere pat on the back accompanied by a reference to one area that needs improvement. In other words, *You're OK—except in this area, where you get a B.*

Leaders give this kind of review because they have been told to conduct a review and because they feel that they need to be able to show followers where they still have room to grow. Leaders leave the review feeling uncomfortable. Followers leave this kind of review not feeling very encouraged but often instead feeling angry. Volunteers or followers tend to forget all the positive things that were said and focus only on the negative areas noted as needing growth. Team members experience such reviews as criticism rather than affirmation. The emotional-relational dimension of leadership surfaces strongly during these times of review. Positive affirmations are empowering, but negative comments can be demotivating. And negative remarks are heard with deeper intensity than positive ones. The way performance reviews are administered touches emotional currents in both leaders and followers, resulting in inspiration (when done well) or resentment (when conducted carelessly).[19]

Leaders should see performance reviews as checkpoints, not as times to criticize. Reviews provide opportunities to help followers develop their skills, expand their contribution, advance their careers, and gain promotion in the organization because they are growing—in short, to become leaders in their own right. All of these outcomes can be accomplished while achieving the organizational goals.

Performance reviews are part of the personal and leadership development system, the feedback loop. They should provide information to the leader and the employee that will enable each to grow in his or her contribution to the organization. Performance reviews mean that someone cares. As I noted earlier, a job description says, *This is an important part of our mission*, and the assignment of a supervisor says, *Someone cares what I do*. The performance review suggests that *Someone cares about me*. It is part of the investment that the leader makes in the growth of the follower. It is a sign of caring.

This was poignantly brought home to me a number of years ago. I was managing an office and, using my preferred model, had been giving

19. Daniel Goleman and Richard Boyatzis, "Social Intelligence and the Biology of Leadership," *Harvard Business Review* (September 2008): 275–77.

performance reviews to all of the team. At that time I only conducted performance reviews with full-time employees. Nancy had worked with me for three years as a senior seminar coordinator. We had been through three reviews together. In her last year Nancy moved to part-time status in our mailroom three months before she was to move across the United States. During this time I conducted performance reviews for all of the full-time team members, but not for Nancy.

Whenever I walked into the office over the next few weeks I could sense that something was wrong. No one said anything, but I could tell there was a problem. Then one day Nancy knocked on my door and asked if she could talk to me. I welcomed her, and she walked in with tears running down her cheeks. I asked her what was wrong. She looked up and asked, "Don't you care about me anymore? You didn't give me a performance review. Aren't you interested in my growth after I leave here?"

Well, of course I cared. But she was right. From that day on, all employees, full-time or part-time, paid or unpaid, were included in the performance review program. It is an investment in their growth and an important way for the organization and the leader to say, *I care.*

Performance reviews are about caring enough to commit yourself to assisting people to do the best job possible. If the work is not up to standard, this is the time to help the person bring it up or, if that is not possible, to help the employee or volunteer relocate to where his or her gifts can be better used. If these reviews are about caring, then they belong in every leadership relationship. If they are about focusing on the mission, then they belong in every leadership relationship. Every member of the organization, every volunteer—paid and unpaid—is owed a performance review as the organization's minimal investment in his or her growth and development.

The heart of the review process is obviously not the particular form or model chosen. The heart of the process is the discussion that follows, the relationship between the leader and the follower, and the action in regard to where we go from here. In fact, it is dangerous to adopt any form that might distract from the relationship, the discussion, and the personal investment of the leader in the employee.

Performance reviews are most effective when they are part of a leadership relationship of continuous feedback. People deserve to know how they are doing all the time, to be able to get the feedback they need when they need it in order to improve and do their job well. Annual feedback is not sufficient; it is too far removed from the moment. To have learning value, feedback needs to be immediate—while the person can still do something about it. If we care about followers and their growth, we will tell them what they are doing wrong now so they can correct it. Or we tell them what they are doing well now so they can keep at it. In fact, I believe that feedback given long after the fact is more a sign of not caring than of true leadership responsibility. If the leader doesn't point out problems along the way so that followers can correct their actions, then he or she loses the right to do so at the annual review.

In the 1980s, the best-selling little book *The One Minute Manager* argued persuasively for continuous review and appraisal, suggesting regular one-minute praises and one-minute reprimands.[20] I completely agree with the principle of continuous feedback that the authors advocated. The technique proposed, however, was a little mechanical, prompting another book, *The 59-Second Employee: How to Stay One Second Ahead of Your One-Minute Manager*.[21] I do not want to argue for a particular technique here but for a principle of relationship—regular conversation and discussion, continuous feedback and learning. I want

---

20. Kenneth H. Blanchard and Spencer Johnson, *The One Minute Manager* (New York: Morrow, 1982).

21. Rae André and Peter Ward, *The 59-Second Employee: How to Stay One Second Ahead of Your One-Minute Manager* (Boston: Houghton Mifflin, 1983).

the people for whose success I am responsible to know exactly how they are doing before the annual performance review.

During the twelve years I was at Regent College, we used the model I will outline here as we conducted our performance reviews each May and June. When I was at Fuller Seminary, I developed this approach that we called the continuous review model. It was one of three models available to managers. The other two were more traditional annual review forms: assessment checklists. We used my model in my department of the seminary. At Regent we set up this model as the institutional model. (There are some privileges to being president!) When I arrived at Regent, I found the usual reluctance to conduct performance reviews. Most managers and employees had had enough bad experiences to resist reestablishing this "demeaning and discouraging" element in our management process. After taking the leadership team through a performance review process, I think they found it reasonably painless, if not helpful, so they then applied the model to their people. We set up the model so employees received continuous feedback about their work, and we found the performance review process to be an opportunity for self-assessment and a time to give feedback to the leadership regarding how we could better support them in their contribution and growth. This is the model we currently use at the De Pree Center for Leadership.

In this model, I provide a list of questions to the person being reviewed about a week before the scheduled meeting. I have eight questions for the management team for whom I am responsible. A similar set of questions is used for the team members without management responsibilities. Each person is expected to come to his or her interview prepared to speak to these questions.

Before conducting a performance review, I write a personal letter of thanks to the person being reviewed, expressing my appreciation for the contribution he or she has made in the past year. If we have been working on a problem area, I might allude to that in the letter; but basically it is a letter of affirmation and thanks. I hand that letter to the individual at the beginning of the interview. Then I listen.

The interview lasts about an hour. For most of that time, the manager being reviewed assesses his or her own contribution by discussing the answers to the eight questions below while I take notes. The questions reveal the direction of the conversation.

1. Assess your contribution to the organization this past year. How does what you did advance the mission?

This is a time for the manager to assess and evaluate his or her strengths, weaknesses, and contributions to the organization. Such self-assessment is much more effective at highlighting areas for needed growth than the leader's assessment. Hardly ever have I had a person give a completely biased evaluation of himself or herself that I needed to correct. If we have had an honest relationship throughout the year, the individual's evaluation will be fairly honest and perhaps more vulnerable.

2. Assess the organization's relationship to you. Have we lived up to our promises? To your expectations?

This gives managers a chance to assess how well they have fit into the team, how well the organization has delivered on its promises. This question can be difficult for the leader because it invites managers to let us know when we have not met their expectations. There have been times when I have had to apologize when a manager pointed out that I had been so preoccupied that year with my work that I had not been there for that person as much as he or she needed. In many ways this form of review puts the follower into the role of reviewer.

3. How have the members of your team grown because of your leadership?

This is a question that the board put to me at Regent and I

now answer to the De Pree Center board. It is a reminder for managers that their work is measured most by the growth of their people. This gives them the opportunity to articulate how they have invested in their people and how they have measured the results.

4. What do you see as your primary objectives for this coming year?

Here the person presents the first draft of annual key objectives for discussion. The conversation will focus on content, implementation, and the support or assistance needed from me.

5. What elements make you excited about your work next year?

Here I want to tap into people's vision, to get them to articulate the vision that drives them into the new year. It is easy for routine jobs to get old—for people to stop growing. Most people need something new and fresh to keep their interest. This is what we talked about under vision. I want those I interview to talk about their vision for the organization and their contribution to that vision.

6. What could you not do next year without harming our ability to achieve our mission?

Peter Drucker calls this sloughing off the old. We cannot keep adding new things to do without creating space by getting rid of some things that we no longer need to do. This does not come naturally to most of us in leadership. This question is designed to force us to consider what we could stop doing in order to make space to try something new.

7. What training or continuing education program have you planned for next year?

I assume that all managers will engage in some form of training to learn their job more effectively or in continuing education to prepare for increased responsibilities. I want them to think about this before the meeting and come with a proposal for their own personal development. In cases where we have promoted a person to a new level without experience, we might build the training into the compensation package. During the time I was at Regent, Mary Lam, the finance manager, became the chief administrative officer of the college. As part of the increased compensation package that came with the position, we gave her a sum of money for attendance at professional training events that targeted her new responsibilities. During the first year, we also set aside funds she could draw on to bring in consultants to advise her in areas where her experience had not yet caught up with her responsibilities.

8. What can I do to support your growth in the job, in your ministry, and in your career?

This is the point where I make myself available as a servant. Can I help this person grow? Sometimes it means getting out of the way. Sometimes it means being more available. Sometimes it means just caring and praying as people struggle to make strategic decisions about their lives.

This final question brings us back to the key element of leadership. Leadership is a relationship. It is an investment of one person in another in order to influence his or her thoughts, beliefs, actions, and behaviors. It is a relationship in which both the leader and the follower should grow.

The questions for persons without management responsibility are similar:

1. How do you evaluate your contribution to the organization this past year? Do you believe you have learned the job? Do you feel like part of the team?

2. Have we fulfilled our promises? Have we fulfilled your expectations?

3. Look at your job description. Do you think it is accurate when compared to what you actually did this year?

> With this question we bring the job description back into focus for review. If there is no discrepancy between the description and the experience, we are probably on target. If there is a difference, either the job description needs rewriting to be more accurate or the work assignments need to be adjusted to meet the design of the position. This question again sees the job in terms of its contribution to the organization's mission.

4a. (optional) Assess your progress on the issues we have been seeking to correct.

4b. (optional) What objectives do we need to set for these areas? With what set review time?

> Questions 4a and 4b allow for the possibility that some negative feedback has been given during the year and a plan is being worked on to correct the problem. The annual review should not ignore that problem but should look at it again, measure progress, and set a time frame for action and further review.

5. What do you want to do next year to make your job more interesting or more responsible?

> This looks for individual vision. While not every proposal that emerges from every employee can be implemented, we have received some very good ideas from the people who are deep in the trenches.

6. What could you not do next year without harming our ability to achieve our mission?

7. What do we agree should be your specific objectives for next year?

8. What can I do this year to help you move toward your goals in this workplace, in your personal ministry, and in your career path?

I have used this performance review model for over twenty-five years with full-time and part-time employees, both paid and unpaid. I have found it to be an affirming and motivating model. It looks forward rather than giving a grade for past actions. When I presented the model at the University of Calgary's Executive Management Program, the faculty member responsible for personnel development liked it but suggested I call it Performance (P)review, because it is driven more by tomorrow than yesterday. I like that.

When the interview is over—whether it is with a manager or with someone without managerial responsibility—I place a copy of my notes and anything the employee gave me in writing in the person's file. If the discussion dealt with anything controversial or negative related to the individual's work, I summarize the discussion in writing and send the person a copy before I file it.

Again, we have found this model to be very effective at strengthening the relationship between the leader and the follower and keeping us working together as a team with shared vision and shared values in pursuit of a shared mission.

Equip for performance and growth

The final principle of people development focuses on providing the training and continuing education needed for followers to grow in their positions. If the performance review seeks to develop employees and volunteers by preparing them for more responsibility, then it should result in some action for that development, supported by additional education. Every person should be learning and growing.

Leaders should think of every person for whose success they are responsible as someone they are training for a better position, for an expanded ministry. What kind of training does that person need? How can we keep his commitment high? How can we improve her ability to serve the kingdom of God? I want to believe that every person who accepts employment at Regent or the De Pree Center, paid or unpaid, will leave better equipped for service and ministry than when he or she arrived. It is part of our investment in the resources that God places in our care.

Leadership is an empowering, individual relationship. *An individual leader*—you or me, with all of our own cultural baggage and experiences, coming with our own level of maturity at the moment and frequently bringing a preconceived idea of the appropriate style of leadership—*in a caring relationship*—that takes the other person seriously and builds trust, cares for the development and growth of the other person, and seeks to empower that person to accomplish his or her task for the mission of the organization to the glory of God—*with an individual follower*—a person with his or her own cultural baggage and experiences, coming with a preconceived idea of the appropriate style of leadership that the leader should exercise—*at a particular level of maturity*—a competence and confidence that varies from day to day and frequently within the same day—*in a specific situation*—right now, today, this task, in these conditions. Effective leaders are engaged in such empowering relationships with the people for whom they are responsible that the appropriate leadership style is an adapted response to CARE-ing for each person in the shared pursuit of vision, values, and service.

Conclusion:
Leadership Is the Use of Power to Serve the People

To conclude this chapter we will turn to another biblical vignette that underscores the role of leadership in the care and nurture of the people whom God entrusts to us and reminds us of our accountability before God, which is the theme of the final chapter.

They were the political rulers and spiritual leaders of a mighty nation, a country blessed by God. They led a nation whose armed forces were respected beyond their relative size on the international scene. This was a country founded on high religious principles—one nation, living under God. This was a country blessed with natural and native resources, strategically positioned for strong international trade. The human potential, natural resources, and spiritual capacity for leadership on the world's stage was great.

And yet these leaders were deposed from their offices. The political leaders fell to internal coups or were defeated in war. The religious leaders were written off as irrelevant to a modern people. The form of their piety and the skill of their rhetoric were applauded, but they made no difference in the lives and behaviors of those around them (see Ezekiel 33:30–33). Why?

One man—a preacher named Ezekiel—stood up and told them why. After the nation of Judah was defeated by Babylon, Jerusalem, its capital, was destroyed, and the people were exiled to other countries. Ezekiel, a prophet and priest living under the authority of his God, addressed the political and religious leaders with a message from God. Take note of his words:

> The word of the LORD came to me: "Son of man, prophesy against the shepherds of Israel; prophesy and say to them: 'This is what the Sovereign LORD says: Woe to you shepherds of Israel who only take care of yourselves! Should not shepherds take care of the flock? You eat the curds, clothe yourselves with the wool and slaughter the choice animals, but you do not take care of the flock. You have not strengthened the weak or healed the sick or bound up the injured. You have not brought back the strays or searched for the lost. You have ruled them harshly and brutally. So they were scattered because there was no shepherd, and when they were scattered they became food for all the

wild animals. My sheep wandered over all the mountains and on every high hill. They were scattered over the whole earth, and no one searched or looked for them.

"'Therefore, you shepherds, hear the word of the LORD: As surely as I live, declares the Sovereign LORD, because my flock lacks a shepherd and so has been plundered and has become food for all the wild animals, and because my shepherds did not search for my flock but cared for themselves rather than for my flock, therefore, you shepherds, hear the word of the LORD: This is what the Sovereign LORD says: I am against the shepherds and will hold them accountable for my flock. I will remove them from tending the flock so that the shepherds can no longer feed themselves. I will rescue my flock from their mouths, and it will no longer be food for them.

Ezekiel 34:1–10

The political and religious leaders of Israel had used their power—the positions and resources that God had given them and their country—for their own benefit, their own gain. They had grown fat off the flock but they had not used their power and authority to feed the flock, to care for and nurture the people for whom they were responsible.

We have been given an awesome responsibility: to feed the sheep of God, to care for the people of God. We are accountable to God for the use of the power he has given us. The prophets are watching. How will we use our power?

6

Influencing with Accountability

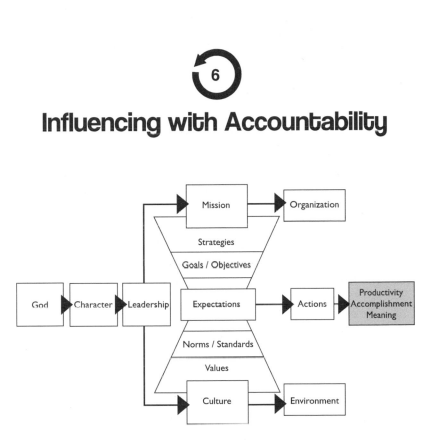

Wandering Stars: Accountability, Accomplishment, and Meaning

With the words of Ezekiel that ended the last chapter still ringing in our ears, we come to this final chapter, looking again to Jude, the half brother of our Lord, for an image with which to launch these concluding thoughts on relational leadership. The fifth and final image that Jude uses of those toxic leaders who were exerting influence in his community is both graphic and sobering: "wandering stars, for whom blackest darkness has been reserved forever" (Jude 13). A flash of excitement streaking across life's stage, swallowed up without performance. No commitment, no patience or perseverance, no long-term investment in the people—nothing to show that leadership was ever there. A burst of energy that calls attention to the leader but makes no lasting difference.

Unlike the previous images, this one carries within it its own judgment. Shooting stars, swallowed up in the darkness of the sky, capture well the shallow and temporary charisma of leaders who disappear from the scene before having any significant impact on the people or the mission. Caught up in their own journey, they are not leaders who care for the people. Note the negative ending of this image. Jude does not simply say they are swallowed up in darkness; he puts a judgmental twist to it. They are people "for whom blackest darkness has been reserved forever." They are accountable! They don't just disappear; darkness is their place. They are swallowed up in darkness precisely because they shine only for themselves. They have nothing to offer the people. They leave nothing of substance behind. Leadership is accountable!

Paul and Philemon: A Relationship of Accountability

One last time we return briefly to our story of Philemon and his important relationship with Paul. Paul is not a flash in the dark. His faith has been called to account. He sits in prison for his love of Christ and his love of people. He has invested his life in the people among whom God has placed him, and he continues to do so—even under arrest. He is in prison because of servant leadership, because he chose to serve the resurrected Christ and the people of God.

And Paul wants to make sure that Philemon also is not all talk and charisma. Paul wants action; he wants Philemon's faith to make a difference. He expects Philemon to practice what he preaches—to live up to Paul's expectations. Paul holds Philemon accountable. Paul is saying to Philemon, "Remember all those sermons and speeches about community? Remember those lessons on forgiveness and reconciliation? Well, it's time to demonstrate that you really believe what you proclaim! Reinstate Onesimus into your home and embrace him as a brother in Christ."

This powerful little letter with its agenda of influence is about accountability. The letter calls Philemon to account: to live out his values, his beliefs. But Paul adds one more layer of accountability. "And one thing more: Prepare a guest room for me, because I hope to be restored to you in answer to your prayers" (Philemon 22). In other words, "I intend to visit and confirm that you have in fact been reconciled with Onesimus." That is accountability. There will be a performance review!

For both Jude and Paul, leaders are accountable. The servant leader commits to the people and pursues a purpose. Leadership makes a difference. It should make a *lasting* difference. Relational leaders are accountable for their personal contribution to the common mission and the growth of the people for whose contribution they are responsible. They are also accountable for their own continued personal growth.

Accountability and Vulnerability

The God whom we follow creates the person we are. The beliefs and values that form our character shape our leadership relationships. As we have seen, leadership serves two purposes in an organization: the accomplishment of the mission and the development of the people. Through the articulation of vision, the planning of mission, and the organization of delegation a trajectory is launched. Its success is measured by the accomplishment of mission objectives and visionary goals. Organizational leadership effectiveness

> Accomplishment and meaning are the measure of effective leadership.

is measured by organizational outcomes, the implementation of vision, and the advancement of mission. At the same time, through the relationships of leadership a culture is embedded in the organization, shaping the environment in which followers flourish or fail.

Through the integrity of lived values, the expectations of corporate culture, and the environment of work a community is formed. Its success is measured by the growth of the people—the realization of their potential. The leadership of people is assessed by the meaning they find in their life and work. Accomplishment and meaning together are the measure of effective leadership. For biblical servant leadership, both are grounded in our relationship with God.

SELF-EFFICACY Belief precedes behavior. Theology matters. It is all connected. When leadership is an expression of the call of God it results in mission, meaning, and legacy that point back to God.

In this concluding chapter I want to look at the accountability and vulnerability of the relational leader. We will look at 1) spirituality—accountability to God; 2) accomplishment and meaning—accountability to the organization; and 3) legacy—accountability for ourselves.

We have been entrusted by God with an awesome responsibility: the management, care, and nurture of his people. We have been given the task of leadership, an audacious undertaking. We know that we are frail human vessels, weak and easily distracted. We need the discipline of accountability to keep us focused on our responsibilities before God.

Because we are accountable, we are vulnerable. It is a risk to lead, to enter into a relationship of interdependency with another person, to offer ourselves in service to a mission and to people. The possibility of failure is high and often outside of our control. Leadership is about accountability and vulnerability. But if leadership is so accountable, why take the risk? Why accept such vulnerability? The only reason I can think of to accept leadership responsibility is because God asks us to and offers us as a gift to his people (see Romans 12:8). And if we lead because God has asked, we have confidence that our vulnerability is wrapped in the hope of forgiveness. Relational leadership—servant leadership—is also about forgiveness.

Spirituality: Accountability to God

This theme has been touched on throughout this study. We are in this business because God has called us to serve. And we know that our impact upon ministry is directly related to our dependence upon God. We cannot do it alone. We will have the kind of impact that Jude and Paul expect only if the power of God works in and through us. We need the continual renewing presence of Christ beside us as we undertake the daunting task of leadership.

Accountability to God is about personal renewal and dependence. I cannot offer a stock formula for our personal development before God. Each of us works out the pattern that is best for us. But I do want to call us back to the resources for leadership that we noted at the end of Jude's letter, as he wrote: "But you, dear friends, by building yourselves up in your most holy faith and praying in the Holy Spirit, keep yourselves in God's love as you wait for the mercy of our Lord Jesus Christ to bring you to eternal life." (Jude 20–21). In particular I want to underline the importance of Scripture and prayer—listening to God.

I have always tried to maintain some kind of ongoing personal relationship with God, some kind of devotional time built into my days, my week. It has not always been easy to find a constant and successful model, however. I hate getting up early in the morning and I am too tired at night. Once the day is underway my mind is captive to the full agenda that calls for my time. I have always had the freedom of continuous informal conversation or prayer with God, but I have not always been successful at setting aside a specific time for listening and talking to God. Not until I went to Regent College! When I took on the responsibilities of leadership there, I knew I was in over my head. I had never been a president before, and I wasn't sure I was capable of the task. I felt the awesome responsibility of the mission and the community that God was entrusting to my leadership. From the day I arrived in Vancouver, I found that time to be with God came much more easily. It came out of dependence and fear of failure!

I knew that I could not do this job without the constant presence and power of God. I could not imagine starting a day of responsibilities without first praying through the day with God and seeking to understand what was at stake. This complete sense of dependence and need drove me to take the time to pray for those for whom I was responsible, to pray for wisdom, vision, and energy as I thought through the agenda for the day.

For twenty years now this has been a fixed part of my day. I begin each morning spending time in the Scriptures and in prayer, trying to listen to God and understand what is important about the day ahead. I have come to realize that, for me at least, there is a direct correlation between being "in over my head" and finding time to spend with God. When I think I have my job under control it is easier to skip the devotional, meditative time with God. But when I am aware of my vulnerability, my complete dependence, that time becomes a priority—so much so that I realize that the reverse of this observation is also true: when I am not spending consistent time with God, it probably means that I am not taking much of a risk in my faith. I believe there is a correlation between recognizing our dependence upon God and investing our time in listening to God. Obviously I still believe that I am in over my head in my current responsibilities!

In this context, prayer is an important part of my listening to God. I find that it is often during times of prayer that my mind sees the reality of my day from a different perspective. I keep paper and pencil with my Bible and allow myself to stop and write down ideas that come during reading and prayer. I am convinced that the meditative mind works differently than the reasoning mind. I see and think differently during times of prayer and meditation. This has become a significant inspirational time for me. I get many of my leadership ideas, sermon outlines, and relational convictions while reading Scripture and praying. While I do lift up others in intercession and place my own agenda before God, I have found these times to be much more times of listening and seeing things from God's perspective.

Leaders, by definition, occupy a risky position. We are responsible for decisions that affect the lives and work of others as well as ourselves. Leadership decisions have to be made when the right choice is not apparent. It doesn't take much leadership when the right choice is obvious. In fact, some would define leadership as the task of making a decision when the alternatives are equal. The *risk* of choosing when the right choice is uncertain is part of what drives me to prayer.

As a middle manager I could recommend decisions, knowing that "someone wiser," with responsibility for me, would correct or modify my decisions if I was wrong. As a president or an executive director, there is no one providing that layer of protection. Thus, dependence upon God becomes more crucial. Because of this dependence, every morning I pray through my agenda for the day. During the day, I pray for wisdom to see things from God's perspective—to look through the eyes of Jesus and understand what is important here, what issues are at stake. In the evening, frequently at the instigation of my wife, I review the day, giving thanks to God for what he has done in our midst.

Prayer for me is more an expression of my weakness and dependence than an expectation that God will make the decision for me. I think prayer brings us into the mind of God so that we understand what is important, so that we discern the values that must be preserved. Occasionally I get brilliant insights when asking for such wisdom, but usually I just sense a reinforcement of the values that are at issue. My prayer as a leader is that I will do no harm, and my final confidence lies in the belief that I cannot frustrate the sovereign will of God.

Listening to God is foundational. *Build time into your schedule for spiritual growth.* This priority for biblical leaders has been a primary assumption of this study. Incorporate worship and nurture. Allow for spending time alone. Build in time with God. Find your Sabbath rhythm—that devotional space where you stop to let your soul catch up with your body. Take time to be with God, not just study God. Leadership is a relationship of service shaped by the God we follow and the theology we live. As Jude reminds us, it begins in relationship with God and leads out of the strength of that relationship.

Accomplishment and meaning: Accountability to the organization

A few years ago I had the privilege of speaking at a conference in which David Breashears also spoke. A world-class mountain climber, Breashears led the expedition that produced the IMAX film *Everest*. He and his team also played a role in the rescue of climbers during the disastrous 1996 climb that took eight lives. He recently completed the PBS/Frontline film *Storm Over Everest*, which reflects on the tragedy of that deadly climb. I found Breashears' presentation at the conference both exhilarating and haunting. He reminded me of the difference between summits and trails, between accomplishment and meaning.

Ed Viesturs, the lead climber of Breashears' expedition, has now successfully climbed all fourteen eight thousand-meter peaks in the world without oxygen—a significant feat of mountaineering. In his book *No Shortcuts to the Top*, Viesturs reminds us that the summit is only halfway; the trail continues, and the expedition is not a success unless you return home alive.[1] Summits are a measure of accomplishment, but meaning is found on the trail. Meaning is found in ascents and descents and continues to unfold long after we leave the mountain.

Because they dominate our horizons, summits are seductive. The intensity of focus and the dedication to the pursuit of the summit can

---

1. Ed Viesturs, *No Shortcuts to the Top* (New York: Doubleday Broadway Publishing, 2006), 207.

easily blind a climber to the decisions necessary for a safe descent and a secure return to home. When that happens to leaders the cost can be significant. The ill-fated 1996 expedition leaders were so focused on the summit that they failed to attend to their people. Hours after the agreed upon fail-safe time when the leader should have turned his team around and led them safely off the mountain, one leader was still pushing for the summit. Because of leadership failures and mistakes, eight men and women died on Mount Everest that May. When a summit looms so large that a leader loses sight of the trail, leadership is a liability.

Summits have purpose, but trails give daily context to the journey. Choosing a trail is a statement of faith, a declaration of vision, mission, and hope. It means embracing a guiding purpose beyond ourselves. The trails we choose determine where we are going and who we want to be.

Summits lure us to the top as though that were the end we seek. When we reach the top we will have arrived. That is only temporarily true. Everyone who climbs mountains understands false summits— places you struggle to reach only to realize that the trail continues to a yet higher point, marking the true summit of the mountain. On the trail of life, most summits are false summits. Most accomplishments are not the end we seek. They are only high points on a trail that continues. When the summit becomes the purpose, depression follows—because the summit only temporarily satisfies. We always want more. Summits are important milestones along the trail, but the trail does not end at the top.

Summits do have an important role, however. They provide specific, visible, measurable objectives. They focus energy and assess progress. They measure accomplishment. Reaching a summit achieves one objective on the trail: it demonstrates progress and maintains momentum toward the purpose before us.

Summits capture our imagination. They stand out as accomplishments when compared to walking for miles in the forest. They keep us motivated and they mark progress. They form the strategies that keep us moving forward. But summits do not replace purpose; they do not provide meaning. The trail we choose will determine which summits we will climb, which objectives will achieve our purpose, and how we will travel together.[2]

Leadership in organizations embraces summits and trails. Through planning and delegation we identify strategic summits—objectives that unfold our mission, accomplishments that measure our progress. Through beliefs and relationships we build community—an environment in which people thrive and find meaning for their lives and work. Leaders are accountable to the organization for both. So how is this accountability implemented?

I want to mention two things here: 1) self-assessment, review, and renewal; and 2) working with a board. A good board will hold you accountable to the mission and the people and expect you to participate in some form of review and evaluation. But as leaders we should be engaged in an ongoing self-assessment of our leadership and growth, including maintaining an appropriate balance of commitments to life outside of our organization.

1. Self-assessment, performance review, and leadership renewal

When I accepted the role of president at Regent, I asked the board for an annual performance review. I wanted to know regularly how I was doing. Was I living up to their expectations? What kind of leadership would the college need in five or ten years? Could I be equipped for that role? A performance review was an opportunity for the college to hold me accountable to the mission and to the community and for me to hold the college accountable for their investment in me.

---

2. This thesis is developed in Walter C. Wright, *Don't Step on the Rope! Reflections on Leadership, Relationships, and Teamwork* (Milton Keynes, UK: Paternoster, 2005), 128–41.

The initiation of this process each year normally came from the chairperson of the board or from me. At an agreed upon time I drafted a five-to-ten-page self-assessment of my contribution to the college. I tried to be honest, reviewing both positive accomplishments and negative realities. I reviewed my strengths and growth and I admitted my weaknesses and disappointments. I evaluated the growth and progress of those for whose success I was responsible. I assessed the relationship between myself, as president, and the board. And I outlined what I was doing for my own growth and renewal. I also highlighted the key objectives for the year ahead. This evaluation was sent to the chairperson, who appointed a small committee of board members to review my performance. Normally I met with them for three to four hours, discussing our relationship. These were important times—not always easy, but necessary for the continued development of the relationship between the president and the board and the continued growth of both.

A similar format is followed at the De Pree Center. At the request of the board chair, I prepare a report that assesses the past year, my performance, the development of each of the principals and staff members, and our plan for the next year. Because this is a smaller context, the discussion takes place in executive session at a board meeting.

Continued learning and growth is critical for leaders. We serve changing organizations in a changing world. The demands on leadership time far exceed the time we have to give. We can easily become so busy leading and serving that we don't take time for renewal and growth. Study, learning, and continual renewal are crucial to leadership. It is hard to sustain vision when we are tired. It is difficult to lead when we aren't growing. New learning is empowering; it creates the energy needed for leadership. That is why we build continuing education into the performance review and assessment process. Leaders must carve out time for their own learning and growth even as they expect it of the people they lead.

In chapter two I identified the Emotional Competency Inventory as an effective tool for coaches to assess and encourage growth. It is also an important instrument for the self-assessment of leaders. Several years ago I completed this 360 degree assessment survey as a measure of my development and as an agenda for improvement. All principals of the De Pree Center also participate in this process of personal evaluation as part of our commitment to provide accurate feedback and opportunity for growth.

Both the 360-degree assessments and performance reviews are helpful instruments for growth and leadership development. The purpose of my reviews is to equip me to be the kind of leader the organization needs as we move into the years ahead. The board and I want to be the most effective leadership team we can be, carrying out the trust that God has placed in our hands.

2. Boards

That brings us to the topic of boards. There is probably no more important and potentially problematic relationship in leadership than the relationship between the leader and the governing board. I cannot begin to do this topic justice in the space available, but I do want to raise it for further thought.

In nonprofit organizations, or, as Drucker calls it, the service sector, leaders are held accountable to their people, to the mission, and to the broader society by volunteer boards of trustees, governors, or directors. The board is the governing body entrusted with the mission. It is responsible for the ongoing vitality and health of the organization or church as it pursues its mission. The board holds the mission and the resources in trust and thinks strategically about the future development of the organization. The board is responsible for selecting the people to whom they will delegate the leadership of the organization and for holding the leaders accountable to live out the vision and values of the community. Boards provide strategic thinking but not day-to-day management.

Richard Ingram of the National Center for Nonprofit Boards identified ten critical responsibilities for governing boards as they exercise accountability.[3]

- **Effective boards determine the organization's mission, culture, and goals.**

  They keep the overall mission of the church or organization in focus and ensure that all programs and services are in harmony with the mission and move toward the accomplishment of the goals. The board is the guardian of the mission; they hold it in trust. This means that the board understands and articulates the theology that shapes the culture of the organization, ensuring that the processes and procedures of the community reflect its values.

- **Effective boards select the leader.**

  Second only to its role as guardian of the mission, the most important responsibility of the board is the selection of leadership for the organization or church. The board recruits, appoints, and determines the conditions of the appointment: expectations, terms, compensation, vacation, study leave. An effective board also facilitates the acceptance of new leadership by the organization and the broader constituency. Once the appointment is made, the board delegates the operational administration of the organization to the leader, stepping back to the policy or "missional" level of responsibility. The board gives trust to the leader and holds him or her accountable to lead the organization.

- **Effective boards support the leader and review his or her performance.**

  As noted above, the board should articulate clearly its

---

3. Richard T. Ingram, *Ten Basic Responsibilities of Nonprofit Boards* (Washington, DC: National Center for Nonprofit Boards, 1988), 3–17.

expectations for the leader and then commit itself to the leader's success. At a minimum this involves annual feedback and performance review. Many suggest that the board initiate an institutional review of the leader every five years using outside consultants. Regent College implemented such a process prior to my tenth year, and it was a valuable exercise for the college and for me. Effective boards monitor the health and continued development of the leader and his or her family, providing adequate opportunity for reflection, renewal, and learning. And I regularly suggest that the board and the leader reflect together on the future needs for organizational leadership and prepare in advance for natural, God-honoring leadership transition. The board is responsible for managing this critical transition in a manner that celebrates what God has accomplished in the past and anticipates what God will do in the future. The relationship between the leader and the board is vital to the health of the community.

- **Effective boards ensure effective organizational planning.** Effective boards establish and maintain an ongoing planning process, guaranteeing that the mission of the organization will be preserved and incarnated in the future. There is some debate over the extent to which the board should be involved in planning. Reflecting on the planning model I articulated earlier, I believe the board should be significantly involved in strategic planning but should delegate operational planning to the leadership team. The board focuses on mission and policy, the executive team on strategy and implementation.

- **Effective boards ensure adequate resources.** This is one of the reasons the board wants to be involved in the planning process. The board is responsible to provide the resources necessary to fund the programs it approves. The board may decide who does the fundraising and delegate the implementation to the leadership team, but the board is finally responsible for the organization and therefore needs to guarantee the securing of the necessary resources. Not every board member can give significantly, nor can every member effectively ask for gifts. But I do believe that every member of a nonprofit governing board should be giving to the organization as he or she is able. A person who votes to shape the church or organization should be investing some of his or her resources in the mission.

- **Effective boards ensure the effective management of resources.**
  An important part of serving the public trust and exercising responsible stewardship is protecting the accumulated assets of the institution and ensuring that current income is managed properly. Normally this is handled by asking the leader to prepare an annual budget for approval, provide regular financial statements that the board can monitor, and submit to an external audit. While the responsibility might be delegated to the leadership team, the board is legally responsible for the use of institutional funds.

- **Effective boards determine and monitor the organization's programs and services.**
  In line with holding the mission and planning in trust, the board normally approves all programs and services of the organization or church, ensuring that they fit the mission, are appropriate to the priorities established by the planning process, and have sufficient funds for implementation. Initiation of programs and services may be delegated to the leadership team, but the board brings critical questions—usually dealing with mission, priorities, funding, staffing, and evaluation—to the fore before approval.

- **Effective boards enhance the organization's image with its constituencies.**

  The board serves as the link between the leadership of the church or organization and the organization's constituencies, promoting the activities of the organization to the public, interpreting its mission and values, and feeding public response back to the community.

- **Effective boards serve as a final court of appeal.**

  Ideally this responsibility will not be exercised, since it potentially moves management from the leadership to the board. However, if a conflict emerges between the organization or one of its members and another party, the board has the final responsibility to adjudicate the matter through appropriate grievance procedures.

- **Effective boards assess their own performance.**

  Unless the board is accountable to another body, the board is the only entity that can assess its own performance and that of its members. Even if it is responsible to another body, such as a denomination, it should be involved in regular assessment. Each member of the board might be evaluated in terms of his or her contribution to the organization at the close of each term of appointment. The board also monitors its relationship with the leadership team. An important principle that only the board can enforce is that *authority rests with the board corporately when in session.* Individual members of the board have no authority over the leadership and staff of the organization; the board corporately is the final authority.

Leaders must invest in the development of strong and knowledge-able boards that understand the mission and accept stewardship of the vision and resources. This is a major responsibility for those of us who provide leadership in the "service," or ministry, sector. And yet this is a major point of tension for many organizations precisely because it creates two sets of "owners," two complementary and competing points of leadership: the appointed leader and the governing board. Both are responsible, both are vitally invested, both are "owners," both have vision. The board normally has final authority, but the leader frequently has more time invested and more knowledge about the life of the organization.

Working together, boards and leaders provide a powerful team for leadership. Working against each other, they create a nightmare for the organization. On average, college and seminary presidents change every four years. Hospital administrators have similarly short terms. When tensions emerge, the leader leaves. Pastors often have the opposite problem. When tensions emerge, the board members leave or the board is marginalized. Too many pastors ignore the board and try to run the church on their own.

I don't have the answer for this struggle. I think it is endemic to our kind of organizations. But I still believe in the model. Leaders need accountability to keep them focused. The board is the primary agent for this accountability in our kind of community. We need to strengthen the board, to invest in the growth and knowledge of its members, to create lines of communication that encourage the shared leadership that must emerge. Leaders without accountability to the people and the mission, without a structure to keep them focused, are in great danger of misusing power for their own benefit. Dietrich Bonhoeffer's prophetic radio message when Hitler came to power underscores the dangerous tension between exercising leadership accountable to the people and being the leader, *der Führer*, accountable to oneself.[4] The board is the primary accountability relationship for the leader in a church or nonprofit organization. We need strong boards.

---

4. Dietrich Bonhoeffer, "The Nazi Rise to Power," *No Rusty Swords* (New York: Harper & Row, 1965), 190–204.

While the board is necessary, its members must know the difference between their responsibilities and those of the leadership team. Once a leader has been selected, the board must delegate leadership and step back, monitoring strategically. Board members must give their trust to the leadership and be available as needed for expertise and advice to the leadership. The board must learn to exercise responsibility without managing. The leadership must learn to be open and accountable without undercutting the board's responsibility. We are talking about *shared leadership, accountability, and trust.* It is a partnership of shared vision. Leaders can only lead accountably when they are given responsibility and assessed regularly in light of the mission and values of the community.[5]

There is much more that could be said about boards. Books have been written on this subject. But for the purpose of this study, suffice it to say that they are a critically important element of accountability in our organizations, an element that needs work and development as we seek ways to provide the kind of leadership our organizations vitally need.

Legacy: Accountability for ourselves

As I move into what I like to call the "third third" of life, I find myself reflecting on what is important, what lasts. My life continues to be rich with opportunity for accomplishment and caring relationships. Both mark the legacy that the leadership journey has left in me and, I hope, represent the legacy I have left in my path. Both are important, yet I am convinced that, just as the relational-emotional-values track of leadership is twice as important as the vision-strategy-accomplishments track in predicting organizational success, the network of relationships in which I have participated over the years dominates my thinking about the legacy of life. Legacy, Max De Pree reminds us, "is the facts of our

---

5. Max De Pree, *Called to Serve* (Grand Rapids: Eerdmans, 2001), 33.

behavior that remain in the minds of others, the cumulative, informal record of how close we came to the person we intended to be."[6]

In organizations, the leadership relationship exists to implement vision and pursue meaning. But it is fundamentally a relationship that is dependent upon the health of leader and follower. In this study we have explored strategies for developing healthy followers. It is appropriate to end with some thoughts about developing ourselves. The third accountability of leadership is accountability for ourselves.

Two topics need to be touched on here: understanding time and getting a life. Over the years, "time management" has been one of the two most requested workshops. Leaders struggle with time. There is not enough; it seems to get away from us. Yet we are accountable. We are responsible for our use of time and, often, for other people's use of time. It is important that leaders understand time—understand that there are different ways to view time and that leaders and followers may have different perspectives on the time they share. It is also important that they find balance in their investment of time.

This study is about the leadership relationship. That is the focus of attention for servant leaders. But it is not enough. We owe our organizations a larger life. Leaders need vital and nurturing relationships outside of the organization to enrich their thinking and broaden their perspective on life. Earlier we talked about mentors; here I would highlight family and friends.

1. Understanding time

Whenever I am asked to talk about managing time, setting priorities, and living with commitments, I am always a little ambivalent. I am a serious believer in time management, in setting priorities, in articulating values, and in keeping commitments. Accountability for the management of our time is a problem that plagues us all. We all have difficulty managing our time. There is never enough time! Yet

---

6. Ibid., 88.

there is very little I can say here that you have not already heard before or do not already know. The problem is *not* knowing *how* to manage your time. The problem is *doing it*! We don't like to discipline ourselves.

Most leaders have very loose accountability for the use of time. In fact, many times we deliberately choose to manage our time poorly to avoid something. It is also hard to talk about time management without being reminded of how poorly I manage my own time! Time management is about being accountable for ourselves. It is about managing our lives before God—being stewards of our time—choosing meaning.

Time is a fleeting resource slipping through our fingers, like sand in an hourglass. *Or is it?* That brings up another problem in the management of time. People see time differently depending on the culture in which they were raised and the personal assumptions that have formed in them over the years.

Researchers tend to identify two basic views of time: monochronic time and polychronic time.[7] But I don't need the research to know that there are different views of time. I have been married to Beverly for forty-six years—that is enough to convince me! You cannot get more divergent views of time than the views that Beverly and I have. I set my watch with precision, wanting to know exactly where I am on the world's time continuum. Beverly doesn't like to wear a watch; and when she does, she deliberately sets it five to fifteen minutes off—she can't remember how much!—so it cannot control her life. You can imagine the many points of conflict that occur like "clockwork" in our relationship. People see time differently depending on their culture, their education, their style of thinking, their logic, or their creativity.

Monochronic time is seen as linear, incremental, sequential, and predictable. The focus is on goals, objectives, and deadlines. Time is seen as a resource to be expended. There is a tendency to focus and

---

7. Ann McGee Cooper, *Time Management for Unmanageable People* (New York: Bantam Books, 1994), 21.

narrow our thinking, to do one thing at a time.[8] *Polychronic time* is seen as layered, almost spatial. It is normal to be multitasking, doing many things at once without regard to a linear passing of time. The focus is on values and relationships. Because many things are going on simultaneously, it is not unusual for a person to diverge off, in and out of various tasks, with no visible logic to the pattern—at least from the perspective of monochronic time.[9]

I believe we live in a world that requires us to draw on both views of time. Yet our starting point is influenced by the culture we were raised in, by our style of thinking, by our left brain/right brain mix. These are not hard and fast categories, but more like overlapping tendencies. In general, Western cultures like that in North America value monochronic time more highly than polychromic time, while Latin, Asian, and African cultures tend to value polychronic time more highly.[10]

Within both sets of cultures, however, we find people who tend toward convergent thinking—focusing and concentrating—and people who tend toward divergent thinking—looking at the big picture. People whose style of thinking is more convergent, more focused and concentrated, tend to be more comfortable in monochronic time. People whose style of thinking is more divergent, looking at the big picture, tend to be more comfortable in polychronic time. Similarly, research suggests that left-brained people who prefer structure and logic move toward monochronic time, while right-brained people who prefer creativity and spontaneity move toward polychronic time.[11]

Why do I bother with any of this? Because I believe we need both views of time to carry out the responsibilities of leadership by serving as relational leaders in our Christian communities. Also, in most of our organizations we serve a community that incorporates a variety of

---

8. Ibid., 25.
9. Ibid., 25–28.
10. Ibid., 29.
11. Ibid., 41.

approaches to time. At Regent College, in any given year about half of the community will be more comfortable with monochronic time and about half will look at time as polychronic. We have differences—and that's OK. That is what community is all about. We cannot expect the person sitting next to us to view time the same way we do. But we should take the opportunity to learn what others see because we must cultivate both perspectives.

Here's a quick illustration from the world of education. If monochronic time draws on time frames and deadlines, it is clear that education is basically monochronic. Students have nine months to complete the academic year. They have identifiable amounts of reading, papers to write, and deadlines when those papers are due. Regardless of their culture or orientation, they are undertaking a program of study that operates in monochronic time. The polychronic people must adjust to that reality. At the same time, Regent College stresses community. Community cannot be programmed. Twenty minutes a day given to relationship building does not necessarily build friendships. Community building and the nurture of relationships are polychronic. They cannot be scheduled. The monochronic people must adjust to that reality. We live in a world that requires us to blend our approaches to time. But because we believe in community, we can learn from one another.

We can see how this fits with our leadership agenda. Leaders are responsible for accomplishment and meaning, for leading organizational strategy and nurturing a community—two sides of the same coin of leadership. Leaders are responsible for vision and values. We translate our vision into action by monochronic thinking, by focusing our energy and concentrating the resources of the organization on our mission. Our planning processes are a monochronic, linear way of looking at our organization. Yet we are also responsible for the values system. Leaders reinforce the values and culture of the organization. This calls for polychronic thinking, involving creativity, divergent thinking, and a holistic look at the big picture of who we are and what is important to us.

Leaders must be able to work with both perspectives. Mission accomplishment requires a monochronic approach to time; building a culture of community requires a polychronic approach. Neither is right; neither is wrong. They are two ways of looking at who we are and what is important. But it is critical to remember that most of us are more comfortable with one approach than the other. It is important that we know ourselves, that we understand which approach to time we find most appealing. We will need partners in our organization who work comfortably with the other approach. Together, in community, we can provide the leadership our organizations need in these times of rapid change.

2. The legacy of a life

The demands of organizational leadership can consume us. Supporting the network of relationships that make up an organizational community is a never-ending assignment. Leaders are vulnerable to burnout when they let the organization become their life, and organizations can consume any leader. There is more to be done in any organization than any leader can possibly do in one life. That is why we have shared vision, shared values, teams, and delegation. But we owe our organizations more than that. We owe them a healthy life.

Leaders need commitments and relationships outside of the organization to give them perspective and energy—to enable them to bring something to share with the organization. We have looked at the leader's relationship with God. We have pointed to the importance of mentors. There are also the relationships of family and friends. Leaders owe it to themselves to keep balance in their lives, to invest themselves in these critical relationships outside of the organization. They owe it to their family and friends. And they owe it to the organization. Leaders must have a whole, or balanced, life if they want to bring life to their organization. It's part of their legacy.

(1) Family commitments. I have very strong feelings about family commitments. They are a top priority for me. I believe that if you have chosen to marry, you have made a lifetime commitment to the well-being and growth of your spouse. That becomes a very high priority. Graduate students have a notorious track record of shattered marriages because they spend all their time in the library and ignore their spouses. Theological students can be worse because they are living this way "for God." Patterns set early in our lives will shape our priorities for leadership. Too many families in the circles of Christian leadership fall apart because the leaders are so busy serving God that they fail to attend to their families. This is inexcusable.

Leaders need to balance their commitment to relationships. If we have entered into the commitment of marriage, we have been given and accepted a priority field for ministry. If we cannot minister intentionally and effectively at home, I have serious questions about our ministry anywhere! Beverly and I have struggled with time and many other things over the years, but our relationship has been a top priority for both of us. That has meant investing time to communicate. In addition to all of the normal time spent together over meals, in the car, at church, we usually spend a minimum of an hour every day in face-to-face talking and listening, without doing anything else. It takes time to nurture a relationship!

We did the same with our two sons. From the time the older was five until the younger left for college, over and above all of the normal family time I took one of them out for dinner every Wednesday evening, just to talk about them with them. For sixteen years! I still enjoy their company, and they still like to have me buy dinner. And now that I am a grandparent, there is a new layer of relationships with four wonderful lives to encourage. Think about it. How much quality face-to-face time do you spend each day talking and listening to the members of your family?

(2) Friends. Leaders need *friends*—men and women outside of the organization with whom we enjoy life, with whom we learn things not related to the organizational mission, with whom we play and get the exercise necessary for health, with whom we discover new things and grow in our walk with God. Friends add to the maturity that a leader brings to the organization. Friendships should be a priority for any leader.

One winter Beverly and I were vacationing on the beach in Mexico. We watched three men in their seventies laughing and talking, swimming and bantering. Their wives were sitting up in the shade. As I watched them, I found myself thinking about the later years of my life. Would I have three friends with whom to swim on the beach or to hike in the mountains? I realized that if this was going to be important to me then, I would need to be investing in those relationships now. We don't attain that level of friendship without a lifetime of relationship! Leaders cannot allow their organizational responsibilities to so narrow their focus that they fail to invest in the broader network of friends in the various communities in which God has placed them.

This remains another priority for both Beverly and me. For the past thirty-eight years we have committed ourselves to small support groups that have met each week. And we stay in touch with many of those in whom we have made such an investment: the Beckers in San Diego, the Partens in Minneapolis, the Whites in Los Angeles, and others that I could name—people with whom we pick up a conversation in mid-sentence even after lengthy absence and geographical distance.

And then there is my mountaineering group. Don Bosch, Brent Stenberg, Rich Butman, Don Dwyer, Newt Malony, Steve Sittig, and I have been climbing mountains, sleeping in snow caves, and canoeing rivers together now for nearly thirty-four years. We went on our first hike together on Thanksgiving weekend in 1975 and have taken at least three trips together every year since. Not only do we enjoy sharing the wilderness together, but over the years we have come to realize that these are important relationships—six other men that we trust with our lives—men with whom we have shared nearly thirty-four years of life and personal growth as well as wilderness trips. This is friendship. They are people who know me thoroughly and like me anyway! They provide balance and perspective outside of the pressure of organizational responsibilities. There is nothing we cannot talk about, nothing we do not talk about. We come from different worlds and have different responsibilities.

These men greatly enrich my life. We get together now as much for the relationships as we do for the mountain climbing. This has become an important priority for me. I build into my life time to climb mountains with these friends, time to call them and see how they are doing. I plan trips through Los Angeles, Memphis, and Chicago, and they come to Pasadena. We want to be doing this together when we hit eighty, and we are making the investment in that future now![12]

These are polychronic commitments. We cannot make relationships happen in our time frame, but we can build friendships into our priorities and make sure that we save time for the people in our lives. Twenty years from now the relationships we have formed will be more important than the accomplishments of our leadership. Being accountable for my time means making time for friendships that reach beyond the borders of leadership responsibilities; it means finding a balance between leadership relationships and life relationships. In the end, I believe the meaning of our lives and the legacy we leave is centered in the relationships we form.

Accountability and Forgiveness

Leaders hold followers accountable to the organizational mission and their own contribution and growth. Boards hold leaders accountable

---

12. The leadership lessons learned in the mountains with this group of men have been developed in *Don't Step on the Rope!*

in the same way. But leaders and followers alike are accountable to God, to one another, and to the mission that brings them into relationship. *Biblical leadership is an interdependent relationship of accountability, grounded in a relationship with God in Christ.* It is the final clause of this sentence that gives us hope. Leadership is accountable. Relational leadership is vulnerable. In relationship with God, because of Christ, we have hope. When God calls us to leadership—when God calls us to life—that call includes forgiveness. I do not believe there can be leadership without forgiveness.

Earlier I mentioned the tragedy that struck the world of mountaineering in May of 1996. Near the summit of Mount Everest two leaders lost their lives, as Rob Hall and Scott Fischer died in the pursuit of their vision. So did six other men and women in one of the worst climbing disasters in Mount Everest's history. You may have heard about it in the news, have read Jon Krakauer's bestseller, *Into Thin Air,*[13] or have seen the television special *Mountain Without Mercy* or the IMAX film *Everest.*

Mountains don't forgive. This principle has long been part of the lore and literature of mountaineering. People make mistakes; people can forgive. But mountains are not a forgiving environment. Everyone knows this, and climbers know it especially well. We still react with shock and outrage, however, when it happens. The margin for error at twenty-nine thousand feet is very slim, but we still scream with pain when the price of a decision is death!

No one knows exactly what went wrong on May 10, 1996. There has been much speculation and there will be more as climbers, sponsors, families, and spectators reflect on the Everest tragedy. Some see it as an error of vision. No one in their right mind would undertake such an objective, let alone pay sixty-five thousand dollars for the opportunity!

---

13. Jon Krakauer, *Into Thin Air: A Personal Account of the Mount Everest Disaster* (Topeka, KS: Topeka Bindary, 2003).

Some view it as an error of values. The interdependent community of climbers caring for one another was replaced by a collection of individual egos pursuing their own dreams. Some see it as an act of God, as a beautiful morning deteriorated into a hellish hurricane of freezing wind and snow. For many, however, it all boils down to an error of leadership—leadership at multiple levels: governmental leadership that failed to control the number of climbers attempting to ascend; organizational leadership that allowed expeditions to compete rather than cooperate, putting twenty-three climbers in each other's way on the final push to the summit; and individual leadership that allowed personal aspirations to set aside the rules of the climb. Mistakes were made. And mountains are not forgiving.

Rob Hall was a seasoned leader, an experienced guide who organized and led commercial climbs to the top of the world. Widely respected, he was known as a solid and conservative leader, a good man with whom to climb. He was a leader whom people chose to follow. He understood leadership as a relationship of trust. He was trusted.

Rob Hall understood the relational components of leadership. He knew about *vision.* He knew where he was going. He had stood on the summit of Mount Everest before; in fact, Hall had led thirty-nine climbers to the top of Everest over the past few years. He knew precisely what he had to do to reach his objective—for his clients and for his company. And it was a *shared vision.* When his climbers paid their fees, they accepted ownership and responsibility for that vision. They were ready to live and, as it turns out, die for that vision. They had a shared vision, but they made mistakes in the pursuit of that vision. And mountains are not forgiving.

Rob Hall also knew about *values.* He understood teamwork and cooperation as he competed with the other expeditions. He knew how to care for his people. He gave them their sixty-five thousand dollars' worth. He worked for their safety and health first, the summiting of Everest second. He understood human drive and human dignity. He knew how to manage fear and conflict under pressure. He knew the value of life and of relationships and he drilled the rules of the climbing community into his people. They shared these values and agreed to be accountable to live by them. Unfortunately, they did not always follow them. Mistakes were made.

Rob Hall also knew about *vulnerability*. He understood the risk of roping to another person and exposing himself to that person's weaknesses as well as his or her strengths. He knew that the shared vision and the shared values were only as strong as the weakest person on the mountain. A mistake on their team could take down others. An injury on another team could direct time and attention away from their own mission if rescue became necessary. He knew that mistakes, bad judgment, poor decisions, physical limits—his or another's—could abort the mission, defeat the vision, even end in tragedy. Climbers are human. People make mistakes. Vulnerability requires forgiveness. On May 10 mistakes were made. Lives were lost.

Rob Hall was an exceptional leader. Did he know where he was going? Unquestionably! Did he know what was important? Absolutely! Did he understand his vulnerability? Of course. Then what went wrong? No one can say with certainty, but it does seem clear that his values, his commitment to his climbers, caused him to stay behind with a stricken climber desperately needing oxygen. In the end, his values killed him. Vulnerable now to a series of questionable decisions, deteriorating weather, and a crippled climber, Rob Hall called his wife on his satellite phone and said goodbye. Mistakes happen. And mountains do not forgive.

Vision, values, and vulnerability: three crucial components of leadership. Rob Hall knew this on Mount Everest. Vision expects responsibility; values call for accountability; vulnerability requires forgiveness. Leadership is about vision, values, and vulnerability. It is also about responsibility, accountability, and forgiveness.

We have talked about vision and values. We have looked at responsibility and accountability. But what about forgiveness? There is very little in the management literature about forgiveness. This may well be the crisis of leadership today. I am becoming increasingly convinced that there can be no leadership without forgiveness. Leadership requires forgiveness, and forgiveness nurtures leadership.

> There can be no leadership without forgiveness.

Forgiving one another

One day the editor of a weekly newspaper called to ask me to write an article in response to the accusation that there was a crisis in leadership in higher education in Canada. A scholar had noted the number of advertisements for deans and presidents and concluded that there must be a crisis. I wrote the article, responding that there might in fact be a crisis, but not the one the scholar had imagined. I noted that, as advertised, there was no shortage of opportunities for leadership in higher education. I also suggested that there was no shortage of capable people ready to serve organizations and work hard for the vision and values of their institutions. But I did acknowledge that leaders do not last long in higher education. In the field of theological education, for example, on average presidents last four years and deans less than three years. Having served twelve years as a president, I am considered one of the veterans—a frightening thought!

The crisis of leadership, I believe, is a crisis of forgiveness. Leaders are expected to lead without mistakes. There is very little tolerance for error in our organizations, very little acknowledgment of the human limitations of leaders. Organizations want leaders whom they can place before them to bear the burden of decision without error. Errorless leadership is an oxymoron.

You may have heard the story of the young executive who sought out the crusty old corporate leader and asked, "How can I become a great leader like you?" The senior statesman looked at her and said gruffly, "Two words: *good decisions!*" After pondering this wisdom for a minute the young executive asked, "How do I learn to make good decisions?" The veteran leader paused and responded, "One word: *experience!*" Persisting, the young executive asked, "But how do I get this experience?" And as you can already guess, the leader turned to her and said, "Two words: *wrong decisions!*"

Leaders lead by learning from their mistakes. And leaders develop other leaders by giving the people for whom they are responsible the space to fail and to learn.

Toward the end of my hiring interview with the board at Regent, I was given the opportunity to ask them some questions. I asked, "What will you do when I fail? I have never been a president before. I will make mistakes. Will you toss me out when I fall on my face, or will you dust me off, stand me up, and encourage me to try again?" They did not really have an answer for me at the time, but perhaps the pondering of that question is part of the reason I served twelve years—leading, making mistakes, and learning from them.

Organizations must create a context of forgiveness if they expect to have quality leadership. And leaders must embrace their own vulnerability and offer forgiveness to followers if they want to contribute to that context of forgiveness, create healthy organizations, and nurture the leadership abilities of their people. The research that underscores the tight connections between relationships, emotions, and health demonstrates that forgiveness has a biological benefit. "It lowers our blood pressure, heart rate, and the levels of stress hormones and it lessens our pain and depression."[14]

---

14. Daniel Goleman, *Social Intelligence: The New Science of Human Relationships* (New York: Bantam Books, 2006), 308.

Forgiveness may be the most important gift an organization can give to its leaders and the most important gift a leader can give to the people for whom he or she is responsible. Forgiveness offers people the chance to take risks, to learn, and to grow in their own leadership within the organization. Given their own vulnerability, leaders need forgiveness; and they must offer forgiveness to others, even though the failures of others increase the leaders' vulnerability.

Forgiving ourselves

But there is one more thread in this tapestry of leadership, vulnerability, and forgiveness. *Leaders must be able to forgive themselves.* This may be the hardest of all. All of us are haunted by the dumb things we have done, the mistakes we have made, the failures of yesterday. Our ability to lead is directly proportional to our ability to forgive ourselves and risk failure again. If our actions are circumscribed by fear of failure, we cannot lead. Failure must be forgiven, and we must learn from it. And there is no one harder to forgive than oneself.

> Our ability to lead is directly proportional to our ability to forgive ourselves and risk failure again.

In 1928 General Umberto Nobile led an Italian expedition to the North Pole. With the famed explorer Finn Malmgrem, Nobile and his men flew the airship *Italia* from Kongs Fjord in the Norwegian Arctic to the North Pole. The expedition succeeded in reaching the Pole but ended in a tragedy similar to the Everest expedition of 1996.

In 1969 this story was retold by Hollywood in the dramatic feature film *The Red Tent*, starring Peter Finch, Sean Connery, and Claudia Cardinale. I use this film in my leadership classes. Though forty years old, the film is still dramatic and engaging, and it is all about leadership. A court sits in judgment on Nobile's leadership, and all the witnesses are conjured up again in Nobile's mind as he looks back on the expedition as an old man. In his fantasy Nobile reviews the story through the eyes of each of its characters as he seeks to pass judgment on his leadership and his failure. It is a very powerful film. As I show the movie in class, I stop the film at three critical points where the general must make a decision and ask the class what they would do. At the end, before the summary judgment is given, I stop again and ask the students to assess his leadership. If they truly wrestle with the decisions along the way, they are much less certain how to evaluate him at the end.

From the beginning of the movie Nobile has a vision, a dream, of landing on the North Pole. He is captured by his vision and exudes his sense of purpose at every point. It is contagious, and his men are caught up in the pursuit of this vision. I stop the tape and ask my class, as I would ask you: Do you have a vision for what you want to accomplish? For your life? For your organization? For your department? Do you live your vision with such vigor that your people have caught it and share your enthusiasm?

As the movie continues, Nobile and his crew arrive at the North Pole and prepare to land. At that moment, however, the weather turns—again like Everest—and Nobile must make a hard decision: Does he land and accomplish his mission for his country, or does he abort the landing and return to Kings Bay (as Kongs Fjord is referred to in the movie) to guarantee the safety of his men? His second-in-command, Major Zappi, states it clearly: "A leader's responsibility is to his mission—you must land." But the explorer Malmgrem counters, "No, a leader's responsibility is always to his men—you must return to Kings Bay."

Again, I stop the tape and we decide. Vision or values? What would you do?

General Nobile makes his decision and crashes on the Arctic ice, killing several members of his expedition. Huddled on the ice in a red tent, the story becomes a chilling tale of survival, heroism, and rescue, with more critical decisions for the general. In the end Nobile is judged for the decisions he makes. But the judgment of history does not haunt him. It is Nobile who cannot forgive himself. Forty years later he is still having nightmares about that trip, about his leadership, about his failures. Only when he faces this harsh reality in a poignant and powerful conclusion can he admit his failure, affirm his accomplishment, accept the judgment of history on his leadership, forgive himself, and sleep again.

This is a powerful movie about the vision, values, and vulnerability of leadership, a strong statement about the critical relationship between leadership and forgiveness. Relational leadership is a risky business. We are entrusted with a vision; we are entrusted with the dreams and gifts and hopes of the people. We are accountable to God and to the organization. We will fail and others will fail us.

Without the hope of forgiveness, we would never have the courage to take up leadership—to offer ourselves as servants of the shared vision and the shared values of our organizations. Without forgiveness, we would never commit ourselves to the interdependent relationships of our communities. But forgiveness comes with the gift of leadership. It is the empowering side of accountability. And forgiveness flows from the heart of the leader's relationship with God.

Conclusion: Prayer and Benediction

As you take up the responsibilities of leadership, as you give yourself in the service of the people whom God has entrusted to your care, as you join them in the pursuit of a shared vision and shared values, as you surround organizational mission with community life, I pray with Paul and Jude:

> We have not stopped praying for you. We continually ask God to fill you with the knowledge of his will through all the wisdom and understanding that the Spirit gives, so that you may live a life worthy of the Lord and please him

in every way: bearing fruit in every good work, growing in the knowledge of God, being strengthened with all power according to his glorious might so that you may have great endurance and patience, and giving joyful thanks to the Father, who has qualified you to share in the inheritance of his people in the kingdom of light. For he has rescued us from the dominion of darkness and brought us into the kingdom of the Son he loves, in whom we have redemption, the forgiveness of sins.

Colossians 1:9–14

To him who is able to keep you from stumbling and to present you before his glorious presence without fault and with great joy—to the only God our Savior be glory, majesty, power and authority, through Jesus Christ our Lord, before all ages, now and forevermore! Amen.

Jude 24–25

Index

Entries for book and journal titles are shown in italics. References to footnotes are given in parentheses following the page number: e.g., 171 (n 21).